Themes in the
Social Sciences

*Communes, sociology
and society*

DATE DUE			
Apr24 79			

Themes in the Social Sciences

Editors: Jack Goody & Geoffrey Hawthorn

The purpose of this series is to publish discussions of general interest to anthropologists, demographers and sociologists, and to those economists, historians and students of politics who are concerned with issues that extend beyond the conventional limits of their disciplines. The books will be both theoretical and empirical, and often comparative. They will deal with non-industrial and industrial societies, and with those in transition. They will not necessarily be introductions to their subjects, but should appeal to more advanced undergraduates as well as to graduate students and teachers.

First books in the series

Edmund Leach   *Culture and communication: the logic by which symbols are connected*
   An introduction to the use of structuralist analysis in social anthropology

Anthony Heath   *Rational choice and social exchange*
   A critique of exchange theory

Philip Abrams & Andrew McCulloch   *Communes, sociology and society*

Communes, sociology and society

by Philip Abrams
Professor of Sociology,
University of Durham

and Andrew McCulloch
Senior Research Officer,
University of Bath

with Sheila Abrams
and Pat Gore

Cambridge University Press

Cambridge
London   New York   Melbourne

Published by the Syndics of the Cambridge University Press
The Pitt Building, Trumpington Street, Cambridge CB2 1RP
Bentley House, 200 Euston Road, London NW1 2DB
32 East 57th Street, New York, NY 10022, USA
296 Beaconsfield Parade, Middle Park, Melbourne 3206, Australia

First published 1976

Typeset by Vincent B. Fuller Typesetting Inc., Philadelphia, Pennsylvania
Printed in the United States of America by R. R. Donnelley
& Sons Company, Crawfordsville, Indiana

Library of Congress Cataloguing in Publication Data
Abrams, Philip.
Communes, sociology, and society.
(Themes in the social sciences)
Bibliography: p.
Includes index.
1. Collective settlement–Great Britain.
2. Individualism. 3. Solidarity. I. McCulloch,
Andrew,   joint author. II. Title.
HX696.A27   301.44'94'0941   75-40985
ISBN 0 521 21188 3 hard covers
ISBN 0 521 29067 8 paperback

Contents

Preface

The work that led to the writing of this book was supported by a grant from the Social Science Research Council and carried out by the authors together with Sheila Abrams and Pat Gore. Andrew McCulloch, Pat Gore and Sheila Abrams did most of the work of visiting communes while Philip Abrams studied the literature and tried to maintain a proper academic distance from the real world. At regular intervals we all met to pool and review our insights and observations and to sift them so far as possible into an agreed account of what we had learned. From time to time one or other of us would be moved to write a fairly substantial piece of analysis in an attempt to develop a theme or resolve a difference – thus Andrew McCulloch wrote a paper on the 'key problems' of communes, Pat Gore drafted an essay on 'mystical influences' in communes. One of these pieces of work (Abrams & McCulloch 1974) became a paper presented at an Annual Conference of the British Sociological Association. And so we built up a file of reports and commentaries on communes and the Commune Movement which turned into the raw material for this book. Not all of the work we did is represented here, however. Sheila (who had the idea for the research in the first place) spent a great deal of time making sense of the results of a questionnaire we had distributed to all the members of the Commune Movement and keeping track of the actual organisation of that Movement and its entanglement with other projects for 'social change and cultural diversity'. Pat became involved in a very close study of religious communities and of a number of attempts to launch women's communes. It would have been very difficult for us to understand the groups we have written about in this book without this further work on the wider alternative society movements, and although this is not fully used here it will, we hope, see the light of day in separate publications. But we had to make some strategic decisions about the sort of book this was to be; and, as we did so, much of the work we had done had to be sacrificed for the time being.

When we began our research there were no easily available substantial accounts of contemporary British communes. It seemed reasonable to think that the most useful book we could write would be a rather practical one of the 'what it's like and how to do it' variety – a down-to-earth guide to the conditions for successful communal living with perhaps one or two more academic articles spun-off in suitably scholarly journals to take care of our more abstract professional leanings. But others moved faster than we did, and by the time we were ready to begin writing in earnest both a practical and a descriptive literature of communes had been created. Clem Gorman (1971) and Mark Broido (1970) had published informed and carefully argued accounts of the practical difficulties facing would-be communes. Andrew Rigby (1974b) and Richard Mills (1973) had produced graphic descriptive studies of the communes and quasi-communes that had sprung up in Britain in the 1960s, placing them in the broad context of a counter-cultural youth movement. In a more challenging way an analytical literature had also appeared. In particular Rosabeth Kanter (1972) and Benjamin Zablocki (1971) had, from the basis of profoundly perceptive studies of American utopian communities of an earlier period, advanced a general analysis of communes as a type of social enterprise which could claim to be rooted in sociological theory of the most sophisticated kind. Somewhat to our surprise, however, we found that the accounts of communes that prevailed in this literature and the sociological analysis that was built upon them, stressing powerful and ideologically elaborate mechanisms of social bonding and commitment, bore little resemblance to what we ourselves seemed to be observing in the communes we visited. At this point we decided that the important thing to do was to follow Kanter and Zablocki in treating communes as a phenomenon of importance for social theory but to do so specifically in the face of the humanistic, non-utopian communes that had been created in Britain and which the American studies simply did not help us to understand. So this is a book about the way in which modern British communes as a serious attempt to construct the social speak to social theory and about the capacity of social theory to make sense of such an attempt. It is not a book for communes, and in a sense it is not even a book about communes. Rather, seeing communes as a peculiarly adventurous and in Max Weber's sense 'transparent' effort to make the social, it is a book about the possible dialogue between social science and society. We would like to think that insofar as it belongs in any particular sociological tradition it is written in the spirit of C. Wright Mills. That is to say, it seeks to relate the personal and the public and to locate the conjunction of the two in a particular cultural and historical milieu. If it explains anything it does so by trying to understand the intersections of history and biography.

We have had a great deal of help. Richard Lloyd and David Nellist, members of the Department of Sociology at Durham who decided to live in communes rather than examine their interest in them, were the

viii

first to convince us that a sociological observer could be honestly welcome in the home of a communal family even while they insisted that the world they had created was beyond the apprehension of the sociologist. Sarah Eno, Patty Dorman and Bob Matthews, secretaries of the Commune Movement at different times, all took great trouble to make our research easier, as did John Thornton. Their good will and support were decisive in gaining us whatever access we have had to the real world of communes. Almost without exception the members of communes and of the Commune Movement whom we met treated us with patience and generosity even when they despaired of our own humanity. The members of Findhorn and of the communes we have called Family Farm, Fern Hill, Hillside and Red Dawn were especially kind, interested and helpful. The students at Cambridge and Essex who allowed us to lecture to them about communes destroyed at least the more schematic of our notions about other people's lives with just that incisive enthusiasm which is a lecturer's most satisfying fee. The SSRC fed some of us and sustained and advised us all for two years in its own uniquely supportive way. The Centre for Middle Eastern and Islamic Studies at Durham made us a grant to finance a visit to Israel, and the members of Givat Brenner and Ein Harod kibbutzim convinced us that despite everything we had seen in Britain, communal values could be realised even in a capitalist industrial society. Ted Benton, Stanley Cohen, David Holbrook, Dennis Marsden and Peter Townsend talked us through a variety of puzzles our experience of communes had thrown up. Colin Bell, Geoffrey Hawthorn, Harvey Teff and Patricia Williams read some or all of what we had written at various stages and made many sensible suggestions for which our book is the better. Alan Waton read and meticulously criticised our work as a whole, highlighting its ambiguities and forcing us to relate it to larger questions of social analysis. Our children suffered in a way they might not have done had we been living in communes.

P.A.
A.McC.

March 1976

COMMUNE

5 couples planning to buy a country estate 22 miles from London to set up a commune need 3 more interested couples. Our interests are: Wanting to live together in a larger social unit, women's lib., alternative technology, community involvement and alternative education. Most of us are lecturers, teachers or artists. Capital or earning power required. Box 1057S.

The Times, 16 October 1975

CHIMERA

A mere wild fancy; an unfounded conception (the ordinary modern use).

Shorter Oxford English Dictionary

1. Communes and sociology- alternative realities?

'Forcing, adjusting, abbreviating, omitting, padding, inventing, falsifying, and whatever else is of the essence of interpreting.'

Nietzsche, *On the Genealogy of Morals*

'All science would be superfluous if the outward appearance and the essence of things directly coincided.'

Marx, *Capital*

The ideal of communal living is ancient and universal. Whatever one may think of the argument that finds the origins of society in a state of primitive communism, it is plain that the process of human specialisation, and the experience of moral pluralism that accompanies it, had hardly begun when groups such as the Essenes felt it necessary to withdraw from the society around them into a communal world of their own where the values of mutuality could be cherished. Since that time bursts of enthusiasm for a communal reaffirmation of a simpler social solidarity have punctuated the march of the division of labour at frequent although irregular intervals. The self-conscious separation of the self from the social which has become one hallmark of the progress of civilisation has called forth attempts to reintegrate human experience communally so regularly and persistently that it is surely right to see communes as tapping a fundamental dilemma of social life. One such burst of enthusiasm occurred in Britain in the 1960s, and that is the immediate subject of this book.

A good deal is made of the fragility and failure of communes. To some observers they are self-evidently absurd; Marx and Engels, for example, dismiss them in a well-known passage as 'duodecimo editions of the new Jerusalem' (1951, I: 59) – although both write with considerably greater respect in their less polemical works; see, especially, Engels' account (1951, II: 118) of the 'sublime man' Robert Owen. We shall make no attempt to hide the fragility and failure of many of the communes created in Britain since 1960. Yet communal experiments and the critique of existing social life which they imply have been a constant and significant theme of British society for a thousand

1

years. However many particular communes perish, communalism lasts. W. H. G. Armytage (1961) has traced the history of communal experiments from the Reformation to the middle of this century, and what is at least as striking in his account as the endless founding and collapse of particular communes is just this persistence of the communal effort. When he wrote, many communes dating from the last high tide of enthusiasm around 1930 were still in being. Immediately afterwards a new movement of interest brought a host of fresh communes to life. And although Armytage chooses to take the publication of More's *Utopia* as a convenient starting point, the continuity of communes could have been traced back through monastic orders and societies of heretics and outlaws to a very early date. Communalism, the idea of a withdrawn fellowship, is a principle of wide and diffuse appeal that can be invoked in the name of many different ends. We find it in one aspect in the group of artists and craftsmen that gathered round Bede at Jarrow, and in another in the band of scholars who made their way across England in the thirteenth century to found an alternative university at Cambridge. Any given commune may be seen as a concentrated expression of some particular values. We shall have to produce some definitions later on. But taken as a whole communalism must be seen as a movement which is very common as well as very old, an instinctive popular sentiment almost. Viewed in this way communes in general catch up a broad range of themes and concerns which have ramified widely and curiously through a great deal of British society. The theme of community of property runs steadily from John Ball and the medieval utopia of the Land of Cockaygne – where 'al is commune to yung and old/To stoute and sterne, mek and bold' (Morton 1952: 219) – through the Diggers, Thomas Spence and William Morris to the present. It has always been a radical theme, of course, but that does not make it less enduring or less native. Or consider the importance we attach to co-residence and still more to commensality as symbols of the unity of groups; soldiers, dons and lawyers all take solemn eating together at least as seriously as the members of communes. Or consider craft work and agricultural labour as images of an unalienated life; the smith and the ploughman were life-asserting figures in our folklore long before they were taken up in fantasies of escape from industrialism. More distant echoes can be found in the symbols we associate with the idea of home. Closer links have been discovered between the scope and character of the cooperative and trade-union movements and the work of the great commune-builders of the early nineteenth century. But there is no need to force our point at this stage; communes are not as we see them an alien or freakish, nor a peculiarly modern feature of British society. Each particular commune is indeed a peculiar bundling together and selection of some more widely shared

2

themes of our social life. And only in that sense are communes odd. The claim of some members of a commune we visited in the Forest of Dean that the great bowls of hill country there are 'commune country' in the sense that communal experiments have had a continuous life in that part of the world since the Iron Age may be far-fetched. But communalism touches our culture closely enough for any study of communal withdrawals from British society to be also a study of the values and structure of that society itself.

Our sense of the commonness of communes is important in another way, too. Communes have had a curious press, being presented alternately as deeply sinister and as wildly exotic. The outsider's imagination has conjured up visions of communal life with an amazing dramatic inflation. Even if nothing is known the worst is usually imputed. Henry Sanders' famous report on the activities of the Diggers on St George's Hill in April 1649 set the pattern: 'all . . . began to dig and sowed the ground with parsnips and carrots and beans . . . they invite all to come in and help them, and promise them meat, drink and clothes . . . it is feared they have some design in hand' (Hill & Dell 1949: 383). The design that is envisaged today is of course almost always a matter of sex or drugs rather than of property; but the approach is essentially the same. It is as though we wanted at one and the same time to convince ourselves that our most licentious fantasies could really happen and to stigmatise those who suggest, however modestly, that social life might be possible on terms other than those of our own tightly constrained system. Academic writers have contributed as much as others to making and perpetuating a myth of communes. It is almost always the transcendent, tranformative, magical properties of communes that they stress. Communes are written about in the context of 'ecstasy and holiness'; of a 'return to Dionysus'; they are of course 'utopian'; their problems are problems of 'mortification', 'renunciation' and 'sacrifice'; they are 'mystical', 'counter-cultural', 'alternative realities' (Musgrove 1974; Cohen 1974; Zablocki 1971; Kanter 1972; Speck 1972; Melville 1972; Rigby 1974a). To conceive of communes as levelheaded, quietly enjoyable practical projects is quite difficult after all this. Of course myths are not untrue; they are simply misleading. To approach an understanding of communes through the veils of this particular mythology is to guarantee that the encounter itself will be a terrible anticlimax. Communal life probably is more intense and coloured in stronger shades than a great deal of everyday existence elsewhere but the differences are subtle, and a delicate balance of difference and similarity has to be struck. When people are happy in communes, are they really euphoric in a way that people in families are not? Are their conflicts really sharper than those in many factories or more self-absorbed than those in many university departments? However many

3

moments of mind-sharing a commune may achieve, it will know just as many moments of washing up. Whatever the truth about orgiastic trips and group gropes, the significant reality of communes is a good deal more familiar, mundane and down to earth. Serious changes in the nature of social relations are being attempted, but the mythology of communes gives us a difficult problem in setting a tone for discussing these attempts. Communes always *do* have a design in hand, but the nature of that design is not necessarily caught in the fantastic meanings imputed to communes by outsiders.

The study of communes came to appear especially appropriate in the late 1960s when an interest in communal living which for many years had been an active part of a complicated and very extended cultural underground broke surface in the form of a Commune Movement, formally organised and speaking as a vehicle of social change directly and critically to society as a whole. The Movement had an impressive resonance. By 1970 it had achieved a reasonably well-defined and stable public identity (Gorman 1971: 12-14). Although the majority of communes remained unaffiliated to the Movement, and although few of those that were affiliated did much to further the organisation or aims of the Movement beyond subscribing to its journal, *Communes*, a point of contact broadly accepted as legitimate by communes themselves had been established between communes and the straight world. (Henceforth we shall use the term 'commune movement' to refer indifferently to all those living in or actively sympathetic to communes whether or not they are members of the Commune Movement). Our own initial discovery of the revival of communalism was made through the pages of *Communes* and through membership of the Movement. Reflected thus, the commune movement of the 1960s seemed to be taking up with great promise and practicality many issues which had come to be defined as distinctive social problems of the day. It is not our view that what are commonly called 'social problems' are objectively given. Rather, they are culturally achieved *as phenomena* by particular societies in particular epochs. Only in this sense were the seven problems we are going to discuss peculiarly problematic in Britain after 1965. As phenomena they did for a time dominate public attention in ways which, say, the problem of wealth did not.

The only formally stated object of the Commune Movement, 'to create a federal society of communities wherein everyone shall be free to do whatever he wishes provided only that he doesn't transgress the freedom of another' (Commune Movement 1970: 7), does not immediately indicate this larger resonance of communes. But it is quickly felt in any closer study of the pages of *Communes*, which give the impression of a many-sided movement of direct relevance to at least seven familiar social issues. First, there was the problem of the generations,

4

both a universal problem and a pseudo-problem in many respects but one which had certainly seized the imagination of most of the people able to communicate publicly in Britain around 1970 as peculiarly ours just then. Recruits to communes were primarily and assertively young, and the rhetoric of the Movement was one of innovation and the rejection of established orders. Second, there was the problem of the family. Although most people living in families at that time would have thought of their existence in that respect as entirely natural and not at all problematic, a remarkable array of moralists from the Provost of King's College, Cambridge, to the leading champions of radical psychology had ruled otherwise. The Commune Movement saw the social relations of the family precisely as setting in which people were bound to transgress one another's freedom and to offer in communes a reconstruction of intimacy of a kind which would not entail the constraints and perversions these moral authorities had stigmatised. Third, and partly within the problem of the family, there was the problem of women. Few if any communes were explicitly concerned with 'the woman question'. But implicitly, and as though aptly responding to the account of female exploitation advanced by the Women's Liberation Movement, communes in general were widely represented as societies in which women would as a matter of course live as individuals in their own right rather than on terms mediated by a man's class and status. More substantially perhaps, communal living was seen as possibly realising a blueprint drawn by Engels: 'With the passage of the means of production into common property, the individual family ceases to be the economic unit of society. Private housekeeping is transformed into social industry. The care and education of the children becomes a public matter' (Marx & Engels 1951, II: 234). In a narrower sense it also became clear that, whether they wanted it or not, communes were being treated as relevant to a more conventional social problem of women – the situation of the unmarried mother. Not that communes put themselves forward as alternatives to the welfare state, but their existence was certainly seen as a possibility of that kind by large numbers of young women who hoped to find communally the support their children's fathers were not giving them. Fourth, in a society dominated by work, communes announced that play was a no less important part of living, perhaps more important. Indeed for many groups the whole point of communal living was to inject play into all life including work. As Gorman (1971: 91) puts it, 'Play is at the centre of communal life . . . [it] is all directed toward the one goal of creating a collective environment in which people can freely play.' Fifth, communes were about identity; specifically they were about the *social* construction of identity. Here at least members and observers of communes were nearly unanimous: what was going on was the collective

5

making of a more authentic type of self. Many different particular images of identity stressing many different values were presented. The expansion of consciousness, love, freedom, spontaneity, union with nature or with God, autonomy, mutuality, unalienated work were all prominent among the qualities emphasised by various groups. But everywhere there was the sense that by withdrawing from a society founded on competition and bureaucracy to one based on sharing and informality communes offered the prospect of a wholeness of identity not possible elsewhere. Sixth, communes were, obviously, about community. The idea of loss of community having slowly made its way to the centre of the most platitudinous but in some senses also the most keenly felt stereotype of industrial society, here was a suggestion that people could, just by an effort of will, break out of the isolation, estrangement, impersonality of their lives and recapture togetherness, an immediate life with people in place of society's mediated life of roles. The term 'intentional community' was often and increasingly used as a better term than commune to describe a group's meaning and purpose. And finally, in an oblique but unmistakeable sense, communes had something to say about the politics of revolution. Appearing in the context and the aftermath of some spectacular failures of direct political action, and against the background of many sobering demonstrations of the power and unresponsiveness of institutionalised politics, communes suggested the possibility of a political detour. Whatever one might have thought of the practicality of the object of the revolution proposed by the Commune Movement, the federal society of communities, the method of that revolution could only seem supremely worth trying. Communes would change their own members. The demonstration of that possibility was surely within reach, however resistant to change the French Communist Party or the London School of Economics or the Mayor of Chicago might have proved. Communes were to be demonstration projects for a gentle revolution of the individual.

No doubt there were many other ways in which communes responded to the concerns of the time, many other themes they expressed and projects to which they were devoted. Musgrove is surely right to see them as symbols of the whole diffuse counter-culture movement (1974: 90); and so are those who regard them as a rational breakthrough in the social organisation of accommodation, a logical development of the division of labour in housing. Nevertheless, it was these seven themes that seemed to us, as they seemed to many reasonably sympathetic observers at the time, to express as concisely as possible the distinctive relevance of the burst of commune-making that occurred in the 1960s. And such a pattern of relevance for society suggests in turn a striking relevance for social theory. It was of course this underlying meaning at least as much as the practical significance of

6

communes that provoked our interest. Like it or not, communes are a challenge to sociology.

Explicitly sociology has a poor reputation in communes. Implicitly communes ask to be seen as an attempt to make nonsense of many of the ways in which sociology conventionally treats the social. They are experiments in social solidarity based upon hypotheses which are, from at least some sociological points of view, incredible. They assert the possibility of relationships between the self and the social which the normal terms of thought of sociology make it difficult for us even to think about. Not only do they refuse to be defined in terms of any of the familiar classifications of sociology but they pronounce those classifications useless artefacts of a self-estranged world – positive obstacles to an understanding of the human qualities of the social. As a species of what has been called the anti-institution (Punch 1974: 312-25), they were bound to seize the interest of those who, whether as followers of Durkheim or of Mead, saw themselves practising the science of institutions. Could there be a form of solidarity which subjectively and objectively abolished the distinction between the self and the social? And which did so without structure, organisation or hierarchy, without our being able to catch it in the interpretive nets of class and status, compliance and domination, sect and church, collective behaviour or ritual process, action and order, mechanical solidarity and organic solidarity, community and association, the crowd and the cult? Was it, in V. W. Turner's terms (1969: 127-31), possible to freeze the moment of transition from 'Communitas' to 'Societas' and make it a social world in its own right? A world beyond the grasp of sociology? Some of the most articulate members of communes certainly believed this to be so.

Academic as these issues are, they do in one sense at least lead back towards questions about the practical meaning of communes. The ability of communes to cope with the immediate social problems to which they are felt to be relevant can be seen as a matter of the degree to which they can in practice deny the reality of the constraining dichotomies and alternatives imposed on social life by social science. In this sense communes are relevant to sociology, however irrelevant they may find sociology to themselves.

Yet at the outset the antithesis between our sense of the social and theirs raises a problem of research for the would-be sociologist of communes which many commune members told us we should find insuperable. In the face of a commune the sociologist's problem of adequate explanation on the level of meaning becomes acute. Are the two orders of reality perhaps so far apart as to make a sociological understanding of communes a contradiction in terms? The heart of the problem is of course the dualism on which social science is so firmly built. The distinction of subject from object, of being from consciousness, of the self

7

from the social, of reason from feeling are essential taken-for-granted tools of scientific thought. Dualism of this kind is indeed celebrated as a powerful and indispensable source of the particular capacity of western civilisation for scientific, technical and economic growth. The history of western science is in one aspect a history of an increasingly unself-conscious assertion of the adequacy of dualistic accounts of nature (see, for example, Burtt 1932: 303). Dualism is already implicit in early Christian theology, increasingly manifest in the Protestant versions of Christianity; and the world created by Descartes and Newton has become an unequivocal celebration of the power and reality of dualistic thinking. Boyle's move from alchemy to chemistry, Locke's move from enthusiastic to reasonable religion, confirm and elaborate the effectiveness of dualism whatever reservations individual thinkers might have had about the violence done thereby to the real unity of nature. Sociology has been a conspicuous vehicle of this type of thought, holding out the prospect of a more conscious mastery of society in return, specifically, for a more conscious alienation from it. The thought-world of sociology is deeply dualistic, a universe of social actors and social facts, of meaning and structure, observer and observed, at its most blatant of researchers and respondents. Of course the best sociologists, Simmel in particular but also Durkheim, have always made it clear that this is a constructed world, a strategy necessary for interpretation but belying the actual dialectical integrity of society. But it is remarkable how often this recognition, as in Durkheim's case (1938: liv), is a matter of a footnote which leaves the main account intact in its own dualistic terms. Indeed, sociology in its present form, the 'two sociologies' and all, would be inconceivable without this type of externalisation (Dahrendorf 1958; Dawe 1970; and especially Corrigan 1975), without our willingness to treat the dichotomised world we have constructed as an adequate reality. Traditionally sociologists used to do this in the form of either–or arguments (either conflict or order, either structure or meaning); now they do it in terms of both–and arguments. The development is not particularly significant. Durkheim's beautiful analysis of the possible bases of social solidarity (1933), quite apart from the sense in which it is of particular relevance to the study of communes, is a classical work of sociology in this respect as in others. The question around which that whole book is organised, about how a person 'can be at once more individual and more solidary', is a problem only *after* one has first assumed a fundamental dissociation of the individual and the social. The division of labour has to be conjured up to work its miracle of combining individual autonomy with social solidarity only because those two states have to be contradictory in Durkheim's initial philosophy. Thus the first agreed masterpiece of sociology is also the perfect demonstration of

8

sociology's ability to solve only those false problems its own dualistic consciousness has invented.

We shall come back to this antithesis of meaning between communes and sociology again and especially in chapter 6. Meanwhile communes may be regarded as one among many attempts to deny the validity of dualism. Along with marxism and some of the more contemplative religions they embody a serious attempt to reassert the plausibility of monism. In trying to talk sociologically about the issue of solidarity in communes one is thus faced unavoidably with a problem of using terms of reference which, seen from within the world of communes, grossly distort one of the most important things that communes are about. This gives both them and us serious problems of communication – problems which are perhaps caught by those members of communes who found our questions about the sorts of personal qualities needed to make a commune a success 'bloody silly', or who answered by saying 'only humanity', or 'a commune is its members'. Viewing sociology's withdrawal from society from the standpoint of their own withdrawal they see very plainly the violence done to social experience by social analysis. To many members of communes the issue is perhaps quite simple: 'academics are anti-life' (*Communes*, 38: 26). And at least some academics have in the same manner treated members of communes as simply anti-rationalist. Such impressions are easily confirmed. We were not the first to experience the difficulty; Dick Fairfield has reported the following typically frustrating interview with two leading members of one well-established commune:

Dick: In the United States there is a lot of experimentation with group marriage and this sort of thing. Are you more conventional than this?

John: We're not more conventional; we don't have that sort of theoretical approach to the problem. What happens, happens.

Dick: How do you deal with emotional aspects?

John: We don't sort it out as an emotional problem in this way.

Dick: You don't isolate it?

John: No, you've just got to live here. Naturally we have these kind of problems, but our attitude to them is that they are the problems of life in any case, really. You've got to deal with them in some way or other. Or move away.

Dick: Right! How do you deal with them?

John: They are not dealt with. They're not thought of in that way. We don't have a formula which is applied to them.

Dick: What I'm really trying to get at is that people in the United States who are interested in a more radical family structure, they want to know how best to approach that sort of thing.

Alan: The best we can say is come and live with us for a bit.

9

Dick: Another thing I'm not clear about is the economic aspect. You say money's not a problem. Is everything pooled? Does one person handle the money or how do you –
Alan: What we do is –
John: I was just going to say: this is a bloody good illustration of the difference of the approach. I mean you assume that we have got some theory, don't you? You assume that we've got some theoretical structure?
Dick: Well, maybe some kind of approach –
John: We don't have a theoretical structure of behaviour on the financial front, which is the sort of way that the Americans would talk about it, which is applicable to the way we live here. So sometimes it happens one way and sometimes another.

(Fairfield 1972: 82)

The anti-rationalism here reflects a profound belief that the analytical and emotional aspects of life are out of balance, that the former is stifling the latter and that an important task of communes is to redress the balance. But another set of ideas is also hidden in such conversations. The commune is not seen, typically, as having an existence of any meaningful kind other than that contained in the personal relationships within it. But these are constantly changing and change anew with the addition of each new person – even a sociological visitor. Consequently, to say what the commune is is to reify and falsify it; it is the experienced realities of all who are involved in it which can *perhaps* be rendered in a narrative but not analysed. Commune members' doubts about the meaningfulness of sociology were in this respect merely the particular form we encountered of a larger reservation about science. The fundamental belief which we found to be very common in communes is that there are ways of knowing which are at once entirely real for the individual and entirely beyond the grasp of science, and that the inability of science to master this kind of knowing in no way invalidates the experience of the individuals in question. At Findhorn, for example, where the attempt to allow the possibility of magic is strong, we were told quite bluntly 'science is always wrong'. More generally we found as a plainly important part of the setting of communal life a suspension of disbelief about magic, an effort to maintain the adequacy of the intuitive response – caught perhaps in the constant and thoroughly opaque use of the word 'vibrations' as an all-purpose means of explanation.

The significance of communes must be found in the quality of their practised relationships. But the overt medium of those relationships is a language which denies the meaningfulness of social analysis. What sort of bridge can be built across a gap of this kind? The aversion to

10

theory in modern British communes is almost a matter of principle. The pages of *Communes* are filled with histories and descriptions of particular communes, but they are vitually bare of reference to any of the writers who have discussed speculatively the problems with which communes are struggling in practice; there is no Freud, no Jung, no Reich, certainly no Skinner. But this is only the edge of the problem. Sociologists are after all quite used to giving accounts of unsophisticated populations. The problem here is to give an account of a highly sophisticated population which has organised its life as a deliberate rejection of, and as a prickly barrier to, one's own style of thought. How does one respond to the claim that the communal alternative is so intimately part of the process of happening that it cannot be adequately separated out in thought at all but can only be known by being lived?

What lies behind such claims, and it is evident in conversations of the kind we have quoted, is a refusal to typify. To the extent that that refusal can be kept up, the common ground between the subjective world of the individual and the world of science is eroded. If one wishes to get beyond the conventional dualities of the self and the social, of internal and external orders of reality and so forth, the existence of some such common ground is vital. Many social philosophers, especially phenomenologists, have found it precisely in the element of typification supposedly involved in all accounts of the world, whether the mundane talk of naive individuals or the abstract elaboration of ideal types in science. Thus, Natanson (1970: 74) writes: 'From the standpoint of the individual, typification is the fundamental means by which the social world is grasped; from the standpoint of the social scientist, the construction of models is the procedural means through which both actors and action are comprehended.' And on the basis of this essential similarity of procedure it is possible for him to envisage a situation in which the scientist can apprehend the self: 'He must arrange a rendezvous between the system of typification of mundane reality and the principles of typification disclosed by science.' Natanson's account of how this might be done is quite full and subtle. But how far does it get us in the face of individuals who, having sensed the possibility of just such a threat to their privacy, order their lives on the basis of an idiom which is fundamentally a matter of refusing to typify?

Of course such an idiom is never sustained with complete success. One can even provoke breakdowns – as when our questionnaire moved one commune member to write in block letters across the form: SOCIOLOGISTS ARE PARASITES – a much more valuable 'response' in many ways than the more usual return of scraps of biography and fragments of material detail about particular communes. But whatever stratagems one might in principle invent to draw out underlying typifications (and that was *not* what we were doing), the simple possibility of being outsmarted when studying any sophisticated and broadly anti-sociological group is bound to remain. Thus, we found ourselves increasingly perplexed about what has been called the 'up-frontness' of communes (Berger, Hackett & Millar 1972: 275). A property of communal life that often seems to go hand in hand with the belief that 'what happens, happens' is a sense of openness, a sense that the process of happening can and should be naively displayed. Candour and spontaneity are valued in relationships within the commune; the curious outsider is typically received in a frank and welcoming way. A readiness to tell it how it is is the dominant tone of *Communes* and of the way in which most communes receive visitors and prospective members. Such encounters are nevertheless also carefully staged. News of the arrival of a visitor is commonly posted on notice-boards and is likely to be intensely discussed both before and after the event. The 'problem' of visitors is also much discussed in the journal, and having returned ourselves from a visit to one commune where we had been, as we thought, received with great warmth and honesty to discover that a leading member of that same commune had just published an article affirming that 'of course . . . people doing studies on the communal family . . . get short shrift' from that particular group, we began to wonder. How much of the impression of up-frontness is in fact impression-management? On another occasion we were fortunate enough to be able to compare our notes on a particular commune with another field-worker and discovered an outstanding coincidence in the way we and he had been received. We had both met the same people at the same times in the same sequence, and they had repeated themselves almost word for word. Was this a gratifying confirmation that we had seen the reality of that commune? Was there not also a suggestion that the problem of visitors had been solved in this case by the production of a smoothly performed communal show? In yet another case our relationship with the members of a commune was all but destroyed by the discovery that our reports on the commune had been seen by an outsider. In that situation it became clear both that the members of this group at least were extremely reluctant to have anything but their own version of how it is made public, and that there were dimensions of the life of the group to which we had not been given access, a level of reality that had been carefully protected from scrutiny because of a fear that to recognise it would pull the commune apart.

It is only the ideology of communal openness that makes the discovery of such protective measures, if that is what they are, surprising. In studying any other intimate social milieu a gap between members' publicly offered accounts and the fragile texture of unspoken meanings

12

and conditions supporting the relationships and the behaviour that are observed is what one would expect. Much of what we think we know about the tensions and conflicts of ordinary family life comes not from the observation of ordinary families but from accounts of the worst pathological possibilities of family life constructed in clinical situations by patients and therapists. Few researchers have ventured to open up the quality of relationships in ordinary families in the way many researchers have presumed they can do in communes. Perhaps the viability of any close relationship depends on a substratum of possibilities that are known but not acknowledged, on an element of not recognising the threatening or the outrageous. The screening of this substratum in communes is odd only in that it takes the form of a claim that everything is in the open. Nevertheless, this claim introduces a fundamental uncertainty into the business of observing communes. In one case when we had found the openness of a particular commune quite impenetrable (that is, we had been convinced by what we had been shown), we subsequently met two members of long standing who had left the commune, or been thrown out, after a period of deep and virulent conflict and who gave us an account of it as a system of fraudulent personal domination which was of course wholly at odds with anything we had experienced during our own visits. On the basis of the communal principle of the equal integrity of every individual's reality, what does one conclude in the light of this sort of evidence? In addition we ourselves compounded our own problems of access to communes by our own unavoidable but manifest lack of commitment to their purposes or meanings. We will come back to this problem shortly.

Without wanting to overemphasise the theatrical quality of communal life we cannot help noticing the similarity between our sense of the difficulty of grasping the reality of a commune and Erving Goffman's account of the realm he calls the 'backstage' area of social interaction (1959: 109-240):

> Within the walls of a social establishment we find a team of performers who cooperate to present to an audience a given definition of the situation. This will include the conception of own team and of audience and assumptions concerning the ethos that is to be maintained by rules of politeness and decorum. We often find a division into back region, where the performance of a routine is prepared, and front region, where the performance is presented. Access to these regions is controlled in order to prevent the audience from seeing backstage and to prevent outsiders from coming into a performance that is not addressed to them. Among members of the team we find that familiarity prevails, solidarity is likely to develop, and that secrets that could give the show away are shared and kept. (p. 231)

13

Communes may be thought of as establishments in the making, and it is likely that for that reason their members, saddled as they are with values that commit them to a constant show of openness to outsiders, will feel the need to construct and protect a back region of communal life in an especially acute and complicated way. It is even possible that one function of the stream of visitors, and one reason for welcoming them, may be found in the very fact that visitors do provide an audience for whose benefit commune members can perform a consensual account of the commune, developing their own solidarity in the course of producing the performance. Visitors would thus enable communes to separate the indeterminate and often rather fraught backstage realities of communal life from the onstage presentation. At the same time of course the onstage presentation is also a positive account of the commune which the members themselves may find helpful in their subsequent dealings in the back region. Fanciful as this sort of interpretation may be, we could if we followed Goffman one stage further also find in it some sort of explanation for the curious ambivalence of many commune members about sociologists:

> One basic technique the team can employ to defend itself . . . is to develop high in-group solidarity within the team, while creating a backstage image of the audience sufficiently inhuman to allow the performance to cozen them with emotional and moral impunity. (p. 209)

We have seen at least one commune prepare with calculated finesse to do just this for the benefit of a visiting television crew; and presumably the inhumanity attributed to journalists is about on a par with that attributed to sociologists. On this particular occasion the process of cozening did not stop with the careful preparation of a suitable performance; the members also decided to ask their would-be visitors for a substantial cash contribution to the Commune Movement funds. The whole encounter, in other words, was a clear moral victory for the commune.

More reasonably, perhaps, one might suggest that much of the reserve we sensed in many communes had to do with our status as visitors rather than as sociologists. Whatever functions visitors may perform for the communes they visit, they unavoidably raise the problem of their own possible permanent membership. Most visitors are in some degree interested in the possibility of becoming members, just as communes are normally interested in the possibility of offering membership to their visitors. But in every case this is a matter of very delicate screening. The commune must both reveal its merits and protect the unity of its existing members on which those merits depend. On a number of occasions we have watched visitors who quite plainly badly wanted an invitation to join a commune become thoroughly mystified

14

as they were at once made thoroughly welcome as guests and denied the offer of membership they so eagerly hinted at.

We have dwelt on these difficulties of access not to justify any thinness in the findings we shall report, nor to excuse the brutality with which, in spite of these difficulties, we went ahead and interpreted communes, but because they raise some interesting questions about the technical and ethical implications of a certain kind of social research – research on people who actively don't want to be researched and who know how to baffle the researcher. A peculiar invasion of privacy is involved here. At the same time research becomes an altogether more polemical activity. Typically, the social researcher has studied populations who have accepted his notions of the nature of social reality with at worst a passive indifference. Not only have the alien cultures not answered back, they have tended to submit quietly to the assault to social science, to accept the meaningfulness of scientific accounts of themselves, and even to try to learn from them. Researching communes is an altogether more strenuous business, a matter of maintaining the credibility of an estranged typifying sense of the world in the course of trying to understand people who themselves well understand the intellectual system within which the researcher is moving and who regard it as nonsense. The probability is that more and more of the groups the social scientist wishes to study will be of this kind, sharing with communes an educated capacity to *enact* their disbelief in the possibility of a scientific understanding of social relations. At one commune we were told that we were welcome to stay not because we were likely to understand the members but because through staying with them we might begin to understand sociology. On another occasion it was put to us that 'verstehen means understanding the poverty of your lives through the richness of other people's'. Generally we came to think of research as a struggle to maintain the singularity of meaning.

A study of communes

Having decided to persevere, how does one proceed? Our original research interest was concentrated on just one or two of the more practical problems with which communes were said to be concerned. We were interested in the possibility communes perhaps offered of separating the social process of mothering from the exploitation of biological mothers. We still take this interest seriously both in terms of its policy implications and as a point of view for talking about the family, gender relationships and the sociology of childhood. And although we quickly discovered that this sort of concern carried with it a serious distortion of what communes were understood to be about by their members, it was on this basis that the Social Science Research Council agreed to subsidise our curiosity. Our SSRC grant was the source of a great deal of amusement among the people we wanted to study (to be *paid* to live in communes was quite a trick). It also served to confirm their view of social science. Why should the government be spending good money to investigate communes? To some this was obviously a manoeuvre in the war of bureaucratic rationality against spontaneous living, a piece of blatant counter-insurgency. The question was, were we innocent dupes or did we know what we were doing? Justifying our research in the field became a major research task. It was, after all, far from certain that the sort of report we were likely to produce would be of any service to the groups we were studying; there is an important sense in which the most helpful thing that could happen to communes would be for them to be left alone for a while by both academics and journalists. However, our research grant and our visits were seen in many communes as having a further and more positive meaning – as confirming the seriousness of the commune movement. Plainly we did take the movement seriously and on this basis, despite the agreed difficulties of any real understanding, most communes were willing to take us seriously, too. And if some commune members perceived us through the inflated imagery of what we have called the myth of communes, with its implications of a basic alienation between us and them, we for our part designed our research in very much the same terms. We envisaged communes as exotic counter-cultural enclaves which we should have to approach with great care. It took many cups of tea to dispel this mutual expectation of strangeness.

Few communes are formally affiliated to the Commune Movement at any one time. Fifty-seven groups or would-be groups committed to various communal projects are listed in the 1970 edition of the *Directory of Communes* (Commune Movement 1970: 14-35). Many more are mentioned in the successive issues of *Communes*. In almost all cases it is indicated that these groups will receive visitors provided that they write in advance to make suitable arrangements for their visit and do not just turn up. At the same time it is well known that the groups that are publicly available through this literature constitute only a small part (and it is said, an unrepresentative one) of the commune movement as a whole. We wanted our work to be as representative and as comprehensive as possible; but its main concern was plainly with the practised relationships of communes in their natural environment, and our main problem was therefore to effect a relatively naturalistic entry to that environment and once there to contaminate it as little as possible. Although we did decide later on to fill out our basic information on communes by presenting all seven hundred members of the Commune Movement with a questionnaire, our main approach had to be both more direct and more piecemeal than that. To research

16

communes at all beyond the level of mythology, rhetoric and self-advertisement, one must develop a field relationship with commune members that has a defined meaning and preferably a positive value for them. The stereotyping that is common in communes of sociology as a rather desperate form of human estrangement makes this quite difficult for the sociologist to achieve.

Our choice of a research style to deal with this problem was much influenced by the advice given by Polsky in *Hustlers, Beats and Others* (1971: 115-47). In several respects we learned for ourselves the soundness of his precepts. Quite early in the research, for example, we were compelled to abandon the use of a great deal of conventional research apparatus – tape recorders, interview schedules, note-taking and certain kinds of questioning – and to teach ourselves to remember conversations and encounters and write them up at night in diaries, in order to maintain the naturalness of our presence. Similarly, we had to learn and then to distance ourselves from the distinctive language, the argot and speech-styles of communes; one has to know what, say, a head-shop is, but at the same time to be alert to the question of what the quality of this language does for its users – that is largely where the practised relationships are. And we also learned, sometimes painfully, the wisdom of Polsky's 'first rule of field research'; to 'initially keep your eyes and ears open *but keep your mouth shut*'. Only once were we thrown out of a commune, and the occasion for that was that we had naively started talking about encounter groups before discovering that to the people we were with even to show interest in encounter groups was 'symptomatic of the sick mentality of the drop-out communes' (L.137; an explanation of our system of referencing our own research materials is given in the appendix). Of course this bit of talk was being seized on as a way of bringing a slowly accumulated unease into the open as legitimate hostility. Nevertheless, keeping quiet would have taught us more. But the core of Polsky's discussion of the problem of field research has to do with the account the researcher gives of himself to the people he wants to study; and here our difficulty was if anything greater than his because the people we wanted to study were mostly convinced that they already had a quite adequate account of the sort of people we were. The other half of the problem of making clear who you are is, as Polsky says, to make clear who you are not; that is, to establish as firmly as possible just where your involvement in the values and ways of life of the people you are studying stops. From the outset it was our intention to deceive our informants as little as possible, but the research encounters were almost always such as to involve some confusion – springing of course from the ambivalence of our interest in other people's intimate domestic circumstances. We always presented ourselves as sociologists and made it clear that our

17

immediate interest was academic. Great as the merits of this approach were in terms of candour it had the effect of causing too many commune members to freeze over in a way we could not hope subsequently to thaw. In one group where we introduced ourselves in this way to the commune as a whole at a meeting our announcement had the effect of dispersing the meeting with muttered apologies and averted eyes in a matter of seconds; some members told us later we had ruined their day. We had, then, to soften our identity a little. Fortunately the 'sympathetic outsider' is a familiar type in most communes; indeed, such people constitute the pool from which the usually badly needed new members of communes must be recruited. And on this basis we could, without loss of candour, modify our account of ourselves a little in the direction of acceptability. We could and did make it clear that the research was not just an idle exercise for us, that we personally took the promise of the commune movement entirely seriously, that we shared many of their views of the defects of contemporary society and of the inadequacies and strains of contemporary domesticity and that in that sense we were authentically involved in wanting to know what communes could achieve. But there is a difference between interpreting the world, however sincerely, and changing it. The practical test of the extent of a sympathetic outsider's sympathy is his willingness as a visitor to a commune to treat his own private life as negotiable within the context of the commune's system of personal relationships. Unhappily, for it obviously militated directly against the success of the sort of research we wanted to do, none of us was willing to be that participant. At critical moments we were forced to make it clear that although we wanted commune members to share everything about themselves with us we had no intention of putting ourselves equally at stake. On at least two occasions we declined serious and considered invitations to give up research and join a commune. When challenged we found that our idea of participant observation extended to making beds but not to making love. Having made it clear that we were in the last resort paying guests and not relations we can hardly complain if some of the inner life of the family was kept from us. However genuine our sympathy, we were committed outsiders; worth talking to because after all we might do something to establish the truth about communes in the straight world or to let members of any one commune know something of what was going on in others (many members of communes wished us 'good luck with the project' for just that sort of reason), but not sufficiently involved to be allowed very close to what was happening, because after all we had made it clear that we didn't want to be very close in that sense.

This refusal to assume the role of genuine participants may have reduced our 'data-gathering' capacity somewhat. It certainly confirmed

18

some commune members' prejudices about sociology. On the other hand we do think that we gained some credit as ethical persons (being true to oneself is valued, too); and that identity was in any case virtually forced upon us by the very close overlap of the academic and communal circles in which we were moving. In the event, the role of naive seeker after truth turned out to be perhaps as successful and frank an approach to the private lives of sophisticated alien groups in one's own society as one could hope to find. One of us was already a member of the Commune Movement (an organisation of sympathisers as well as of participants), and we began by using that meagre but genuine resource. We visited or wrote to a few other members of the Movement, told them of our interest in the question of mothering and asked them to help us explore the possibility that communes might have a better answer to that question than society as a whole seemed to have produced. On that basis we were put in touch with two communes which seemed particularly worth attention as experiments in domestic relationships and which were themselves willing to be looked at in this way. After staying with these two groups we found that we had made contact with members of a number of other communes which, on the basis of more or less explicit references from our original hosts, were also willing to be visited. Despite their reservations about us, most communes received us with almost unfailing kindness and responded to us firstly as people and only secondly as sociologists. A snowball developed. At the end of two years the four of us had visited sixty-seven communes. We were in no position to advance generalisations based on an empirically secure study of a cross-section of communes; but we were fairly confident that we knew some communes really well.

At the same time the focus of our interest in communes had shifted. For a number of reasons, which are developed in chapter 5, and which result in a typically small and unstable population of children in most communes, the possibility which certainly exists within the set of ideas commune members have about communes of a different social organisation of mothering is very rarely realised in any substantial way. This became clear very quickly and our attention moved to the problem of explaining why such an important opportunity was not in fact being seized. This led us of course to a study of the dynamics of communal life in general. And at this point we became aware of the problem of separating communal reality from communal myth. The communes in which we were staying were in some important ways startlingly unlike the communes we had read about; they were altogether less distant from society, less mysterious, less esoteric, more tied down in everyday practicalities and more interesting. The more exhaustively we read the literature (whether produced by academic writers, by journalists or by members of communes), and the more carefully we compared it with the fraction of the commune movement we had encountered directly, the more puzzled we became. The ecstasy and transcendence, the mini-apocalypse (Hedgepeth & Stock 1970: 184) of the counter-cultural myth materialised as fleeting moments in a catalogue of strangely domestic excitements (Sunday dinner), problems (keeping warm) and aggravations (cleaning up).

The myth of communes is assiduously cultivated (there are so *many* books and articles) and deserves explanation in its own right – what does the sense of magical liberation do for all those professors? One of the clearest presentations of it is to be found in *The New Families*, where we are offered the picture of a system of 'variant values' starkly contrasted with those of the non-communal world (Speck 1972: 151-5). Speck suggests that we should confront communes with questions about five fundamental concerns around which all systems of values have been said to be built: 'What are the innate predispositions of man? What is the relation of man to nature? What is the significant time dimension? What is the valued personality type? What is the dominant modality of the relationship of man to other men?' (Kluckhohn 1965). We shall find, he argues, that in each case there is a radical opposition of values between communes and straight society. Thus, in the communal world man is innately good and cooperative, the relationship of man to nature is one of organic unity, time is essentially time-present and if measured at all is measured in terms of experience, the valued personality type is above all peaceful, intuitive and loving and the dominant mode of relationship is sharing and giving on an informal basis governed by a sense of collective solidarity. By contrast, the outer world, whether judged in terms of its public religions or its private practice, sees man as innately evil and competitive, treats the relationship between man and nature as one of antithesis and exploitation, engulfs the present in both the past and the future and measures time mechanically, values rationalistic, assertive and calculating persons and rests on dominant relationships of personal having and taking in the context of formal organisation and individual ambition. One could vary the details of this particular set of contrasts, but the sense of contrast, of a polarity of values, is almost universal. The question is, are these writers talking about what communes achieve or only about what they intend? Or possibly just about what some people would like them to intend?

The idea of a revolution of values of the kind mapped by Speck plainly does excite the imagination of both members and observers of communes. But can communes provide the sort of structure, the sort of relied-upon social relations in which such a revolution could be carried through? It was at this point that we began to feel that most previous

20

studies of communes had perhaps remained trapped in the myth. Of the communes we visited, about one-quarter were gathered on the basis of common activities which required a more or less forcible insulation from society for their effective pursuit: a search for the curiously private and elusive sense of transcendent unity offered by drugs or intense mystical communion, for example. Another quarter were means to the more effective pursuit of social or political projects in the outer world. But a good half were simply this-worldly ends in themselves. This is not to say that their members did not have a distinct morality or view of life. They usually did see some mixture of freedom and sharing as an ultimate point of value. But this ideal was not usually worn on the sleeve. Rather, it tended to emerge quietly in the way in which successive situations were lived through. On the surface the commune was much more likely to be justified as simply making life more interesting or more stimulating or even more comfortable than it could have been for any of the members on their own. Emphatically these groups were not living in the hot flood of the counter-culture. The special quality of their lives has to be found in their efforts to shift the implicit values of their experiences step by step towards their ideals through such simple, difficult things as forcing themselves to face up to the meaning of quarrels, of demands for privacy or of the failure of some to contribute what others consider their share. What distinguishes them from families is not the absence of such episodes but the effort that is made to treat them as occasions for serious self-questioning and collective change; their willingness to treat the structure and design of the group as problematic, debatable, alterable. It is this property, of course, that makes it so hard to give an adequate account of the structure of a commune; communes are an interactionist's heaven – in principle everything is negotiable.

Much of communal living is indeed dominated by the wish to make communal values a reality. But at least as much demonstrates the overwhelming pull of the practice of life in an opposite direction. The importance of communes may indeed lie in their image of revolution. But the importance of studies of communes should be sought not so much in their celebration of that image as in their attempt to work out what happens in fact when the concern for sharing and loving and for a fusion of the self and the social which everyone has observed runs up against the possessiveness, intolerance, jealousy, waywardness and varying capacity for domination of actual individuals and against the constraining and oppressive power of actual societies which became evident to us in communes.

In other words, communes must be taken seriously but not at face value. In one quite important way they are certainly a good deal more serious than the army of well-wishers, academic observers – with or

21

without SSRC grants – apologists, part-time beats and weekend hippies they have attracted would suggest. Unlike these hangers-on, the members of communes have realised that the alienation, fragmentation and one-sidedness of life that disturb them are not problems that can be *thought* out of existence. Rather, they have to be lived away. Philosophical dualism is not to be mastered in their eyes by new attitudes or better philosophy and certainly not by better sociology. It is to be denied in practice. This insight is not in itself particularly new. It emerged, for example, at the height of the great tide of communal enthusiasm of the early nineteenth century:

> It will be seen how subjectivism and objectivism, spiritualism and materialism, activity and suffering, only lose their antithetical character and thus their existence as such antitheses in the social condition; it will be seen how the resolution of *theoretical* antitheses is possible only in a *practical* way by virtue of the practical energy of men. Their resolution is therefore by no means merely a problem of knowledge but a real problem of life. (Marx 1959: 109)

It is their move from theory to practice and from individual practice to social practice that makes communes serious. The question is, how much can this particular kind of practice achieve – in practice? This issue, curiously muted in the mass of existing literature on communes, will be the organising thread of our work. We shall look at the experience of life within communes and at the relationships between communes and the society around them and we shall interpret communes as more or less successful attempts to achieve a practice which, in however inexpressible a way, negates the realities of British capitalism, intellectual dualism and sociology.

Within this framework we shall treat each of the social problems and sociological puzzles for which we have suggested communes may be seen as peculiarly relevant. In the next two chapters we shall define more carefully what we are talking about, distinguishing communes from a family of related social forms with which they may be compared and presenting some basic information about the context, extent and character of the commune movement at the time we studied it. We give an account of the rudimentary structure of communal life and of its distinctive processes and problems. And we present in descriptive form some accounts of the pattern of communal life as we found it. Chapter 4 takes up the ways in which communes manage two of our seven social problems, those of identity and youth, treating these questions largely in terms of what might be called the phenomenology of communal self-seeking. Chapter 5 considers communes as possible solutions to the problems of the family and women. In the sixth chapter the communal assertion of the primacy of play and the bearing

22

of communes on the problem of community are considered in the context of a discussion of the issue of social solidarity in communes. The last chapter compares the sorts of communes that emerged in Britain in the 1960s with some other types of communal project and in that context takes up the questions of the practical relevance of communes for the problem of revolution and the intellectual relevance of communes for the problems of sociology. We end with some proposals for a social policy for communes.

This is, in other words, a highly selective study of communes. We shall be concerned mainly with only one type of commune, which we will call the secular family commune. And we shall be dealing with only one range of problems and issues of the many in terms of which communal living might be thought interesting or important. We hope to show, nevertheless, both that our particular object of study has an intrinsic significance which has been overlooked in much previous writing about communes and that it can be studied in a way which is of use in a more general social analysis.

2. *The nature, structure and problems of communes*

A social relationship will be called communal if and so far as the orientation of social action – whether in the individual case, on average, or in the pure type – is based on a subjective feeling of the parties, whether affectual or traditional, that they belong together.

Weber, *Economy and Society*

When a friendship is founded on the expectation of some advantage to be received, what the friends are thinking of is their own good; when it is based on the expectation of pleasure they are thinking of what is pleasant to themselves. Their affection is not for the object of their affection as such. These two forms of friendship, then, are grounded in an inessential factor . . . So parties are ready enough to dissolve their association when they are themselves changed.

Aristotle, *Nichomachean Ethics*

The idea of a commune

The definition of a social phenomenon is an extremely difficult business, and our search for an adequate definition of a commune proved both tortuous and haphazard. We scurried backwards and forwards among what we thought we saw happening in communal ventures, the modern literature on them, works of social theory and the utopian literature, especially that on nineteenth-century American communities. Gradually we came to some realisation of what we were interested in attempting to explain and of a theoretical strategy that might help us to complete the task. The definitions we used changed and sharpened as our work developed. It is no accident that although we produced numerous typologies of communal ventures and many papers on definitions during the course of our research, this chapter was the last to which we turned our attention when writing this book; definitions come after analysis not before it. This chapter puts forward a definition of communes, but it does not attempt to be a shining example of sociological method. Often such chapters make ritual obeisances to rules of method, say little and mislead monstrously by omission. In the standard textbooks of methodology, defining the object to be explained is commonly seen as a first step which must be achieved before satisfactory progress can be made. Our experience leads us to the belief that this is a fanciful and simplistic view. Definition is not extrinsic to explanation; it is intrinsic, and the development of an explanation of a social phenomenon through empirical research and theoretical development is a complex and many-sided process about which we know little – even while we claim to be doing it. Accordingly, this chapter attempts two things at the same time: to record our search, detours and bewilderment; and to work towards a definition of communes meaningful within the context of our research experience. We do this not out of a sense of intellectual heroism but in the hope that it will make the book more useful. The use of definitions as we understand them is at once practical and rhetorical. In defining a commune in this chapter we do not believe that we are grasping reality or even achieving any sort of independent basis for the observations and interpretations we are going to present. Rather, the definition is itself caught up in the whole process of observation and interpretation. What this chapter does, therefore, is to indicate some of the ways in which we in practice separated what was problematic to us from the whole universe of communal phenomena, and to formulate more concretely than in the previous chapter the questions we shall try to answer. A definition is a delimitation of questions, not an account of the world.

What we try to do first is to seize the essence of what communes are about for those who are seriously and actively concerned with living in them. That we do so does not mean that we believe that this is necessarily the most significant level of analysis of communes. However it is important to examine *their* beliefs as a first stage, and especially when those being studied are so self-conscious and assertive about the importance of personal belief.

Communes belong within an enormous family of forms of social life and are hard to distinguish from other members of that family. One can observe in communes a sort of communion (as envisaged by Schmalenbach), a sort of community (as envisaged by Nisbet), a sort of family (as envisaged by Parsons) and a sort of establishment (as envisaged by Goffman). They are a species of association and a species of encounter. They may be seen as a type of primary group and as a type of collective behaviour. They share many of the properties of clubs, of revitalisation movements, of therapeutic groups, of crowds and sects. They have features typically associated with the folk village and features typically attributed to the total institution. Few if any of the concepts devised to further the analysis of social institutions fail to illumine some part of the nature of communes. Put another way, the commune is one of those 'typically mixed' social phenomena which, as Weber regularly reminded himself, make the habit of thinking about the social in terms of formal types and models so inadequate. There is perhaps no one model of social organisation to which any actual commune will entirely conform. And communes differ from one another and resemble one another in ways as numerous and complicated as those in which any given commune differs from and resembles any given model of social organisation. Andrew Rigby (1974b: 5) distinguishes between six types of commune which he calls self-actualising communes, communes for mutual support, activist communes, practical communes, therapeutic communes and religious communes. Plainly, these types are not mutually exclusive, nor do they exhaust the possible range. Carter (1974: 56) suggests that one should recognise some eighteen varieties of commune, differentiated in terms of the members' own view of the principal purposive activity of the group. Thus, we might distinguish craft communes from mystical communes, group-marriage communes from agricultural or social service communes. We ourselves began with a simple distinction between the idea of the commune as an end in itself and that of the commune as a means to some extra-communal objective, and with the intention of concentrating on the former. We have, loosely, maintained that distinction, but in practice we found it constantly blurred by the restless actuality of communal life; we, too, found ourselves rapidly inventing a host of subtypes only to end up wondering whether any typing at all really made sense. Many members of the commune movement certainly insisted that the whole attempt to type communes was a mistake; there were as many types of commune as there were communes. Yet we were almost as frequently told that a particular group, or perhaps a particular type of group, was not 'really a commune'; and our intuition confirmed such feelings. Within the field of innovating or counter-cultural or 'underground' living arrangements one comes across many projects which are just as clearly not quite communes as a few quite clearly are. There are student houses and crash pads, squatters' projects and housing associations, and even some kinds of housing estate, colleges and monasteries, workers' cooperatives, networks of swinging couples, floating hash parties, intentional villages and embryonic religious movements. The commune has a fleeting and elusive existence in the midst of all these forms of activity – related to them all and yet significantly unlike them all.

Definitions and classifications of communes abound. Most of them are based on supposedly observed structural or ideological properties of groups calling themselves communes. We, too, began our research by agreeing to accept as a commune any group that chose to call itself a commune. But we quickly found ourselves uneasy about regarding all these empirically given groups as the same sort of project; and we found that there were some groups we did want to treat as communes despite their own resolute resistance to being labelled in that way. Our immediate experience of communes and quasi-communes was implicitly constructing a model for us. Before long we had elaborated a notion of what we wanted to study – the secular family commune treated as an end in itself, distinguished in what we hoped was both a specific and a systematic way from other types of association. We had arrived at our own version of what Jerome (1975: 54) calls 'the Great Commune in the Sky'. We arrived at it, so far as we can tell, not by observing the formal properties of communes, nor by attending to accounts of what commune members said a commune was, but by interpreting and synthesising what people who take communes seriously seemed to us to be trying to do. By the same route we arrived at a notion of the significance of that type of project and of some problems and contradictions which were likely to be consequential for it. Reversing the order of our own research experience we can therefore begin by setting out an ideal–typical conception of a commune as a type of social project. It is inevitably the usual 'one-sided accentuation'.

The secular family commune, which is the empirical variant we have wrenched from the whole range of communal activities for particular attention, is an attempt to cultivate friendship. Friendship has not been a significant issue in social theory since the sixteenth century, and this perhaps explains some of the difficulty social theorists seem to have in understanding what communes are about. We shall try to make sense of the ambiguous existence of communes by seeing the commune as trapped in a paradox well known to ancient and medieval social thought, the paradox of the attempt to institutionalise friendship. At

26

the same time the attempt to treat friendship as an ultimate value is overlaid by attempts to realise a variety of essentially self-oriented ends peculiar to individual commune members. The incompatibility of these personal purposes with friendship as a collective purpose is not entailed *a priori*. It is therefore an empirical question whether friendship can or cannot be institutionalised on the basis of the particular individual purposes brought to communes by the type of people interested in communal living in contemporary capitalist societies. Nevertheless, what one makes of the idea of friendship does have implications for the way in which one decides that the empirical question must be answered. And here it seems fair to say that unfortunately for themselves contemporary family communes are committed to a notion of friendship of a peculiarly ambitious and idealistic type. Why they demand this kind of affective solidarity should become clearer as the book unfolds. Unfortunately for the rest of us, that same notion of friendship also seems to embody a very positive image of human social relations not realised elsewhere in contemporary capitalist society. Sartre's bleak statement that 'the bourgeois has no friends, only competitors' has a compelling force. Ours is surely one of the very few types of society which have not created distinctive institutions of friendship: our pubs, clubs and the rest are rather substitutes for them, havens of created sociableness without real and lasting substance. Perhaps it is after all not so strange that the very terms for serious friendship used by the Greeks, *philia*, and the Romans, *communicatio*, are ones we find it difficult if not embarrassing to translate. Were all these people Socrates talks about really 'lovers'?

Aristotle (1953) devotes two books of the *Nichomachean Ethics* to a discussion of friendship as one of the fundamental and natural types of human self-realisation. He is talking about a relationship of great closeness which is at once natural (in the sense that it is spontaneously sought) and difficult to attain (in the sense that the ways in which it is sought themselves put it in jeopardy). The defining properties of friendship are intimacy ('a friend is a second self') and activity – doing something together, not just being together.

Already friendship defined in this way is beginning to be contrasted with Aristotle's other fundamental form of association, government. By the thirteenth century the theme had been developed sufficiently for Aquinas to speak of an established distinction between public and private societies, and to see friendship as the distinctive mode only of the latter. Thereafter serious social theory concerned itself more and more exclusively with government and the problems of public societies; friendship as a discussable form of social relationship survived only as an occasional and trivial theme for belles-lettrists. Communes are of interest if only because they are seriously attempting a revival of friendship as a form of public association. In the absence of any more recent guides to the sociology of friendship we will perhaps be excused for spending a little more time considering what Aristotle had to say about that sort of project.

He distinguishes between three bases of friendship which he calls utility, pleasure and goodness. Friendship involves finding one's happiness in the happiness of another – 'loving is more of the essence of friendship than being loved' – but the reciprocity of friendship means that one gets back what one gives. Friendship thus defined may exist within any form of social relationship; between husband and wife, parent and child, teacher and pupil, ruler and subject, between fellow students, fellow workers, soldiers or travelling companions. It need not exist in any particular relationship. Whether it does so will depend on the satisfaction of a number of conditions of which the most important are equality and activity; where friends are in a position to contribute equally to the reciprocity of the friendship, and where the friendship is enacted in a common project over and above the relationship itself. It follows that friendship is a matter of practice, not will: 'wishing to be friends is quick work, but friendship is a slow-ripening fruit'. Where the basis of the relationship is utility or pleasure – a self-regarding rather than an other-regarding value – the process of ripening is constantly threatened by the tendency of each party to interrupt the ongoing activity by impatient calculations of personal benefits and costs. So, too, when would-be friends relate on a basis of inequality.

What is required then, seems to be activity, equality and goodness. Goodness is an idea even harder to render in modern English than friendship. But what Aristotle seems to have had in mind in this context is that the relationship between friends is mediated by the attachment of each party to objective values which he or she finds embodied in the other. The insight that follows from this idea is that enduring friendship is based on self-love; 'the good man feels toward his friend as he feels towards himself'. In other words the communion of friendship presupposes self-knowledge and self-respect – a sufficient understanding of and confidence in oneself to love others for their own sake insofar as they display qualities which match or mirror or complement the qualities that are the anchor of one's own identity. To be capable of friendship one must first know and esteem oneself. Then one must engage on terms of equality in an active relationship through the enacting of which one experiences the goodness of others while demonstrating goodness to them. Whatever the difficulties of catching Aristotle's precise meaning here, the broad tendency of his argument contains psychological and sociological insights which seem to have stood the test of time. And because the conception of friendship that he advances – a non-utilitarian communion of strong selves vigorously

28

enacted on a basis of equality – is one which is echoed in strikingly similar ways throughout the contemporary commune movement, we may fairly take that conception as an essential statement of what communes are about. For the most part the commune movement has not found ways of talking about love that are as matter-of-fact or as empirically substantial as those of Aristotle. This is no doubt because of the spectre of romantic love which looms reproachfully over almost all our intimate relationships, particularly over those that attempt to substantiate the notion. Aristotle's conception of friendship falls somewhere between our idea of romantic love and our idea of friendship. The prime difference between romantic love and great friendship is that romantic love can only have one person as its object; friendship need not. It is a dissatisfaction with both that has led those in communes to seek the middle ground described by Aristotle, but this leads to considerable problems. Thus, Jerome (1975: 158) speaks of love as meaning 'that one trusts and forgives beyond reason', but has a hard time explaining just how people achieve that condition. Many members of the movement are frankly shy of making too much of 'the love bit'. On the other hand, as what they value is plainly stronger than what is meant in contemporary English by friendship, there is a difficulty in spelling out just what is meant without sounding silly, and it is one that baffles almost all advocates of communes. So Clem Gorman (1975: 41) ends an exceptionally careful and perceptive search for the secret of communality by abandoning analysis and saying simply: 'and at the bottom of it all, when all theories have been tried, there must be love'. The Aristotelian notion of friendship does seem to come closer than any other 'theory' we know to identifying what such statements mean.

But if it is fair, as we believe, to see the realisation of a classical idea of friendship as one of the distinctive and defining purposes of contemporary communalism, it is equally fair to take note of some of the obstacles to friendship which were also recognised by classical writers and to ask how far contemporary communes might be able to surmount them. Aristotle for one saw friendship as a highly precarious relationship. It was, as he understood it, threatened to the extent that the parties to a relationship were moved by utilitarian or hedonistic motives; it was threatened to the extent that their own selves were insecure; and it was threatened to the extent that their statuses were unequal. One might well consider that in the real world, and especially in the real world of modern capitalism, the prospect of any relationship's not being beset by some at least of these difficulties would be remote. In later chapters we shall consider the ways in which they do indeed beset, and are faced by, the members of communes. But there is one further obstacle to friendship which is hardly hinted at by earlier writers and yet which seems to us implicit in the classical notion of friendship and very explicitly realised in communes as a result of the distinctive way in which they seek to institutionalise and live that notion. This is the danger of treating the activity through which friendship is cemented and achieved as an end in itself and more important than the relationship or individuals that it is expressing: to use an obvious example, the achievement of remaining *married* becomes more important than being *together*. This danger of reification in which the essential content slips away to leave a prison-like form is one to which communes are especially vulnerable as a direct result of the way they go about institutionalising friendship. They do this through the peculiar medium of making a place to live together. Whatever else goes on the activity of place-making is indispensable. In the Aristotelian notion the 'essence of friendship is living together'. It is a measure of the commitment of communes to the idea of friendship that the making of a place in which to live together, and the ordering of the place so as to permit and express a particular way of living together, must be ranked first among the necessary conditions for the existence of a commune. But just as place-making, whether in the form of the city or the home, has always been a prime way of stating and embodying shared values, purposes and relationships, so it has also always been a peculiarly seductive way of reifying relationships and of imposing some people's values on others. The problem of friendship in communes is in large measure a question of at once devoting great energy to place-making and preventing place-making from becoming what it is all about.

The externality of places makes them peculiarly easy objects of reification. As Weber points out in his discussion of medieval cities (1968: 1212), spatial artefacts such as towns are brought into being architecturally, morally and legally in order to establish the social reality of particular strongly valued relationships; and the effective power of those relationships in relation to an outside world is enshrined in the place. Within the place the relationships that the place-makers want are made inviolate. But inside the town there are also relationships of power, and very quickly we find that the idea of the town, enacted in ceremonies, rituals and symbols of all kinds and enforced in the fiction of the town's legal personality, is being used by some town-dwellers – the *patricii* of Venice, the *Richerzeche* of Cologne, the guild-masters of Norwich – to establish new kinds of domination. The place is both an appropriation of freedom and a context of oppression; its structures and the accounts that its members give of it embody both. Place-making as a mean of liberation and self-expression required the objectification of the place – in the form of ramparts, charters, guildhalls, rules of membership, the cultivation of civic pride. But the further members went in such objectification, the more they found they had created a power over themselves; the forms of the place they had made were

30

increasingly used to limit the free flow of their activity – which is why in the end the medieval towns were *not* the scene of the industrial revolution. Towns and homes are the extreme and familiar examples of the hazards of place-making. But because communes are deeply and by definition engaged in place-making we would expect them to face them in almost equal degree. The danger is indeed often realised quite explicitly: 'The difference between the commune and the family has always been obvious. The commune is a *place*, an "alternative institution", which must of necessity give way to a more important and absolutely intrinsic social structure based in *individual people* and their relationships to each other . . . Place must always be second in priority to the people, otherwise the magic stops' (Diamond 1971: 98).

So much for formalities. We suggest that communes may be thought of, first and foremost, as attempts to institutionalise friendship on the basis of place-making. And that insofar as that is what they are doing they will face certain major problems – of hedonism, utilitarianism, inequality, self-consciousness and reification. We shall treat communes as though they were indeed this sort of project and trace the ways in which these difficulties occur and are successfully or unsuccessfully met. However, this view of communes is not entirely formal or fanciful. It emerged from our research and was only retrospectively imposed on it. Empirically it does seem to be what was distinctive about the commune movement that developed in the 1960s and in particular about the secular family communes that appeared within it. So we would say that for the purposes of understanding the commune movement the modest typification we have sketched will be useful both on grounds of simplicity and on grounds of pertinence.

One of the more dubious elements of our attempt to study communes was the questionnaire which we sent to seven hundred members of the Commune Movement late in 1972. Just over two hundred of these forms came back to us, and even though most of the people who replied did so very fully we are not going to pretend that anything we think we learned from the exercise has on its own any substantial value or should pass as knowledge. Nevertheless, even in this superficial skirmish with the world of communes, the emphasis on friendship, in the way we defined it, as the point of the commune movement, the emphasis on place-making as a condition for and expression of such friendship, and the emphasis on the connection between such a project and difficulties of the particular sort we have mentioned were powerful. We asked of course what people thought communal living had to offer. Four-fifths of those who answered stressed what we have called friendship: 'companionship', 'sharing my life with people I love', 'love, peace, companionship, togetherness', 'sharing at every level of existence', 'love, genuine interpersonal interaction', 'a family, but with people I've

chosen', 'a place where I can have real relationships', 'a genuine pooling of personalities', 'mutal development, particularly interpersonally'.
In the same measure it was understood that the troubles of communal
life would spring directly from the dialectics of friendship: 'Relationships between members are the only real difficulty'; 'People get on
each other's nerves'; 'anxiety, restlessness, personality conflicts'; 'Everyone has an ego; unless people are really *very* close it won't work';
'Many members don't feel sure enough of themselves to give much to
the rest of us'. Conversely: 'The difficulties of this way of life are the
lack of privacy and not being able to get away from the interrela-
tedness of it all'; 'Sometimes I feel the furniture in this place is as holy
as it was in my home'; 'A lot of the younger people who come here
can't bring themselves to put the place before themselves'; 'fear of total
loss of personality sometimes'; 'my selfishness and others' selfishness';
'conflicts due to trying to keep others happy and concealing one's own
negative feelings'; 'It's difficult to give as much as one knows one
should without wondering what's happening to your own identity';
'The people who want you to love them aren't always very lovable';
'There are times when I wonder what *I'm* getting out of it all.' What is
wanted is a self intimately involved with others and yet intact in itself;
the 'possibility of deep relationships with a number of other people,
self-discovery in a situation where one can experiment and develop'.
No one doubts that this is a difficult enterprise. Commonly a realistic
but positive attitude is taken to the prospect of a rough passage. The
Scylla and Charybdis of 'being eaten up by others' and 'untogetherness'
were seen as a challenge as well as a hazard: 'the interpersonal relationships which I expect to be valuable will be so partly because of the
difficulty in establishing and maintaining them; I see a correlation
between difficulty and value'. For a decisive majority the successful
navigation of this passage was just what communes were about.

One apparent difficulty for our approach should be mentioned
before we move on. It gave us a good deal of trouble for a time. We
found, both in the questionnaire responses and in our more substantial
work, an extraordinary emphasis on the *suppression* of ego. This is of
course quite at odds with the Aristotelian idea of friendship and also
with the widely held belief that the value of communes is that they
somehow allow one both to have a self and to be with others. Nevertheless, the idea of the need for a suppression of self, 'I-death' as
Jerome (1975: 162) and others call it, has emerged very strongly as
one conclusion from the practical experience of communes. It is much
stressed by both observers (Zablocki 1971: 239) and practitioners
(Mungo 1970: 114) of communalism. We make sense of it not by
modifying our view of what communes are about but by suggesting
that what happens in communes is that members discover how pro-

foundly disqualified they are, as a result of their pre-communal lives, for the friendship of equals in Aristotle's sense. In effect, the talk of I-death is not an indication that communes are about something other than friendship but a recognition of a very severe obstacle to friendship generated within contemporary capitalist society: 'most people, me included, are not ready to live communally . . . selfishness and hang-ups are inbred in all of us whilst in this present social structure' (Q.037). For all the mysticism and melodrama with which members of the commune movement speak of I-death – Jerome talks about 'composting the ego' and suicidal leaps, Mungo writes of chopping off his head in order to clear his throat – what is envisaged is not in our view that ultimate surrender of the self to the social that marks the sect or the secret society but a step towards the creation of selves strong enough to sustain friendship. Whether this can be done and how it is attempted are questions we shall consider at length. A great deal turns on the specific structure of the groups within which the attempt is made.

Structures and problems of communalism

Of the communal groups known to us only about half are communes in the sense we have defined them – groups devoted to communal living for its own sake as a way of institutionalising friendship within and around a chosen domestic place. What we call a commune is therefore only one variant among a multitude of diverse communal projects, even though it is a variant we would consider uniquely representative of the contemporary commune movement as a whole and uniquely indicative of the dilemmas of contemporary British society. Within limits it is possible to generalise about the structural forms developed by such groups. With reservations and allowance for a great many ambiguous cases it is possible to distinguish them from other types of communal enterprise.

There is to begin with an enormous penumbra of what may be called quasi-communes. The hallmark of the quasi-commune is its acknowledged transience; from the point of view of the members its existence is a matter of short-term pleasure or utility. It is this type of project that is so effectively described by Richard Mills: 'the flat was characterised by a relative informality of relationships and by the sharing of some property; like most of the situations in which hippies live it had an essentially *accidental* character; people stayed there when it was convenient to do so, moving in and out without plan or purpose; as the group was characterised by a lack of deliberate form and structure over time, so also through space' (Mills 1973: 113). Frank Howard, the self-appointed leader of the communal gathering on Eel

Pie Island, has explained in similar terms why that was not really a commune:

> This is a jumping off point for a lot of people. When I first came here a year ago I used to think it was important for people to have a place to get it together themselves. I still believe that. If people can come here and not have to do too much work like in the regular outside, then in a short space of time they can sort out what they want to do with their lives. They can come here and over a period of a month or so slow down; then they can go back into the society but not to a position they were in before. This is not a commune in the sense that it's not a place where the people are really together. Lots of people pass through this place on their way to the country to set up other communes or to travel elsewhere or just go it on their own or whatever they're going to do. This is okay. So we're just a stopping off point here, a reception centre for people until they find where they really want to go. (Fairfield 1972: 42)

Although we were aware of a great number of these quasi-communes we made no attempt to study them directly. In fact their main features and functions are quite easily discerned. It was noticeable that the members of communes often had a certain contempt for the members of quasi-communes and would draw our attention to the pattern of grandiose and irresponsible ideals combined with depressing practical incompetence which seemed to haunt the latter. Certainly it is the case that the members of communes tend to be young-middle-aged professional people in the first stages of family-building while the members of quasi-communes are most commonly much younger, without ties or formal skills and of working-class parentage. If a quasi-commune does begin to aspire to develop more lasting relationships (and we know some that did) the attempt almost always fails for lack of adequate financial resources. If a windfall should occur, such as the gift of Dorinish Island to Sid Rawle and his group of Diggers by John Lennon, superhuman results may be achieved – the hardiness of Rawle and his group drew admiration even from a reporter from the *News of the World*. But there are ideological as well as material and social differences. Quasi-communes have what might be called a deliberate sense of impermanence, a belief in living for the moment. They live in a surfeit of spontaneity which blocks any construction of permanent structures, negates the very idea of permanence. The one possible exception, suggested by Mills, is perhaps provided by those pop groups who coexist in a tightly, commercially and semi-permanently organised form for the paradoxical purpose of promoting a culture of living for the moment. More clearly within the ambit of quasi-communes are those countless groups which are communes while their members are students and those groups cohering atomistically around the consumption of hallucinogenic drugs – possibly very numerous in the United States (Speck 1972) but either rather uncommon or very successfully invisible in Britain.

Quasi-communes seem to have three main functions. They are frequently the first refuge of those who have rejected, for the moment, the social definitions thrust upon them by their background. They are often a haven for those who for whatever reason have lost faith in, or the ability to tolerate, permanence, routine and stable social organisation. And they serve as a testing-ground, an incomplete point of induction, for many who are trying to decide whether to join a commune. It would not be inappropriate to call them sites of passage.

Communes differ from quasi-communes in the deeper level of investment of their members and the greater intensity of their organisation. Because they are older, and because they are more frequently middle-class, commune members have more to give and more to lose, and they wish their lives to be more rooted – rooted but not tied down and rigid. Because the dividing-line between communes and quasi-communes is vague and shifting, a distinctive problem for communes arises from the constant influx of people who may be looking for a commune or may be looking for a quasi-commune; such people must be welcomed, but if they fail to pull their weight (that is the sort of phrase that is used) there must also be ways of getting rid of them. At the same time communes resemble quasi-communes in the essentially individualistic basis of their existence. The members of communes have made a different calculation about the conditions under which self-realisation is possible. Intuitively, rather than in an explicit, reasoned-out manner, they have decided that self presupposes some sort of society; their project is to create the right kind of society, a society of friends, in order to be themselves. They see a symbiosis of self and others where the members of quasi-communes see an antagonism or at best a utilitarian opportunity. But their individualism, which links them to quasi-communes, also separates them from a further type of communal project which may be called the utopian community. Some of the best writing about communalism has in fact been almost exclusively concerned with this type of project (Zablocki 1971; Kanter 1972 and 1974) and has tended to engulf all communal experiments within the experience of the utopian community. Yet communes are profoundly unlike utopian communities just as they are unlike quasi-communes.

The idea of friendship envisages an enrichment of self through interaction with others who are in effect second selves. The utopian community seeks to create an instituted social order existing over and above its individual members and on the basis of the willed subordination of their selves. Kanter's account of such communities strikes us as

35

very apt. She emphasises their ideological and social elaboration and completeness and their sense of a mission to establish a new social dispensation. What strikes one about communes by contrast is that the common theme of individual development is *not* elaborated into an inclusive ideology which relates all aspects of life, giving the group an adequate framework of action for all situations, an ontology, epistemology and a sense of where the group is going. There is a groping, tentative quality about social interaction in a commune which suggests the encounter rather than the establishment, a continuous testing of others indicating that the unity of meaning within the group is uncertain, fluid and problematic. In the utopian community the individual does not relate directly to other individuals in a sea of uncertainty of this sort but indirectly by way of an already achieved and known account of what relationships should be like. As Kanter puts it:

> A utopian community seeks self-determination, often making its own laws and refusing to obey some of those set by the larger society. It is identifiable as an entity, having both physical and social boundaries. It intentionally implements a set of values, having been planned in order to bring about the attainment of certain ideals, and its operating decisions are made in terms of those values. Its primary end is an existence that matches the ideals. All other goals are secondary and related to ends involving harmony, brotherhood, mutual support and value expression. The utopian community may also be a centralised, coordinating organisation, often combining all of life's functions under one roof. (1972: 2-3)

Accordingly, the bonding of members of a utopian community is not a matter of conditional negotiation, exploration, tentative affirmation or withdrawal, but of strong and deep commitment, self-denial and renunciation in the name of higher purposes. Above all, the utopian community is one that has been established socially as 'an entity' with strong boundaries and strong identity – in other words, it is a place that has become a thing, a social force separable from its members. Its essential features, like those of the quasi-commune, are ones the commune seeks at all costs to avoid.

Not surprisingly, Kanter recognises that her analysis of the utopian community has little grip on the contemporary commune movement. What we observe today, she notes, is a proliferation of groups which do indeed 'share property, close relations and a livelihood' but which lack an ideology of the old sort and which 'resemble an extended family more than a utopian community – a family of brothers and sisters without parents', and which 'develop from friendship rather than groups welded together by an ideology' so that 'the personal and the intuitive define the quality of life'. Here then, midway between the quasi-commune and the utopian community, is the commune, or more specifically the secular family commune, a phenomenon to be studied and explained in its own right. One might say that the quasi-commune takes its force from the conventional idea of friendship, whereas the utopian community attempts to inspire in its members an emotion towards it akin to romantic love. Advocates and interpreters of the quasi-commune find its viability and value in the way in which it embraces the accidental and the impermanent. Advocates and interpreters of the utopian community find its viability and value in the commitment of its members to an instituted transformative social order. The commune proposes a viable and valuable existence which dispenses with both of these qualities. Neither the literature on quasi-communes nor that on utopian communities would lead one to think that such a proposal could easily be made good.

When we have set aside utopian communities and quasi-communes, there is still a great deal of communal activity left. At this point distinctions related to the specific focus of activity or to the degree of ideological commitment or to the relative importance of internal and external interests are commonly introduced. Thus Jerome speaks of creedal and non-creedal communes and of internally and externally oriented communes. Skolnick (1973: 140) distinguishes between religious and secular communes and between urban and rural communes. Our own modal commune is plainly one that has a relatively strong internal orientation; the cultivation of relationships within the commune tends to be the most important thing in the lives of the members; and it is secular and ideologically undeveloped rather than religious, creedal or ideologically elaborate. We can thus distinguish it not only from quasi-communes and utopian communities but also from a further general type of communal project which we will call the purposive commune. Many of the communes we visited were groups of people who were living together in order to do something else, to promote a cause or realise a faith or effect a cure. Communality was for these groups a significant means, perhaps even a necessary condition, of succeeding at this purpose. But in the communes in which we became most interested communalism was its own purpose; the groups lived together simply in order to live together, on account of the goodness of living together. Whatever projects of an economic, moral or political nature might be devised to sustain the group were in principle subordinate to the existence of the group. In religious communes and communities, in therapeutic communities and in groups such as the women's communes we found in several large cities, it always seemed to be understood that in the last resort communality was subordinate to the interests of faith or therapy or liberation. In practice the distinction between family communes and purposive communes is hard to maintain; the question of what constitutes being cured in many therapeutic communities is remarkably akin to the question of what constitutes a true mutuality of self and others in many family communes; many of the religious communities we visited make helping others the test of faith to such an extent that their religion often seems to depend on their relationships. Nevertheless, we feel that the distinction is important. In principle at least, the purposive commune is equipped with an idea which counts for more than its members and can be used to guide, transform and discipline them in a way that the family commune is not and cannot be. To this extent the purposive commune does not have to face all the implications of pure communalism as the family communes do. They can indeed, as Sugarman has shown in the case of some therapeutic communities (1975: 141-61) avoid them very effectively by imposing their purposes on their members in thoroughly authoritarian ways. The advantages of making purposes more important than people from the point of view of stability, collective achievement and the well-being of the powerful are great, and most family communes are chronically tempted by them. Not quite surrendering to that temptation is a hallmark of the family commune.

We thus envisage four general types of communal project, the quasi-commune, the utopian community, the purposive commune and the family commune. Because communalism is for the latter an end in itself, or, to put it another way, because there are some groups in the contemporary commune which exist precariously by treating communalism as an end in itself, we have chosen to concentrate on this one type. But it is largely through implicit or explicit comparison with the other types that we shall understand the distinctiveness of the type that interests us. Within this framework it is possible at the outset to say a number of things about the ecological, economic, moral and social characteristics of such groups.

The most complete commune would be one in which the group shared a single dwelling or tightly integrated cluster of dwellings and the basic services within it. All areas of activity would be common and so would property. The group would earn its living together and divide all that it earned equally, and all surplus would be available to all members. The group would constitute the circle of best friends for all its members, and the functions of the family would be concentrated within it; the depth and range of emotional interaction between the members would be great. Stable couples would not be recognised, and many different lines of relationship would be possible. Children would be regarded as children of the group as a whole, and everyone, including the children themselves from an early age, would have an equal say in their upbringing. The ethos of the group would not be formulated ideologically but would be strongly supportive of its life-style and of the values of mutuality. Decision-making would be achieved through universal participation and assent. Leadership would be an irrelevance. The members would see communes as an answer to many if not all of the social problems they considered important in the outside world. The commune would be felt to be a lifetime undertaking. Needless to say, we know of no such communes.

On the other hand, all the communes we know may usefully be seen as seeking to approximate to such a condition. There may well be considerable retention of private ownership; members may have their special, personal areas within the commune; clothes and even consumer durables may continue to belong to individual members; they may not pool their wealth but pay an agreed amount regularly into a common fund; pair relations may well be not just tolerated but the emotional backbone of the commune; beliefs about the value of communalism may well be modest and highly personalised – the commune provides *us* with better and richer relationships and is vaguely 'good for the children'. What is essential is that there is a sense of group identity, that the members want to be the best of friends and that the group is expected to function as a household and a family; but also that it is expected to function as a world in the sense that the majority of each member's social interaction, or at least that part of it which is felt to be deeply important, takes place within the group.

So far as size is concerned, it is a well-confirmed observation that in practice communes of this type tend to have between five and twenty-five adult members both in this country and in the United States. Perhaps five is the minimum number required to break the conventions of monogamous pairing and private life and to sustain a sufficient variety of relationships for the issue of mutuality to become both important and challenging. Certainly twenty-five seems to be the limit beyond which the diffusion of intense relationships among all members of a group ceases to be possible. So long as friendship is what a commune is about it will remain firmly within this range of membership. Both quasi-communes and utopian communities can manage to be very much larger, being institutionalised either on the basis of a lack of enduring investment in the personal relationships between the members or on the basis of ideologically autonomous power.

Communes do not achieve their optimum size naturally. What tends to happen – and this may be the most important single feature of the structure of communes – is that a small group of members who may be the founders but may equally well include latecomers who have proved exceptionally devoted to the spirit of the commune, constitute a core around which many other would-be members come and go. The basic structure of a commune consists of a core and a fringe. At Lee Abbey, one of the largest religious communities we visited, the structure is manifested quite blatantly in the wearing of lapel badges: red for full members, green for probationary members and white for visitors. This degree of distinction is exceptional, but the structure it symbolises seems unavoidable. And this is one of the many respects in which purposive communes find social structure easier to live with than family communes. For the former the pattern of core and fringe can be interpreted as expressing the successful pursuit of the communes' purpose. For the latter the appearance of persistence of such a pattern can only be problematic. It is doubly problematic because the pattern does seem to persist even when the situation of particular individuals within it changes. The fringe changes constantly, and the core may also change as original members become disenchanted or caught up in new projects or as newcomers slowly make their way from the fringe to the core. Outright usurpation may also occur—we know of at least one case in which the entire group of founding members found the 'demands' of six newcomers so unbearable that they all moved out, leaving the erstwhile fringe in possession. Given the structure of core and fringe, however, it follows that communes will develop procedures for joining and leaving. There must be entry arrangements, however implicit, which allow new members to win the approval of the existing members. And there must be mechanisms of extrusion which will enable the group to make the continued membership of a difficult individual impossible. The fact that communes are neither legally nor ideologically firmly sanctioned and defined (unlike marriages on the one hand and utopian communities on the other) means that, essential as these procedures are, they are characteristically vague and fluctuating. Members find it difficult to describe them and may not in any conscious sense know them. Insofar as the criteria governing these processes are perceived, they will tend to be economic, ideological or personal; but the more nearly a commune approximates to our idea of a typical commune the more strongly purely personal factors will be emphasised. The failure of rapport between the group and a particular individual has to be laid at the door of the individual as a person; non-admission or expulsion will be interpreted in terms of selfishness, irresponsibility or hang-ups. Any other account would involve the group in recognising the rather severely conditional nature of its own practice of mutuality. The decisive consideration in relation to both joining and leaving will be to interpret the event in ways that affirm the relationships within the core of the group. Because this cannot be done through an appeal to rules or even to the agreed principles of a formally stated and apparently independent ideology, communes often seem to be extraordinarily harsh in their dealings with individuals; what matters has to be what is good for those who are there when the newcomers arrive and who remain when the ex-member has left. Thus, since a departure cannot be the fault of the group, there can be little question of any sort of 'reasonable compensation' for the time, skill, involvement and energy a departing member may have given a commune. Typically, departures are arranged in such a way as to be more painful for those who depart than for those who stay.

There must also be procedures for affirming the identity of the group and for establishing its 'goodness' (to use Aristotle's term) over and above the particular relationships which from moment to moment make it up. Here again, the relative lack of either an overt ideology of the kind that defines the utopian community, or the machinery of myth and enforcement, the fairy tale and the divorce court, that turns social relationships into social facts in the case of marriage, leaves communes to manage the task of establishing the group in a distinctively tentative, informal way. When a commune is working well, the mechanisms in question will be experienced simply as some of the more obviously pleasant and pleasurable facets of communal living, the sort of thing one readily points out to visitors. The two that occur again and again are the group evening meal and any sort of common project for improving the place. The importance of the shared making and eating of meals is obvious enough; it acquires a special value as a context of solidarity when a group has little other institutional definition and when so much of the rest of the members' lives is based on personal rather than common skills and resources. The pursuit of a common project 'for the place' rather than for any particular members, whether it is converting a disused barn to make more rooms, redesigning and re-equipping the kitchen or trying to raise a crop of beans for the market, manifests togetherness still more effectively. Conversely of course, the actual quality of interaction (and food) at the common meal and the extent to which common projects actually get accomplished are in our experience two of the best indicators of the real moral state of a commune. Insofar as we had a clear sense of method in our research, one strand of it involved 'situational analysis' of the kind advocated by Van Velsen (Epstein 1967: 129-49). That is to say, we tried to be particularly attentive to the issue of normative conflict beneath the surface of communal life and hence to take particular notice of disputes, quarrels and other episodes of tension and dissensus in the belief that we could in that way hope to glimpse the submerged structure of communal society and understand it as a system of more or less well-managed contradictions arising from more or less unacknowledged conflicts of norms. In this respect we believe we did learn substantially both from the tone and style of communal meals and from the progress or lack of it of collective place-making projects.

What we gleaned from a great deal of conversational sniping, sarcasm, non-participation and accusations of selfishness ('coverting the left is clive's ego-trip, it's got nothing to do with the rest of us') was a

41

sense of a fundamental structural fault in communes which can be described as a conflict between the idea of friendship as being and the idea of friendship as having. We develop this theme at length in chapter 4 and again in chapter 7. Having is possibly the master trait of middle-class personality in our society. The fact that it is illegitimate within the ethos of a commune means, not that it is in fact abolished, but that every member is constantly suspicious of being taken over (had?) by others even while failing fully to suppress his or her own tendencies to take over them. In this sense communes express a curious revulsion on the part of at least some middle-class people from the civilisation which is distinctively that of the middle class. The revulsion itself is not new. It was Rimbaud who said, 'For the civilised individual all that matters is *to have*. And what the *I* has must be taken by it *from others*.' The attempt to use communal living as a way of leaping into a new moral order in this respect does, however, face people who have been made within such a civilisation with a certain dilemma – the dilemma of at once being and not being themselves.

Beyond this point the common structural features of communes are difficult to specify. Plainly there will be some sort of common economy. The simplest thing would be for each member to give everything he or she has or earns to the commune, drawing on the common fund according to need. This is only superficially easy. Possibly, again, it is a result of the extent to which personal identity is bound up with personal possessions that communes must make some sort of serious effort at economic sharing (to demonstrate the authentic communality of the commune), but almost always stop short of a complete communism and instead devise a variety of elaborate schemes which establish the principle of common contributions and common benefits while actually leaving substantial resources in the private control of those members lucky enough to have them. Again, there will be at least a loosely agreed scheme for the sharing of work. Strict egalitarianism is perhaps more important or more possible in this respect than in the case of income and ownership; certainly communes devote a good deal of care to the creation of such schemes, and equity if not equality is meticulously sought and on the whole achieved. Similarly, and despite the great variety of houses communes occupy, there are the rudiments of a common internal ecology. Buildings are made over to allow all members to participate in the cooking and eating of meals and to spend leisure time together. Conversely, personal private space tends to be reduced to a minimum. Generally communes develop more facilities such as libraries, workshops, studios, play areas, music rooms on their premises than are found in even the largest private home; a sense of spaces being defined for collective use tends to emerge. In any commune there appear to be three such areas of essential importance, the kitchen, a sitting room where everyone can chat, play records or simply be together, and a place for eating. Even if people have their own bedrooms these rooms may not be regarded as private space but be open to anyone during the day. The problem implicit in these arrangements is of course the problem of privacy. The constant giving that is called for in communal relationships is an exacting business, and members of communes, especially members of the core groups, never tired of telling us how much they needed, or if they had it, appreciated, some corner of private space to which they could retreat to rest, think and renew their energies.

Finally there will be some arrangements for common decision-making. These may involve the belief that decision-making has been abolished and that what happens to the commune merely happens – although it will be conceded that things are, for example, 'talked over' at the common meals. Or they may involve a well-formalised system of regular meetings, with or without voting, organised discussion and the keeping of minutes. Encounter sessions or other kinds of mutual discovery experiences may be seen as an essential part of this process. The less ideologically self-conscious a commune is, the more it will tend towards informality in decision-making, although there are exceptions, because what is striking about communes is the variety and pace of their changes in structure in the area of decision-making. This protean character must reflect a basic uneasiness with any version of the process. Formal or informal, however, the problem that must be accommodated by the procedures of decision-making is the problem of leadership. The easiest way of solving most of the other problems of a commune is to allow a structure of leadership to emerge in which one or two members, either because of the unique understanding they are held to enjoy of the communal ethos or because they are willing and able to monopolise certain essential tasks or resources, are allowed to mediate the flow of relationships and with increasing authority to shape the course of events. Unfortunately, although common, this restructuring of the commune is bound to threaten the principle of mutuality as other members, especially those on the fringe of the commune, understand it. Probably the commonest reason given for leaving a commune is somebody else's dominance. Yet communes are again and again driven to evolve leadership. At worst it is less undesirable than surrendering the direct experience of other people to the indirect experience offered by a mystical ideology. At best one will find the sort of leader whose leadership is experienced not as dominance but as an invigorating and expansive energy. At least the dilemma is well understood. Steve Diamond speaks for many groups when he ends his account of the Chestnut Hill Commune by saying:

What is required is that we unite with others, in order that all may complement and aid one another through holding together. But such holding together calls for a central figure around whom other persons may unite. To become a centre of influence holding people together is a grave matter and fraught with grave responsibility. It requires greatness of spirit, consistency and strength. Therefore let him who wishes to gather others about him ask himself whether he is equal to the undertaking, for anyone attempting the task without a real calling for it only makes confusion worse than if no union at all had taken place. (Diamond 1971: 174)

But to understand the issue is not to be able to solve the problem. Most of the communes we visited were struggling with the question of leadership. Few had mastered it. Those that had given themselves to a leader were without exception remarkably intolerant places.

There is in fact a double problem here. The absence of leadership can generate a demoralising sense of aimlessness as easily as leadership can create an impression of domination. Younger members, particularly, sometimes feel that their idealism is draining away into the sands of endless discussions and evasions of decisive action. Thus, one member of a well-established commune who left and then joined the Divine Light Mission explained how the deepening impatience that had led him to leave had reached a point where he no longer had any idea why the commune existed or what the members were doing together. Again, given that the resistance to ideology means that a commune has little or no clearly defined vision to hold on to, minor personal shortcomings and trivial organisational failures escalate into major crises of meaning and purpose. In such situations the need for leadership is often keenly felt. People do need help in determining how self-interest and common interest can be reconciled in such situations, if not from a book of rules or a creed then from a respected and sympathetic third party. But the leaders that arise, whether to mediate these crises or to implement decisions that have been consensually approved but remain unenacted, cannot base their leadership upon a constitution or doctrine independent of themselves. They must rely, exhaustingly, upon their own personal qualities. If they become personally disliked they have no refuge in appeal to the idea of their position or to the argument that they are good at the job. In a commune, being good at the job of leadership means being personally liked. The affective and instrumental tasks of leadership are completely fused, and the affective side is paramount. Commune members are in the unenviable position of at once seeing the need for leadership and making it all but impossible for leadership to be provided. In such a predicament leaders either wear themselves out in the attempt to lead in ways that are compatible with the ethos of the communes or they

44

tend to stabilise their authority on the basis of economic or ideological power of a kind that profoundly subverts that ethos.

A commune, then, is a relatively and intentionally stable group of between five and twenty-five adults with whatever children they may happen to have, recruited from more than one nuclear family and strongly, but conditionally, committed to living together and sharing as much as possible of their lives. They share the work of the common household or complex of households in which they permanently live. Ideally, group life has primacy over all other except, possibly, that of couples of mixed or the same sex, and their home is designed to further this group life and allow many collective activities and at least communal eating. The group is bound together morally and economically, and interaction in both these respects will proceed in a spirit of tentative and exploratory mutuality. There will be sufficient resources to maintain group cohesion in the face of considerable internal strain and external pressure. The importance of communes lies in the claim they advance that people such as they are in a society such as ours can create circumstances in which it is possible to institutionalise friendship – in a remarkably full and generous sense of that word.

Before we leave this cursory and general account of the object of our research and take up some more specific matters, something should be said about the way in which the members of communes themselves see the world around them. Just as the commune may be thought of as an attempt to do away with social structure, and in particular the structure of the family, and substitute relationships that are open, direct and unpredictable, so the larger world is seen as curiously lacking in structure. We shall come back to this point in chapter 5. But at the outset we want to stress that the same voluntarism that inspires members of communes to undertake the experiments they believe in – the belief that if one tries hard enough one can be different – colours their view of the world as a whole. Thus, capitalism is not seen as a complex, historically produced system of social relations and constraints but as a way of life, something that happens because people are selfish or short-sighted enough to want it to happen; if they could be persuaded to want something different, they could have something different. Changing the world is therefore a matter of changing people's ideas: 'The question is really how best to combat reactionary attitudes' (*Communes*, 35: 14). On this basis celebrations of freedom by champions of capitalist enterprise can be applauded; strike action by organised workers can be deplored. Political attitudes are typically unfocussed and variable; everything is premised on voluntarism and a diffuse underlying belief in other people's ultimate good will. Perhaps the connectedness of such views of the external world to the internal struc-

45

tural problems of communes can be illustrated by mentioning that the one commune we visited which did seem to have a thoroughgoing revolutionary understanding of British society as a system alterable only on the basis of prolonged organised struggle was also characterised by the fact that it had developed an elaborated and explicit ideology to govern its internal social relations and that that ideology included a justification for a high degree of structural closure, a strict hierarchy and strong leadership – all of which were indeed powerfully present. The obverse and more typically communal situation is one in which suspicion of ideology and resistance to leadership go hand in hand with a mildly anarchistic denial of significant structure outside; the corruptness of power rather than the intransigence of interests is what tends to be stressed. Internally, therefore, members are reluctant to let themselves be seduced into positions of leadership – as both power-seeking and the exercise of power pervert true individuality. But the structural gap is not left unfilled. What tends to happen is that as a result of the refusal to contemplate the problem of power structurally, the principles that determine the distribution of power in the larger society insidiously make themselves felt within the commune too. Leadership is not evolved in a random way but concentrates in almost all cases in the hands of those members who would be judged powerful in the crudest external terms – those who own the building or contributed most to buying it or who have the largest incomes or do what is deemed to be the most essential work or have established the widest reputation in the general counter-cultural world. The relationships that would dominate in the outside world insinuate themselves within the group; and they do so the more easily the more resistant the group is to general ideological analysis. In this respect at least the distinctive attempt of the commune to be at once ideologically withdrawn from the world and structurally open or at least indifferent to it is a hazardous if not a doomed enterprise.

Yet there is one way in which the belief in the possibility of ideological insulation is not a fantasy – and it is one that perhaps goes a long way to explain the ideological innocence of most communes. Communes by and large are not persecuted. They have their difficulties with 'bureaucracy' of course, and they share conventional radical attitudes about government and the police. But for the most part they are not themselves victims of oppression. Some communes do get busted and some commune members find themselves serving quite substantial prison sentences for drug offences – and the experience of apprehension, trial and detention tends to have a wonderfully hardening and radicalising effect. But generally the communal use of drugs is above all discreet. Many communes profess not to tolerate drugs, or alcohol, at all. Such use as there is is never flaunted. In this respect at least, an essential feature of the commune is that it really is effectively screened from the world, disengaged. To the extent that their activities are deviant they are deviant in a very untroublesome way – and cushioned by the belief that it is only a matter of time until everyone gets round to seeing things their way. Communes may be at odds with capitalist society; they do not see themselves as being in conflict with it.

This uncertain relationship is well exemplified in the typical economic experience of communes. The communal ideal of work is one that directly reflects the general ethos of the commune movement. As a spokesman for one group put it: 'Our aim is to establish a working example of an alternative to the present economic system – an alternative based on love and mutual aid rather than the profit motive and status-seeking of individuals. Thus we work for nothing and our products and services will be free' (*Communes*, 35: 12). Or again: 'What we are really thinking about is the achievement of a life style in which work for money is irrelevant' (*Communes*, 34: 8). The rhythm of work would be that natural but dramatic pattern envisaged by E. P. Thompson (1967), the fluctuations of lassitude and periods of ceaseless, intense activity indicative of true personal control of one's work situation. The vision of the eventual transformation of Britain into a federated society of communes involves the idea of a barter economy based on cooperative handicraft production – but even barter would be kept to a minimum as all the communes involved would try to be self-sufficient. Many individual communes do indeed engage in handicraft production and sometimes try to live from their products, either producing directly for themselves or for the market. Whichever they do, they are presented with a number of problems, however. To begin with, there are the problems that arise from inexperience. The skills required for effective craft production or even for subsistence farming are formidable, and enthusiasm is not a substitute for them. Even the limited aim of self-sufficiency in food requires deep reserves of skill, capital and time – as it takes about three years to work the sort of land a commune can hope to acquire into any sort of productive shape. We came across many deserted communes where this lesson had been learned the hard way. Ferna Rosa, for example, was an abandoned smallholding perched on a hillside in the Forest of Dean; it had to be approached on foot along a track overgrown with wild roses. Later in the year there would be a riot of blackberries; once the house was reached, the views on all sides were a miracle of space, peace and green. But the ground attached immediately to the house was rocky, barren, a ruin of steep embankments and collapsed terraces; the soil was thin and porous and there was no nearby supply of water. Three different groups had tried to establish a commune there in the two years before our visit. None had been able to mobilise the capital, machinery

47

or energy that would have been needed to restore the land. The latest group had bought the place in October, moved in in November and were destitute before the time came to sow the plants they had hoped to harvest the following summer.

Nor is the actual rhythm of work required by subsistence farming or craft production for a market in any way like the ideal. Both, if they are to be successful, impose an insistent continuous pace; they are, indeed, bound by routine. Bursts of joyous enthusiasm are, again, not enough. Then, too, there are the problems that arise from the commune's unavoidable competition with machine-made produce or agriculture conducted on a business basis, a competition which means that commune members must either charge very high prices or work fearfully long hours or suffer a harshly depressed standard of living, and sometimes all three together. Such experiences are difficult to reconcile with the hope of striking a new and more genuine bond between people and their work. In practice, too, many communes find themselves producing goods that their own members cannot afford. If their economic projects prosper it is because they have found a market among the comfortably off, and the more determined they are to succeed economically the more ruthlessly they are driven into finding and cultivating such markets. Although the oddness of this state of affairs is often appreciated as a rather sick joke, the powerfulness of the structures of the external economy which is implicit in it is seldom realised. What tends to happen instead is that some if not all of the members continue to hold jobs firmly within that economy for the sake of the income that such jobs yield to the commune. This arrangement in turn gives rise to innumerable small but keen anxieties or jealousies centred on the problem of establishing some sort of equation between different members' contributions to the collective well-being. In the extreme case, if all members go out to work, the quality of the life of the group inevitably suffers. If one or two members stay in the commune to look after the place and the children while the others work outside, the people who are left at home tend to feel they are mere servants of the rest. One solution to this sort of problem is to live on supplementary benefit or student grants. Neither is particularly conducive to group morale or to a high standard of living; nor are they indeed easy to come by in the typical domestic circumstances of communes. Another solution is to treat outside work in a highly instrumental way, working when money is needed for the commune, easing off when it is not. Unfortunately, the only category of people who can raise a substantial income on that basis are free-lance professional workers and those without ties or dependents – which rather limits the availability of communal living.

In fact the problems are not as black and white as this; many viable

48

compromises can be worked out. Having discussed the structure and problems of communes in principle, we must now plainly consider the patterns of living they actually revealed to us. In this chapter we have tried to do two things: to identify the commune as an object of study – both as an empirically given phenomenon and as a formal type of social relationship, and to indicate the key structural properties and problems which communes as a distinct object of study present. We have emphasised three general themes: that communes may be understood as attempts to institutionalise friendship on the basis of place-making; that at an immediate, observational level the decisive feature of the structure of communes consists of the combination of a core and a fringe; and that at a rather deeper level an important reality of communes is their effort to be both ideologically withdrawn from and structurally open to the outside world. We suggest that most of the problems of communes, and their prospects of success or failure, flow from these three general characteristics.

3. *Some communes*

If you came this way
Taking any route, starting from anywhere,
At any time or at any season
It would always be the same; you would have to put off
Sense and notion. You are not here to verify,
Instruct yourself, or inform curiosity
Or carry report. You are here to kneel
Where prayer has been valid.

Eliot, 'Little Gidding', *Four Quartets*

It is not only prayer that shames rational inquiry. Eliot's response to the memory of Nicholas Ferrar's community at Little Gidding is evoked even in the sociologist by the integrity of many contemporary communal projects. We have borrowed his words to open this chapter because we are aware of the affront it perpetrates. We *were* there to instruct ourselves and inform curiosity, and in carrying report we shall certainly belittle the validity of the lives we were allowed to witness. The point is emphasised for us by the fact that one of the groups that was most helpful to us in forming our report, the Pilsdon Community in Dorset, is explicitly inspired by and modelled on the experience of Little Gidding. Our difficulty is that we do want to talk about communes in a language for which 'verify' is an important verb – the language of social theory – and we must somehow ground our argument in what was presented to us by actual communes. But we know perfectly well that what was presented to us was incomplete and that what we have made of it has been made by us, not them. What follows is not, therefore, a description of some of the communes we visited but an account of them, our account. Description is the hardest part of social science, and to describe adequately even a single commune would be a task of enormous length and complexity calling for an author who could participate equally in all the different points of view within a many-sided and constantly changing relationship. Nothing of that sort is attempted here. The accounts we offer are meant to be detailed enough to give some substance to our general interpretation of the nature and problems of communes, but they come nowhere near to giving a full or adequate picture of the wholeness of communal experience. They are carefully observed but selective sketches. What is stressed in them is not necessarily what the members of the communes themselves would have stressed but what seemed to us indicative of the processes through which some communal projects were working themselves out.

Many of the communes we visited and discuss in other chapters of this book have been described at length elsewhere by their own members or by other observers. Thus, the Kingsway Community, a Christian therapeutic community of particular interest for the way in which it was reluctantly forced to abandon openness for authority, and the Postlip Hall commune, unashamedly middle-class and hovering uneasily on the edge of genuine communalism, have both been discussed in some detail by Andrew Rigby (1974b). So has the Shrubb Family Commune, which has also been described by one of its own members (Cockerton 1972: 8-12). The commune we call Fern Hill is discussed by Armytage and also in a book by one of its own members. Beshara, the Sufi community in Gloucestershire which we shall also mention quite frequently, has, again, been written about extensively elsewhere and produces a good deal of literature about itself. Purposive communes, especially religious and therapeutic communities, have attracted many case studies and analyses. So, too, have utopian communities and quasi-communes. Family communes have been less subjected to formal observation by outsiders, although they are the main concern of writers in *Communes*. So we see no need here to try to amplify the broad view of what British communes are like which Rigby, Gorman and others have established. Our accounts are intended, however, to suggest the distinctiveness of family communes as compared to other types of communalism and in particular, since a conventional wisdom has emerged – see, for example Whitworth

(1975) – which tends to absorb all communes into the field of religious phenomena or else to dismiss them as epiphenomena, to suggest that there are serious communal projects which cannot be fully understood either as sects or as trips and which are significant on their own terms as attempts to change the nature of private life, the world of family and friendship, within the framework of industrial capitalism. Ideally we should have included accounts of other types of communalism for purposes of comparison. But perhaps the work of Jones (1975) and Sugarman (1975) on therapeutic communities as a species of purposive commune, of Mills on quasi-communes (1973) and of Zablocki (1971) and Kanter (1972) on utopian communities are accessible enough. One source of comparison we felt we had to include, however. At the end of this chapter we give an account of the Findhorn Community. Findhorn has been described and discussed extensively by Rigby and in its own widely distributed publications; it is probably the best-known of British communal projects. Nevertheless, we have chosen to give our own account of it; partly because Findhorn has exercised very real influence on the commune movement as a whole – members of many other groups have passed through Findhorn and been inspired or informed by it; partly because we found it impossible to decide where Findhorn belongs in terms of our sense of the types of communalism and because the way in which it mixes aspects of the family commune with aspects of all three other types serves to emphasise both the uniqueness of family communes as a type of project and the difference between the real world and certain kinds of academic ideas; and partly because there is something irreducibly baffling about Findhorn, at least from our own rationalistic point of view, and our inability to master it, while itself of academic interest, goes some way to rescue the validity of communal lives from the erosions of social science.

When visiting communes we allowed each visit to develop its own pattern. Our accounts are based on diaries, reports and records of conversations written up by ourselves during or immediately after our visits and on letters, histories and other writings sent to us over the period of our research by individual members of communes. Nevertheless, we did know what we wanted to know – observation and interpretation being sides of one coin – and within the pattern of each visit, however it might develop, we tried to organise our observations in relation to a common checklist of questions about the history, ecology, social composition and structure of the commune, its relations with the outside world and its economic arrangements and ideological style. Within the loose discipline of the checklist we instructed ourselves to expect communal life to be, like that of larger societies, incoherent and many-layered. And so we aimed to attend in particular to those patterned or recurring episodes of togetherness or tension which might help us to grasp the complex of inconsistent and vaguely formulated expectations and principles constituting communal society as a whole. To this extent we would argue that the only assumption that can clearly be said to have predetermined our observations was the assumption that communes were societies.

Because the accounts that follow are selective and because publicity is no favour to a commune, we have in all cases except that of Findhorn changed the names and locations of the communes we discuss as well as the names and some other details of their members. In some cases we have gone further than this in modifying the external details of the life of particular groups. But the essential relationships, purposes and situations are presented as we saw them. For this reason the disguises we have used may well be, or seem to be, transparent to readers who are fairly closely involved in the commune movement. But there would have been little point to a chapter claiming to record the actuality of communes unless we had taken that risk. The purpose of a disguise is not to make one invisible but to introduce a significant different, to alienate in a Brechtian sense, not to conceal. And in this case the alienation is unavoidable anyway; our interpretation has to stand between the reader and the reality.

Family Farm

We visited this commune six times over a period of two years. The house is a large, seventeenth-century farmhouse on the edge of a medium-sized village in the heart of Somerset. There are several outbuildings in various stages of repair, including an old barn the roof of which had collapsed at the time of our first visit. All these buildings are designated as being of historical interest, and planning permission for structural changes or even for changes of use had initially been refused – to the frustration of the founding members, who had hoped to use the barn as a workshop for a small precision-engineering enterprise. The house was originally bought for £16,250 by four of the founding members, using their savings together with a gift of over £3,000 from a friend who did not join. The founder-members set up a limited company to own the house so that other residents could later on share in the ownership – at a price of £100 a share.

The house is surrounded by about two acres of land; fruit trees, conifers and shrubs have been planted to the front; most of the land at the rear is devoted to vegetables grown for the household and also for sale through a shop which one of the members owns in a nearby market town. Goats and chickens are kept. On every occasion when we visited Family Farm the horticultural activity was more extensive and advanced than before. Indeed, one difficulty about describing this

52

highly work-oriented commune is that almost everything about it, except for the orientation to work and the composition and ascendancy of the core members, had changed each time we visited it.

The core members are Kate, divorced and in her mid-forties a woman of astounding energy, hard common sense and devotion to the idea of communalism; Ian, her lover, who is younger than she and who is the member most involved in the idea of developing the precision-engineering workshop as an economic base for the commune; Frances, who is Kate's daughter, and who shares her energy and in a quieter way has probably played a larger part both in the Commune Movement and in the holding together of this particular commune; and Gary, who owns the shop and has a stable relationship with Frances. Frances has a young daughter, Samantha, who lives with her in the commune, but Samantha's father, to whom Frances was married before she met Gary, does not. Around this group other members come and go. On some occasions the core group have found themselves on their own; at other times there have been up to ten other adults and up to six other children with them. The intention of Kate, Ian, Frances and Gary throughout the time that we knew them was to create a stable larger group, although it is probably true that the two women are more committed to this aim than the two men. In fact, there has been a constant traffic of prospective new members, and although strong attachments were often formed between the latter and individual members of the core group, none of those we had met on previous occasions were actually living at Family Farm at the time of our last visit. The exceptionally clear pattern of core and fringe which revealed itself in this particular commune was, so far as we could tell, largely a result of the pressure exerted by the core members to put working for the place above everything else. For them, working for the place was a way of demonstrating the solidity of personal relationships; other members tended to want their personal relationships to be more directly attended to and to see the demand for work not as an expression of collective solidarity but as an imposition which separated those securely attached to the place or the core relationships within it from those who were merely seeking an as yet undefined togetherness. During each of our visits discussions were going on and decisions were pending as to whether some newly arrived members were sufficiently committed to be allowed to stay.

Despite this toughness, both the core members and the home they have created are very attractive, and as yet there has been no shortage of would-be new members. The ground floor of the house is dominated by a large, square kitchen which in turn is dominated by an Aga cooking range and a huge, oblong scrubbed table flanked by benches. Most meals are eaten here. There is a smaller table near the range at which

53

the children eat and a blackboard on which a list of jobs to be done is chalked each day. A separate notice-board displays a diary of day-to-day events, including projected visits, outings and meetings, as well as letters and details of the rota for cooking the evening meal. Across the hall from the kitchen is another large room furnished somewhat ambiguously to serve either as a sitting room, with sofas and easy chairs, or as dining room or as a room for meetings when the business to be discussed is too delicate or fraught for the more natural gathering in the kitchen. This room is brightly decorated and has large windows looking out over flower beds. Frances and Gary have placed their hi-fi equipment in this room for everyone to use, and there is a long bookcase full of books donated by various members in the same spirit. On most evenings, at least some members of the commune can be found chatting and relaxing in this room. The other rooms on this floor tend to change their use from time to time, sometimes being occupied by individual members and sometimes being used for different communal purposes; one room at the back of the house was eventually painted in several shades of yellow and made into a children's playroom. Apart from bathrooms and lavatories, there are eight rooms on the two higher floors, and these are used as bed-sitting rooms by whatever individuals or couples may be resident or visiting. Despite a certain amount of general wandering around, privacy is highly valued; people invite one another to their rooms often and easily, but the principle that the rooms are private to their occupants is well established, and some members – individuals who because they are doing a demanding job outside feel that they are already giving enough to the commune or couples who are mainly interested in each other – may, once they have done whatever tasks have been assigned them and eaten their meal, virtually live in their rooms.

Against this background the pattern of membership is fluid. On each of our visits some of the people who were there in addition to the core members were described to us as 'permanent' while others were said to be merely visiting, prospective or possible. Being 'permanent' might mean that shares had been bought and certainly meant that a decision had been taken to admit the member in question fully to the group. It was no guarantee of permanence. Two who came near to lasting the course were Jeremy, who had in fact joined the commune as soon as it was founded, having taken a degree in agriculture, and who worked as a labourer on a neighbouring farm while trying to work out a viable farming project of his own in connection with the commune, and Christine, who had broken with her family after being forced through an expensive private education, had travelled the country for a while before ending up at another commune about twenty miles away and taking a job in Gary's shop; from there she moved to Family Farm, where she became involved with Jeremy. On our last visit, both had left to earn money for a projected tour of communes in America, although Jeremy had kept the shares he had bought in Family Farm, and it seemed possible they might eventually return. Valerie and her daughter Jane were also 'permanent' up until our last visit, although we were aware of a running tension between Valerie and Kate as to the proper balance of work and pleasure in the life of the commune; this issue led to an increasing range of jobs being organised on a rota basis, but even so Valerie failed to appease Kate's demand for work, and it was over this that – much to the regret of other core members – she finally decided to leave. All the other members we knew stayed for shorter periods. Some, indeed, were almost deliberately transient, as they were from the first caught up in plans or relationships which were bound to prove incompatible with the requirement that place-making within the commune should be everyone's first priority. Between our first and second visits, four adults (and three children) left; two, Seth and Karen, because they had found an opportunity to realise a long-term project to set up a swimming school for handicapped children, the other two, Betty and Mick, so we were told, because their idea of a commune was more love and peace than work – as Frances put it, 'Betty expected me to love her just like that and it isn't as simple as that.' The problem of the departure of these members was discussed a great deal by the others; Valerie in particular obviously missed them and stressed how much more relaxed the atmosphere had been while they were in the group; Frances and Kate were more concerned with the difficulties of living with people whose purposes were so different from those which they considered essential to the commune.

A number of young men also came and went, refugees from routine jobs or a pointless education looking for a more natural and fulfilling way of life, for work they could believe in or a woman they could love. One of the most interesting of these unattached men was Tom, who had read English at Oxford with a view to becoming a school-teacher, become disenchanted with the authoritarianism of teaching, taken an office job and hated the routine, given it up to live on social security and drifted into the commune movement a thoroughly unhappy person. When we first knew him he was very silent and withdrawn, not just with us but with almost everyone at Family Farm. He did a great deal of work in the garden but had no outside job or other source of income. When asked if he liked the commune he replied, 'I like the garden'; when asked what he thought of the commune he said, 'I don't think.' Once again the question of his membership was being discussed intensely by the core members of the group. Kate particularly favoured his staying on the ground that 'it might do something for him' and because his work on the garden was valuable; most of the others wondered whether he would ever contribute in other ways. In fact it turned out that Tom was very keen indeed to be allowed to join. He had a sense of finding himself within the commune, enjoyed working with Kate and the others and at the same time 'I can stay in bed or get up when I feel like it or read all day in the library if I want.' He especially liked having a lot of children around. And he offered to take a job doing WEA teaching or similar work if he were able to stay. As he opened up personally, the other members of the commune all came round to agreeing that he should stay. The discussions about his joining had, interestingly, served the further purpose of allowing the others to rediscover and restate their own idea of what Family Farm was about, and Tom was caught up in the resulting renewed sense of solidarity. In the event, he left fairly soon afterwards to take on a rather challenging educational job. But this was plainly a case of a temporary but mutually successful membership.

An equally common category of temporary members is the young mother. The existing members tend to agonise over applications from such people and frequently end up accepting them on a temporary basis, hoping that from the flow someone really suited to permanent membership will emerge. And sometimes, as with Valerie, it almost does work that way. But the issue is always a delicate one and involves a careful weighing of principles and costs. One day during one of our visits Christine, Jeremy and Kate were in the kitchen preparing the evening meal when a telephone call came with just such a request. Christine took the call, and it gave rise to the following conversation:

Christine: I don't think so; she's just left her husband; she's got two kids, she wants a place to live. You know like . . .

Kate: But then life's tough for women. I must admit that some are sillier than others, but life's very tough for a woman and two kids – what do you think she should do, stay with her husband?

Christine: No, not at all, but I'm not going to make a decision by myself.

Kate: My instinct is, well of course we have to invite her because that's just the group of people who do end up in a sticky position, and they really can't be expected to get themselves out of it. It's up to us, isn't it? And I would have thought yes, under the circumstances.

Christine: I mean, perhaps we could send her to some other group. You see, she's got no home, Kate, so it's going to be hard to say come for a bit, isn't it?

Kate: No, come for a bit and see how you get on. We can put her in touch with other places if she looks more like any of the other places – if she doesn't we may have to keep her.

Jeremy: I do sort of object to people using communes and thinking they can stay until they find something better – that sort
of attitude.

Kate: Is that really what she said?

Christine: I don't know, but she said 'a place where I can stay
while I get myself sorted out' and I thought, oh, oh.

The strong pair relationships at the core of the Family Farm seem to
have a further effect on the way unattached would-be members are
talked about and treated. There is a hope that they, too, if they stay,
will become paired off. Arguments such as 'Jenny would be just right
for Dave' are quite common, and although the movement of relationships among the members is in fact quite volatile it does seem that the
core members would be happiest if the pattern of everyone else's relationships was the same as their own, just as they would like other
members to share their enthusiasm for work. One of the things that we
were told had 'gone wrong' so far as Karen, Seth, Betty and Mick were
concerned was that Seth had become involved with Betty, which had
made Mick jealous, and he in turn had then started a relationship with
Karen which left Betty deeply upset whenever Mick and Karen went
off to make love. Rightly or wrongly, this was construed as illustrating
their unsuitability for life at Family Farm. Stable pair relationships are
highly valued, and a devotion to working for the place is seen as a way
of keeping trouble with relationships under control as well as a sign
that one has got one's priorities right. There is plainly a defensive element to this stress on pair relationships as well as a shrewd strategic
understanding of the conditions needed for Family Farm to work well.
So long as the personal relationships of a large number of members are
unstable, the strain imposed on the pair relationships that do exist is
very powerful: 'singles present practical and emotional problems and
space problems; trios and cross-pair affairs cause pain'. Kate and Ian,
Frances and Gary and Christine and Jeremy all found at different
times that the demands of unattached members of the commune for
their sympathy, love and involvement, or, alternately, for a spirit of
'putting the group above private relationships', drained the relationships they valued most. All of them tried to be what they called 'multi-
valued' in weighing the importance of their pair relationships against
the cohesion of the group as a whole, but what it felt like from inside
was well described by one of them as follows: 'It is an awkward trap;
when does one leave off meeting others' needs? The founder-pairs here
have impoverished their own relationships in order to do what they
could see others needed. It is acute for pairs in groups; the problem,
not necessarily fatal, is one of one's responsibility to one's pair needs
versus group needs.' So, ideally, other members of the commune would
be stably paired as well.

57

Like everything else, the pattern of work varied a good deal from visit to visit; only the sense of its importance was constant. When we first arrived, Kate, who had left school at sixteen and attended a horticultural college, did no work outside the commune but worked enormously hard within it. She would get up before six in the morning, work all day in the fields or the house and afterwards make the evening meal as well as doing a few chores before going to bed. By contrast, Ian held a quite senior position in a scientific instrument company where he worked full-time earning the money to provide both his and Kate's contributions to the commune. When he came home in the evening he was not expected to take on household work, and more often than not he would retire after the evening meal to work on his project for developing his own workshop as a communal enterprise. Frances and Gary worked at raising produce for the shop and with Christine at looking after the shop. Frances and Karen, with Valerie, tended to divide the business of looking after the children, but apart from that there was no clear division of labour so far as household chores were concerned. At times the men cleaned and cooked and the women worked in the garden or looked after the animals or worked on structural repairs to the buildings. This sharing of tasks became more marked later on when Kate took an outside job doing interior decorating and a system of rotas was developed to equalise the load. A striking feature of Family Farm is that new work projects are constantly being planned and launched. At the time of our last visit planning permission had finally been obtained to use the barn as a workshop and work was energetically in hand on the conversion. A little earlier Frances had secured a weekly stall on the market at Yeovil and plunged into organising the preparation of home-made bread, herbs, eggs and organic foodstuffs generally. All this made Family Farm seem a dynamic and exciting place to the visitor. But we can understand why Christine once complained that 'no one seems very happy here' and why Valerie talked a lot about 'the pressure'. So, too, we can understand the enthusiasm Kate and Ian felt for contemporary China. Their commune was, we felt, imbued with the Protestant Ethic, an ascetic dedication to work – but a *communal* asceticism of mutual development in which the collectivity rather than the solitary individual was the significant moral entity. Theirs was the Protestant Ethic mixed up with an ethic of sharing. When we put this view of Family Farm to its members, it was rather firmly resisted, however. They suggested that we should speak of their 'realistic hedonism' – as distinct from either vague idealism on the one hand or a cramped mania for work for its own sake on the other. We were urged to describe the place 'for what it was: good food, good work, good play, humour, and yet economy and not profligacy'. Nevertheless, while accepting 'realis-

58

tic hedonism' as a better description of what Family Farm was about than our own we *were* struck by the extent to which in practice that involved emphasising deferred gratification and self-denial. Many of the characteristic tensions we noted at Family Farm sprang from this underlying pattern. First, there was the row about the children's food. The ultimate responsibility for each child remained with his or her natural parents. At the same time it was felt that the children should be allowed to make their own world within broad limits set by the general principles and spirit of the commune. Within this framework it was only too easy to create unmanageable three-way conflicts between what the mother of a particular child wanted, what was generally thought to be right for the children and what the children themselves felt. The issue of baked beans, sausages and cornflakes versus organic food welled up in this way and dragged on in a deeply divisive manner for months, perpetuated by the combination of a strong sense of what was right and an equally strong determination that no one should be imposed on. Then there was the trouble about Kate's tools. Christine, needing a spanner and nuts and bolts, had helped herself to the first she could find in the kitchen. They happened to belong to Kate, and when she in turn needed them they were not where she had expected to find them. A very tense and rancorous evening followed, and again no easy solution presented itself. On the one hand, of course, Kate was right, given the way the commune depended upon her work, to insist that the tools she needed should be available to her. But Christine was also right to assume that the resources of the commune were there to be shared; the fact that Kate didn't want other people to use her possessions meant that she didn't trust them. To which Kate replied that in a sense she *didn't* trust them; work on the place had to go on and the tools to do it were therefore all-important; if they were lost or broken who would find the money to replace them. By the next morning the immediate issue of the quarrel had fallen into perspective and everyone agreed that it had all been rather silly and over-dramatic. But a deeper undercurrent of worry about 'Kate's possessiveness' – in which Kate herself was involved as much as anyone else – was not so easily dispelled. The very awareness that the members of the group had developed of the feelings of others tended ironically to deepen and complicate such minor difficulties. Over time the group appeared to evolve a technique for dealing with situations of this sort which largely involved leaving the immediate issue to simmer while trying 'to think out what seems most important for the long-term good of the *place*'. When the simmering process was felt inadequate, someone would call a meeting. These meetings seemed to occur about once a month. We did not ourselves take part in any of them, but the way they were described by several members suggested that their function was not to resolve issues so much as to allow people to relieve their feelings and to reunite the commune through a common realisation of their shared involvement in a system of intractable contradictions which 'had to be lived with'. The alternative interpretation of these meetings was that they were occasions on which 'they' tried to force their view of the commune on 'us' – and people who interpeted the experience in that way did not usually stay at Family Farm very long.

The ethos of the group at Family Farm emphasises sharing and giving as well as place-making, but the core members are well aware of the amount they have already given in using their life savings to acquire the house and in the work they do in and for it to ensure that it is a viable and exciting setting for their lives. They do not take easily to being asked in addition, especially at the end of a gruelling day, to give themselves to the sympathetic contemplation of someone else's emotional state. And they tend to notice very quickly that those who talk a great deal about loving and giving do not necessarily *do* very much to make life richer for others. When we asked Kate what she thought communal living offered her, she replied without hesitation, 'Work; more work; scope for sharing and minimising housework and increasing scope for more constructive work.' And she went on to tell us that the question we ought to have asked was what can people offer a commune, not the other way round. The core members of this commune thus find themselves in the odd situation of being as keen as ever to find others with whom to share their lives while having a conception of sharing which, while it works for them, seems intolerably demanding to most of those who join them, especially the young who had not learned to give themselves unreflectively in the way Gary, Frances and the others expect; 'when all are as busy and hardworking as we are, our togetherness has to be mostly while working'. Over the time we knew them, the members of this group seemed to become less rather than more tolerant of the 'love and peace brigade', to become clearer in their minds about the wastefulness of trying to work directly to produce good or honest relationships and to develop a greater determination not to compromise their projects for the sake of warm relationships with people whose aim in life was a warm relationship. When we last met them they had decided to try to find some 'ordinary people' to join them.

For all its difficulties, Family Farm is a successful and exhilarating group. When we last went there, some things, including the shop, seemed to be going awry: a deep division over the question of whether or not the commune should have a formal constitution and rules had developed and ended with some long-standing members who favoured a more formal structure leaving to join another group. But other things, including the market stall and the precision-engineering project, were driving ahead. Although several members had just left, those who remained were canvassing new prospects as energetically and as hopefully as ever. And beneath it all the core members had grown steadily more attentive and responsive to one another. They sometimes described Family Farm as 'a non-kinship family', but a better clue to their experience might be found by thinking of them as a communal business. Within the core the commune has come to be defined as a matter of working to create an environment in which people can be what they want to be. And we were not surprised when one member of this inner group told us that a main reason for disputes within the commune as a whole was 'guilt in those who don't work hard – the place needs a lot of work; there won't be an environment to be people in if we don't work on it – and resentment in those who do'. The correctness of that judgement does not, alas, help Family Farm to solve its main problem – which is to recruit and retain new permanent members without losing those qualities which have made it, among contemporary British communes, quite exceptionally dynamic, stimulating and economically viable.

Hillside

This commune is distinctive in many ways, but particularly in the deliberateness of its arrangements. It is, with the possible exception of Postlip Hall, the most planned of British communes. At the same time it must contain one of the widest ranges of belief and values within its membership. We visited three times during the second year of their life together.

The group is situated in an extremely favourable rural location. The nearest other dwelling is half a mile away, and the nearest settlement of more than a few houses is over four miles off. The house, which is an extremely large one in its own ample grounds, sits just below the top of a ridge and is surrounded by mature trees on three sides. From the fourth there are wide views of some of the best rolling countryside in England. The large common room, one of the vital areas of communal life, is on this side of the house, and it is easy to be gripped by euphoria by the mere visual consequences of entering it.

In the grounds there are a disused tennis court, terraced flower gardens, a well-tended vegetable garden, a greenhouse, stables, many outbuildings including a dilapidated coach house and a well-equipped workshop where one of the members practises his highly skilled craft at which he has earned a national reputation. A retired couple who live in the house and who are the parents of one member of the commune even though their own membership of it is uncertain devote themselves to the garden. They recompense themselves by selling some of the produce for their own profit. The rest of those living in the house are a little dubious about the morality of this transaction, but in the light of the important role played by the old people in the acquisition of the house, both their deviance and their non-involvement are grudgingly tolerated. For them, living at Hillside is partly a way of affording a rather gracious retirement, and their situation in the group is such that their wish to live there on those terms has to be respected.

Inside the house, which is built on a square of roughly ninety feet, there are on the ground floor five rooms given over to particular people – a living room for the retired couple together with four bed-sitting rooms – a kitchen for the exclusive use of the retired couple, two communal kitchens, one of which was still only half completed at the time of our last visit, a guest room, a common room, a children's playroom, a storage room, a pantry, two lavatories and another guest room. The old kitchen was adequately equipped with two cookers, refrigerator and washing machine. Below ground there were extensive cellars – hardly used when we were there, although it was envisaged that the new kitchen would be connected by internal stairs to the cellars to form an enormous storage, cooking and dining complex. Upstairs there were three bathrooms, the retired couple's bedroom, eight bed-sitting rooms, two empty rooms and the bedroom of two children of a couple living in the group. The other younger children slept with their mother, and one other slept in a room next door to his mother. However, these room arrangements, except for those of the retired couple, were by no means fixed. The use of rooms changed constantly both under the impact of changing and growing membership and the breaking and making of relationships and in the light of reassessments of the purposes and needs of the group. There was never a time during the period of our visits when some architectural project was not in the process of being realised. It is a help that one of the members is a qualified and skilled architect. Thus, at one time there had been two common rooms, but one of these, the smaller with the worse view, had to be given up in order to accommodate some new members. And this room was itself a product of earlier changes when a large room had been divided into two to provide more accommodation. During our visits the main construction project was the new kitchen. This was being made on the side of the house with the view, next to the common room, a change felt to be necessary so that the preparation of food could enjoy the central role it deserved in the life of the group. As the group ate together more regularly and valued eating together more highly, it came to seem increasingly wrong that the one or two members whom the rota had committed to making the meal should be relegated to solitary confinement at the back of the house. In fact what had happened prior to the decision to make the new kitchen was that more and more members were finding their way to the kitchen in order to help out informally with the cooking or simply to be around when such an important activity was taking place.

During the period we were visiting Hillside the membership of the group grew quite significantly. Just before our first visit, a couple with their child and a separated mother with three children had joined the group, the couple eagerly skipping the normally required probationary period of three months. Before that the group had consisted of four men and four women: the retired couple, a young married couple, and two women, one of whom had two children, and two single men. There were two other heterosexual couples who had permanent rooms at the house but stayed there only at weekends. In the following six months one of the single men, much the youngest adult in the commune, left, as did the two women and the mother with three children. None of these people had been among the founding members of the project. Meanwhile there had been numerous additions. The two young couples who had been visiting at weekends, both of whom turned out to be founder-members of the group, had now made Hillside their main home, although there was some doubt as to whether one of the women would stay very long. Another young couple had also arrived, but this was understood by all to be a temporary stay, as they intended to travel to India as soon as they could. A travelling theatre company had also made their home at Hillside – four males and one female – as had the sister of one of the founding members, who had left her husband and arrived with her two children as a permanent member just before our second visit. Thus, in the space of just over six months, the group had lost three women, a man and five children; but the group had grown from a nucleus of eight adults and two children to contain eleven men, eight women and five children. The oldest of the adults were over sixty, the youngest was nineteen and the average age of the adults, excluding the retired couple, was twenty-seven. The children ranged from one to five. Most of the people who were at Hillside by the time of our second visit had professional qualifications, and the majority of the nineteen adults had been to university, although not all of them had completed their degrees. The professions represented at Hillside were dentist, nurse, designer, architect, social worker, actor, musician, editor and, overwhelmingly, teacher – at all levels of the profession.

Only two members earn any part of their living by working at home. All the rest who earn do so by working outside, sometimes a considerable distance away. There are plans to establish a dentist's surgery on the premises, however; and the theatre company rehearse in one of the outbuildings. There is in fact some feeling that the presence of this troupe is a doubtful advantage. They had been introduced to the group by one of the newest members, who had organised a charity concert in which they had taken part. But only two of them seemed to be seriously interested in communal living, and the claim of many of the members of Hillside was that the actors stayed only because the place – close to a motorway, with ample rehearsal space and food laid on – supported them in the face of their own inability to support themselves. They seemed to form a quite separate emotional and work unit within the group as a whole.

It was difficult to establish the details of the creation and founding of Hillside. One of the members, Andrew, answered an advertisement in a national journal appealing for people interested in communal living. Having fired the enthusiasm of Andrew and a group of his school friends, the advertiser himself then vanished. This group, whose relationships were formed at public school, maintained their friendship, sharing flats together, steadfastly throughout that period of leaving home and going through higher education and professional training, during which many middle-class children leave their earlier attachments behind them. They said there was nothing mysterious about this, but did not explain it, and we simply had to accept as a fact that for whatever reasons this commune was in the fortunate position of having a core group that had established deep and tested relationships among themselves before the communal project began. Perhaps this explains the extremely methodical manner in which they were able to go about finding the type of property they wanted. They divided the country up into sections, and each member was assigned a section and the task of contacting estate agents and viewing property within it. They had certain agreed criteria of closeness to towns, size, state of repair and price but, even so, they sifted through thousands of house particulars in this way before making their decision. Hillside was a property that had in fact been considered and initially rejected in favour of another place, but when that fell through they investigated Hillside again more thoroughly and agreed that it would suit their needs. One member of this original group has never actually lived at Hillside, but it is agreed that his interest and involvement in the project are undiminished; his mother is indeed one of the four trustees who provided the £20,000 needed to buy the house in the first place. Before moving in, the core group held a series of meetings to which other prospective members were invited in an attempt both to recruit congenial people and to work out a relatively specific understanding of the principles on which the commune was to work. The meetings were not a success, tending to reveal both personal awkwardness and conflicts of principle rather than to consolidate a larger group. When the move occurred, those involved were still only the original core.

Not all of the trustees live at Hillside. The group of residents as a whole is legally committed to paying them 9 per cent per annum interest together with repayment of their capital over ten years. At the end of that period the house will belong equally to all those living there — an arrangement which plainly assumes a high degree of permanency among the participants. The internal accounting is organised with the same minute care that marked the search for a house. Everyone pays a basic weekly charge and a daily charge for food; beyond that, variable charges have been worked out for each room on the basis of an agreed scheme of amenities. Living in the group could be extremely cheap indeed, but even so, in determining the 'rent' no account was taken of the size of the individual member's income, so that the poorest tended to have the worst rooms. As it became clear that there was going to be more turnover of members than had at first been expected, a further scheme was introduced to enable new members to acquire shares in the ownership of the house. Within the house, by contrast, the sharing of possessions was not extensive, and the standard of living, generally, was adequate rather than luxurious. Heating was erratic and partial, dependent upon an ancient and frequently broken central-heating boiler. The communal parts of the house as a whole were functionally rather than elegantly furnished. Individual rooms, however, varied enormously, from the plush to the avant-garde, from the exquisitely tasteful to the spartan or downright tatty. Some rooms explored the space under the eaves while others had had their floor space increased by half by having a platform hung over the floor space midway between the floor and the high ceiling. In one room this platform provided a sleeping area. In another a piece of 'total furniture' dominated the room – a combined bed, desk, table, seat, store, wardrobe and defensive rampart. In sum, at least as much of the place-making activity that went on at Hillside was concerned with the cultivation of private space as was devoted to the shared areas. Even so, it seemed to us that the members had a lower standard of consumption of consumer goods than their professional peers. The compensation for this was of course the grandeur, beauty and spaciousness of the house and grounds, which would normally have been accessible only to the very rich.

Many members made more than cash contributions to the household, although there seemed to be little pressure applied to make people work, and some plainly contributed little to the commonality. Although the retired couple spent much time in the garden, others helped as well. Sarah, who had virtually separated from her husband within the group, did a great deal of domestic work. Andrew was in the forefront of every structural and decorative transformation of the house – so much so that his enthusiasm was sometimes resented, and much to his distress he found himself accused of being 'pushy'. Others, although

65

not all, had specialist areas in which they made valued contributions. Ordinary household tasks were assigned by a mixture of routine and good will. There was a rota for which people signed up for cooking the daily evening meal and Sunday lunch, but the rota was treated as a guide, not as a rule. The washing up was done by whoever felt most willing or most guilty except that whoever had cooked the meal was exempted. Not everyone joined in these arrangements. The retired couple had withdrawn completely from the common cooking and eating, and their son and his wife and two children had withdrawn partially. The children were almost always fed separately from the adults by their parents. Individual members were deputised to clean particular common areas of the house, and there was a further rota which distributed the responsibility for obtaining the main household supplies to one member per month. Cooks were expected to plan the menus for their meals, however, and to obtain anything extra that they needed themselves. Laundry was a personal responsibility.

In contrast to very many communes, at Hillside decisions on matters of policy and administration were made at frequent business meetings which were efficiently and conventionally conducted. Decisions were normally unanimous, but if someone objected, but agreed to bow to majority opinion, the majority decision prevailed. Really major issues are in principle saved for special meetings at which the trustees are present, but this has never happened. Minutes of the ordinary meetings were typed and displayed on a notice-board. The chairmanship of the meeting moved from member to member in no planned fashion. Between our second and third visits a new development had occurred: it had been decided to inaugurate a new type of meeting devoted to the exploration of the emotional side of living at Hillside. The aim of these meetings was to air grouses and define aims. One of the original members was a social worker who specialised in running this type of therapeutic session. It was perhaps her expertise that helped in the starting of this new venture, and in her view the first meetings of this kind were a great success, but it is against the ethos of Hillside to make a mystique of professional qualifications. In her opinion the most urgent problems to be solved were the relation of personal demands for privacy to communal involvement, and how to achieve a state of affairs in which everyone can contribute as much as he wishes and if his contribution falls below the average not be made to feel guilty – and presumably the converse, how to prevent those who contributed most from storing up resentment. Members claim she did not have a dominant role in these meetings. The contrast between Hillside and Family Farm in their management of this issue could hardly have been greater.

Throughout the founding of Hillside and during its initial phase of

66

existence, the project was thought of in very modest terms. They professed merely to be interested in the possibility of communal living and insisted that they were not influenced by any explicit theories and were reluctant to be thought of as a commune. They moved gradually towards a stronger sense of themselves as a commune under the influence of changing membership. It was not just that the membership broadened beyond the original group of school friends sharing a common and privileged background; it also came to include new people who found Hillside lacking in generosity of interaction and emotional warmth. Complaints were made by members whom the core group wished to keep that the group was too prone to selfishness and too deficient in love. One new member in particular voiced this complaint, and, challengingly, made it clear that what he had in mind was the reluctance of others to share his enthusiasm for communal work. Gradually others, too, came to feel that Hillside could present a cold and unresponsive face, especially to visitors and prospective members. It was discovered that one visitor after five days at Hillside had spoken to no one and seen nothing beyond the room assigned him and the common room. At least some of the core members were affected by these criticisms and moved slowly towards enthusiasm for a more active solidarity.

But others felt that the privatisation of the place was being exaggerated. Certainly the common room was used every evening by a large proportion of the group, not exactly the same set every night, to play records, talk, entertain guests and, if anyone produced any drink, to drink copious amounts of home-brewed beer. It seemed to us that almost invariably the subject of talk in the common room during these sociable periods was not any abstract issue, not politics, the arts or even communality as such, but whether the children needed both parents, whether the people at Hillside could be trusted enough to 'trip' with, whether one of the new members should have left her husband, what made one of the women so neurotic, why Andrew was 'pushy', why Ellen felt it necessary to do so much housework, why Guy and Mary kept themselves apart. Some members claim that communality was a burning issue, seriously discussed, as was music, and that this 'gossip' was the preoccupation of a minority. But talk about relationships often prevailed at the common meals. Meal-times were slightly festive occasions when the events of the day are softened, captured or decorated with light banter as the group relaxed after the day's work in the world outside. In the same way the kitchen would often be packed with people laughing and gossiping while the cooking was done. On one such occasion, Sid, a long-term visitor, was making two huge cheese pies and vegetables to go with them, helped by his girlfriend, and at the same time instructing the child of another female

67

member whose father did not live at Hillside how to make her own miniature pie. It was remarked for our benefit that here was a splendid example of surrogate fatherhood as practised in communes. It was certainly an example of the growing alertness to the issue of communality which the new members had generated. In fact the group is to a remarkable degree a world unto itself. Although members of the group do have friends and associates outside, the majority of their leisure time is spent in the company of people belonging to or living at Hillside.

Only six of the nineteen adults at Hillside were permanently at home, however: three mothers with young children and one retired woman; and two men, one of them retired. The rest worked outside, and some returned home late in the evening very tired after a long journey commuting. Although different combinations of the group came together during the evening on weekdays, the great gatherings were at the weekends, when the whole group might go out together on Saturday evening or to the local pub at Sunday lunchtime. Throughout Saturday and Sunday small task-forces got together to tackle various jobs around the house and garden. There was an attempt, not totally successful, to move away from the normal division of work between the sexes, but this was only within the strictly domestic sphere; outside of that, women worked on the garden or with the animals, and men chopped down trees or did the plumbing, rewiring and carpentry.

Despite this conviviality, privacy has a high value at Hillside. Members' rooms may be used for the occasional visitor if the member is temporarily away, but otherwise the privacy of these rooms is inviolate. Within the rooms the personalities of the occupants are expressed and developed, private entertaining occurs and intimate relationships are nourished. Members may withdraw to their rooms with little or no comment at any time and for long periods. A good many of the difficulties experienced in the more public life of a place like Family Farm were probably simply avoided at Hillside in this way. When we last visited them, the members were still divided and uncertain about just how much of a commune Hillside was. Some of the older members still held that the group should be considered simply as a collection of people who liked living together. But the balance of feeling was moving away from this view towards a more self-conscious concern to be a commune. At the same time there was a good deal of confusion as to just what that meant. The new members were themselves very diverse in their values and beliefs; some espouse no more than a conventional middle-class liberalism; others are whole-hearted devotees of the 'alternative society'. Nevertheless, sexual and social relationships remained quite conventional; the stable couple, married or unmarried, is the norm. The general inhibition against interfering in members' private lives means that pot-smoking, for example, is not forbidden – but neither is there any question of anything like that being a collective activity.

In the course of its short history this group has demonstrated a capacity to evolve slowly on the basis of the firm institutional and relational ground-plan it laid with such great precision and care at the outset. But there have been strains and setbacks. There is opposition to the group's becoming child-oriented. At various times representatives of the two sides, commune and co-residence, declare their intention to leave. Some of the older members are worried about the effect really becoming a commune would have on the value of the property. Some of the newer members complain strenuously about the extent to which older members keep themselves apart and ideally would like to be able to buy them out and develop Hillside more fully on their own terms. And yet the striking thing about Hillside is that in fact all these people go on living together.

Three years later, after the members of Hillside had seen what we had written about them, they invited us to visit them again. They felt that the group had changed so much that some description of their present was essential to an understanding of their past. There has been much physical change. The coach house, which had seemed destined to become a ruin, has been transformed and its value at least tripled. With the roof repaired and the whole building made structurally sound, it now contains three very pleasant sets of living quarters, an extremely well-equipped pottery studio and shop and a very gracious guest room. The main house, however, has become slightly shabbier and slightly dirtier and bears the imprint of a few more not-quite-finished minor alterations. The hall ceiling has been freshly painted in striking and tasteful colours. The projected dentist's surgery has materialised, fully equipped and functional in the old back kitchen. The large kitchen that was being installed in the front of the house during the earlier visits has replaced the kitchen that had been lost. The chimney-stacks which had been in a dangerous condition have been repaired communally, but much of the renovation and building that has gone on has been the result of the efforts of individuals or couples working alone.

The membership of the community has changed considerably. The travelling theatre group has disbanded, and only two of its members remain at Hillside, one having returned to his old profession of accountancy, the other still struggling to establish himself in the theatre, this time as a solo artist. The retired couple have also left, taking with them their share in the equity of the house. Their son and his wife were on the verge of departing. The wife of one of the original trustees who had been expected not to stay when we were there earlier had never really

69

joined. Her husband, Sandy, had left and was now living with someone else, who had also been a member of the group during our earlier visits. The couple who had been staying temporarily prior to a trip to India made their journey and were refused readmission to Hillside on their return. In all, about nine people whom we had known earlier had left. A number of others had come and stayed, all of them either couples, with or without children, or single-parent families. Sonja, a law student, had come with her child, and she forms a couple with Andrew. Caroline, a designer, had joined with her child very shortly after the early visits we made. Two potters had come with their children and another couple, one of whom is a folksinger. Conventional couples are still the norm, and the group often think of each other in couples, but all the couples do not share a room. Four people do not have partners within the group. One of those alone is Simon, a new member who has two children. He is also leaving, not voluntarily but because the group had decided that he did not fit in. This is the first time that they have actually gone so far as to expel anyone living in the community.

Many of these changes reflected a striking organisational upheaval of volcanic energy which one member at least believes is a result of the impact of the 'encounter' meetings that had just been beginning three years before. However, these meetings had not been held continuously throughout the three years and were about to start again after a break. The battle between co-residence and community and the wide differences in creeds had been partially accommodated by the group's splitting internally. Sandy left because he opposed this move. He maintained that he was a scapegoat for the group; but many people at Hillside are said, or claim, to have that role. Those who support the new pattern say that their experience of fluctuating numbers at Hillside has shown that between six and ten people is the best size for a communal group, as it is possible for everyone involved to know everyone else properly. Beyond that number, an elaborate structure is necessary if the group is to function. However, Hillside needs about twenty-four people if it is to be an economic proposition, and therefore the obvious step was to create small groups within a larger structure. Two groups were formed in the house, with separate kitchens and living rooms, and a third group was located in the coach house and the outbuildings. This third group was originally entirely devoted to arts and crafts. The two groups in the house took their names from the colours of the kitchens that they used. Despite exceptions, the members of Yellow Kitchen were united by a common active interest in the Women's Movement and a certain style of community politics. Blue Kitchen as a whole had much less interest in directly effecting social change. It was intended that the three groups would develop in their own directions, seeking

70

members sympathetic to their particular aims. Over the fifteen months that this system has been operating, the differences between the two kitchens have apparently persisted, even though by the time of our most recent visit a bewildering series of movements had taken place between the groups. Almost no one had remained in his original group. Blue Kitchen now consists of only two members, one of whom lamented being 'on the periphery' – his very words. After a period when, as another member said, 'we sat in our different sitting rooms seeing who could make the most jolly noises', Blue Kitchen began to decline in numbers, some going to the coach house, others to the Yellow Kitchen, and some leaving altogether. The Yellow Kitchen, which won a reputation for assertive individuality, had become, in effect, the commune, and there was talk of having a common sitting room with Blue Kitchen again. The coach-house group cannot really be said to be a communal group, as the three households eat as distinct units. The potters, at least, had always intended to be part of a community rather than a commune. One of the coach-house households consisted of a single woman, and she was the most marginal member of the whole community, keeping apart even from her very near neighbours. She was not the only one to feel bitter about the development of Hillside, for the process of recasting the community had generated enormous heat.

Yet the community as a whole does still have a number of real and powerful links including very close proximity of daily living. Most important are the meetings which handle the business of the community and which meet every fifteen days. The odd rotational period ensures that the meeting falls on a different day of the week every time, and thus no one is permanently prevented from attending by outside commitments. Meetings are well attended (which was not the case in the past) and very infrequently cancelled. The groups have a common financial structure, each individual paying into the one fund for the facilities he uses just as before. They all pay into a common fund for food and buy their basic foodstuffs from it, and they nearly all share in some communal duties such as feeding the hens. An indication of the shift of the ideological centre of the community is the fact that in all groups members could be found who supported the move to change the financial structure of the community. Originally there were four trustees who lent the money to the twelve equitable owners of the house. Although some of the people who were living at Hillside bought a share in the equity of the house when they moved in, others did not, and this has led to unhealthy tensions. At the time that we visited them, the community – although we suspect that most of the drive was coming from within the Yellow Kitchen – were exploring avenues through which they could end the perceived differences based on investment, or the lack of it, in the house, and the unfortunate possibility that a small number of the equitable owners could force the sale of the house if they wished. Also, for ideological reasons, they would be happier if the equity was to accrue to some trust that would use it for progressive or enlightened causes should Hillside come to an end. They were finding that the law was not designed to help them. Another indication of this ideological shift is that a greater percentage of the people living at Hillside than ever before work at home. Only five out of thirteen work outside and only two of these full-time. Lastly it appeared that women now do many more of the jobs, such as home renovation, plastering, bricklaying and carpentry, that were previously almost exclusively done by men.

The community is making strenuous efforts to expand and grow in its new form, and throughout the summer they had had a constant stream of visitors. These efforts have not been terribly successful as yet, but their vigour seems unabated.

Red Dawn

In inventing a name for this group we have tried to catch the combination of bounding optimism, practicality and socialist conviction of the name one of the group gave them. Although not all the group were politically committed, the richness of their aspirations stands in stark contrast to the wretchedness of their experience which culminated in the splitting of the group into two sad, hurt and warring factions. We do not describe their experience here out of mischievous prurience or an attempt to undermine the efforts of the commune movement or to mock them; and most emphatically we do not do so in order to confirm the suspicions of those who believe that all communes are messy and emotionally squalid. Indeed, this would be a superficial impression, for despite the strains the group did care deeply for each other. But our aim in this essay as a whole is to write about communes honestly and to recognise their difficulties and failures as well as their potentialities and successes. Many communes do collapse, and most experience to some degree the sorts of troubles that destroyed Red Dawn. The strength of our analysis of the difficulties of communes can only rest on our observation of those difficulties as they are lived, and we would think it odd to make no attempt to describe such an important part of what we saw, especially as it is our view that the underlying principles of social organisation are more evident in crisis than in health.

We should stress at the outset that although the lives of the children appeared to be hard and difficult, it is quite likely, as one of the members claimed, that the effects of the commune softened this and made it more bearable for the children than it would have been had they

72

been isolated with their parents. We should also remember, as Gil has pointed out (1973), that in our culture violence against children is culturally admissible and sometimes actively praised. Nor were the children at Red Dawn angels of innocence. But childhood is at best an almost unmanageable predicament, involving as it does both the loss of the powers of babyhood and the denial of the rights of adolescence, and it is difficult for communes, even with the best intentions, not to aggravate a child's confusion as to whether he or she is a person or an object. At Red Dawn the children were theoretically persons, but there were many times when they were in practice little more than objects.

The commune lasted two years to the day. It fluctuated in size from four to seven adults; three children were there constantly, and a fourth was born during the life of the commune. When we first met them, the people living there were Ted, who was about 40 and had recently given up a highly skilled design job to go to teacher-training college; Sue, his wife, who was 37, a secretary and the mother of Luke, 13, Rob, 10, and David, 9; Maggie, who was a schoolteacher of 23, but not working because she was nursing her three-month-old baby, Jane, whose father was Ted; and Bill, a 28-year-old newspaper worker separated from his wife and two children. Bill's wife was a permanent invalid, and he had found it impossible to continue working full-time and looking after her and their newly born baby girl, so she was living with her parents just north of Manchester. He visited her very frequently at first, but by the time he joined the commune he had allowed himself to lapse and only visited some four to six times during the time he lived at the house occupied by Red Dawn. These four adults had been in the group from the beginning. Duncan, a free-lance language teacher, and Peter, a bookseller, both in their mid-twenties, had joined the commune separately only a month before. Peter had the only car, and it was not used communally. Jerry, a night-time telephone operator, poet and playwright in his mid-thirties, had joined six months earlier.

They shared a large, double-fronted, two-storied late Victorian villa in a lower-middle-class area of Manchester. Over the front door was a sign saying 'Red Dawn'. Off the large hall on the ground floor, which was painted in dramatic colours, were Ted's study, a room shared by Duncan and Luke and a room which was Maggie's and which Ted shared with her as a bedroom. Also on this floor was the large dining-room, a fairly small kitchen with all the standard equipment and a deep-freeze, and a bathroom and lavatory, and their pride and joy, a shower. In the hall there was an extension to the telephone, which was upstairs on the spacious landing. At the front of the house on the first floor was a combined kitchen and communal room with a cooker, a fridge and a sink and draining board, called the 'breakfast room'. Seating was provided for about six people by two dilapidated sofas, and on the floor was a low dais which was used as seating and as a table for chess, draughts and cards, which were frequently played. A small bookcase crammed with paperbacks stood by the door, and the newspapers, the *Morning Star* and the *Guardian*, were kept there. The communal notice-board was in this room, too, and most of the items on it related to the Communist Party, of which Ted, Sue and Bill were members, and to the boys' school. In the summer the board was also used for a holiday project for the boys called 'Farago'. A collage of articles, jokes, drawings was pasted once a week on to a board and put up on the notice board. Everyone was supposed to participate, but it was primarily for the boys. There was no television, radio or record-player in this room, as it was a rule of the commune that these must not be used in communal rooms. Bill, whose room was also off the landing, had an ancient television set which cast a faded picture, and most people watched this, with some difficulty. On the same floor, Sue shared a room with her youngest son, David. The remaining son, Rob, had a small room of his own next to Peter's at the back of the house. Lastly, there was an attic room where Jerry lived – perhaps the most elegant and tidy of the rooms. Maggie's room was also distinctive in its taste and femininity, but most rooms were untidy and not very well decorated, the furniture tending to be old, utilitarian and mean. Being out at work all day, Sue did not have the energy to do anything to her own room, particularly towards the end of the life of the group. The cheerlessness was relieved by the bright yellow paint in the upstairs communal room, the pictures in the dining room and the warmth of the central heating.

There was a wish to give every adult a room of his or her own because it was agreed that some might feel the need for privacy very deeply. However, they also did not wish to move the boys around just to suit the wishes of the adults. This conflict was insoluble and gave rise to several minor irritations.

The paintings in the house were mostly by Paul, an original member who stayed for just under a year. To one of the late joiners it seemed as though Red Dawn had been the result of two entangled couples, Maggie and Paul and Ted and Sue, but in fact this was not the case. Maggie met Sue and Ted when at eighteen she became their baby sitter. Maggie met Paul, with whom she was merely good friends, during a spell of working in a bookshop whilst she was a student at a teacher-training college. Ted and Sue had discussed communal living before they met Maggie, but it seems that the development of a relationship between Ted and Maggie was instrumental in creating the need for living together if Ted was not to abandon Sue. Paul became ill and was taken into hospital, where he met John, who left the group when Paul left. When in hospital Paul had difficulty keeping his accommodation and was therefore invited to stay with Ted and Sue a few weeks before they all moved into Red Dawn. Bill was separated from his wife and child and looking for a new home when he met Sue at a local Communist Party meeting. Against Sue's advice, Bill was invited by Ted to live at Red Dawn. Jerry had arrived from another commune known to the group. There was, and is, disagreement about how Duncan and Peter joined. A simple version is that Duncan had seen an advertisement for members they had placed in an 'underground' journal and his application to join had been unanimously approved by the group. This was not the case with Peter, who had been trying many groups before arriving at Red Dawn. Unfortunately, he had only asked Ted and Maggie before moving in; his arrival was merely announced to the others. The room he moved into had a leak in the roof which he had had repaired at his own expense, placing the commune in his debt. Sue and Bill were enraged by the assumption that their consent was not needed before a new member joined, and Bill was especially angry because the room Peter moved into was really 'his' – he had moved out only because of the leak.

The practical and economic arrangements of the group moved through a number of forms. The inhabitants of a room had the responsibility for cleaning it, and the cleaning of the other rooms was in theory the responsibility of everyone; usually one of the two women did it. There was no washing machine in the house and everyone, including the boys, took his washing individually to the launderette. There was a cooking rota, which itself rotated so that no one cooked consistently on the same days, and turns were posted in the kitchen. In practice a good deal of barter took place over the rota. Normally all the adults took their turn, and attendance varied with the cook. Washing up was distributed *ad hoc* but everyone had to do it at fairly regular intervals. Most of the shopping was done by telephone by Maggie; specially required items were bought by whoever noticed the deficiency.

Near the beginning of each month, a formal meeting was held round the dining-room table. After dinner on an evening when all could attend, grievances were aired, bills and finances gone over and new arrangements discussed. At one time, all the boys were included in these meetings, but the younger ones quickly became bored and were subsequently excluded. The long intervals between meetings were meant to be a safeguard, providing a period for cooling off so that issues were discussed dispassionately and meetings not called on the spur of the moment. This tactic did not appear to be very successful. At Duncan's first meeting, Bill had stormed out in a rage protesting at Peter's having joined the group. He had asked, with the support of

Sue, that Peter be made to leave. Luke had also supported this move, but after making his stand against his father was reduced to tears. The protest was unsuccessful, and Peter stayed with Ted's support. The formal decision-making was supplemented by numerous informal discussions at dinner every evening and afterwards in the common room upstairs. Bill and Luke, and occasionally Ted, played cards, draughts or chess nearly every night.

The financial arrangements of Red Dawn went through many convulsions. The system of which we first had knowledge was that there was a formal treasurer, a rotating post then held by Maggie, who passed all the commune's money through her own bank account, since there was no longer a communal one. Since she was not working, she paid the group only £7 per week, but everyone else paid £10 per week, although there was some feeling that those who could should pay more. The treasurer had a large account-book in which were listed the major items of expenditure: rates, mortgage, gas, electricity, water, food and telephone bills. Less conventionally, the commune, out of its income, also supported Bill's wife and Jerry's and Bill's children, paying out a total of £52 per month, an extremely generous arrangement and unique, to our knowledge, amongst the groups we came to know. There was also a book for incidental expenses. This was a way of coping with cash payments from visitors and the cost of small items of food. All the children were supported by the group, and any purchases for them or small amounts of food bought were credited to the person who bought them. At the end of each month the total was worked out and subtracted from the expected contribution of each member. Any surpluses from visitors were used up, but despite the political commitment of some of the members, money was not given to political causes. The £20, for instance, which was given to the Angela Davis Defence Fund was raised by Sue, who organised a special function for International Women's Day. This system worked for nearly a year; and the post of treasurer changed every three months. All visitors were required to pay a set, but very small, rate or do some equivalent work around the house. The hall had been painted in this way by some visitors.

According to Ted, money had always been a source of conflict. For six months before the group was founded and for some time after, Ted worked in a highly paid job in Paris, and Maggie joined him for most of the period. Most of the group went and stayed in turn for a short holiday. Whilst there Ted sent home £50 per week 'without thinking'. It was his quoted income at this time that enabled them to raise a mortgage with the council, on the understanding that further income was to be raised by letting the house to a tenant, which was officially

76

Bill. The deposit came from the sale of Ted and Sue's previous home, and it was Sue who arranged the sale and the new purchase.

When he was in Paris, Ted claimed the atmosphere back at Red Dawn was free and easy. For instance, he said John and Paul met a couple of Canadians in central Manchester late one night who had nowhere to stay, and who came back with them to stay the night. They told their friends where there was free accommodation, and as the news spread the commune snowballed into a doss house. In the first year, so many people registered for a vote from the Red Dawn address that they were visited by the local inspector responsible for the electoral roll. One night Sue, 'foolishly generous,' according to Ted, cooked and served dinner for twenty-two people. Passing the hat round only raised a couple of pounds, which did not even begin to cover their costs. This continued even after Ted and Maggie returned from Paris, and indeed Ted was instrumental in setting up a joint account to which all the members in the group paid in their income and to which all had equal access. Since not everyone had time to get to the bank, they had a cash bag in the house from which people simply took what they needed when they needed it. Whenever the bag was empty someone went to the bank and took out more money. Despite the fact that the system was not really abused by anyone's taking more than his 'fair' share, Ted felt the scheme had a number of disadvantages and, as one of the signatories, froze the account five months after returning from abroad. As he confessed, money was a subject of great importance to him, and he had probably poured more money into the group than anyone else. Of the crash-pad phase his chief complaint was that money was not treated seriously: 'There wasn't anyone thinking about it concretely; it was all an abstract dream . . . one of the complaints which were directed at me was: "Christ, it was all right until you fucking came back", meaning that there had been a lovely happy atmosphere and nobody bothered talking about that [money].' When they had a joint account it was apparently a tense period of petty jealousies. As Maggie put it 'The main difficulty was that you don't know how rich you are. When you earn yourself you know what you've got. You know how much you have got over so you can spend on frivolous things. Whereas with this [the joint account] you don't really know how much you have got, and it is very difficult to tell how many liberties you can take. You start feeling niggly about other people. You're being careful and you notice that they're not being careful. You start rationalising about it and you say, "Well, why shouldn't they do that? They think we can afford it, why shouldn't they?" To which Ted added: 'And the end of it is that you've lost touch with reality. Someone will buy a new coat, and you think, Christ, if he's going to, I'm going to. That's crazy.

You don't do things like that for those sort of reasons.' The group was not able to safeguard itself from the gullibility of members like Paul, who had handed over £300 to some builders who had promptly disappeared before doing the work; as a consequence a gas bill could not be paid. According to Ted, there was a widespread feeling that there was plenty of money, so why worry, or why work? John and Paul preferred to stay at home painting and not earning money, which Ted and Maggie could not accept. Six sets of expenses were drawn out of the bank account; therefore six incomes must go in.

Not only had Ted put a good deal of money into the group, the Council mortgage for the house was solely in his name, and he began to assert the authority that this gave him. After the post of treasurer was created, Ted increased his pressure on John and Paul to find a job. Bill reported that Ted began a systematic campaign, every two days or so waking John and Paul up earlier than usual so that they could get a good start in their half-hearted search for work. After a month of this they finally defiantly decided, Paul in particular, that they had no real intention of getting a job at all, and Ted threw Paul out, stating, 'This is my house and I don't want you here.' Paul subsequently got a job and occasionally visited Red Dawn, although Ted and he did not speak for three months. John quietly left at the same time, Ted claims, solely out of loyalty to Paul, but Sue says that Ted also commanded him to leave. He did not manage to find a job and visited Red Dawn often and seemed to depend upon the group for friendship and emotional sustenance. Sue said, 'Paul did come back once but he took it very hard indeed that no one really gave him the support he expected, although Bill did make a good show.' Not unnaturally, this assertion of ownership and power caused considerable anxiety to Sue and Bill, who demanded, unsuccessfully, that some kind of document be drawn up distributing ownership of the house. Ted and Maggie and Sue and Bill now shared the house during what must have been a difficult period, although Ted and Maggie always had the upper hand. Bill was a boaster and imagined that he was a match for Ted, but although impressively large and fearsome in appearance, his wild, formless rages were ineffectual and consisted mostly of thoughtless abuse ('Maggie is a silly old cow'). Sue was too intelligent to side totally with him, and neither had Ted's ruthless intellectual intensity.

It was at this point that Jerry joined and was able to ameliorate some of the conflict and stand up to Ted in a significant way. He was attracted by the greater organisation of Red Dawn compared to the group he had left (we did in the course of our research meet some people more than once but in different groups), its urban setting and the sense of reality injected by the need to work; but he opposed Ted

78

on many issues. While we were at Red Dawn a rash of notices appeared in the upstairs communal kitchen signed by Ted. 'Please empty your OWN ashtray.' 'If you must bring' – a characteristic phrase of Ted's – 'pots, pans, cups, saucers, etc., up from the kitchen, take them back again. There is not room for them up here.' This claim for control was thwarted by Jerry's suggesting amongst much hilarity that in the last lines 'Ted' and 'them' should be transposed so that it read 'There is not room for Ted up here, signed Them.'

Nevertheless, Jerry did agree with Ted that the problem of privacy had not been solved, and that perhaps there was too much socialising. As a consequence, he found it difficult to write. Bill and Sue wanted greater closeness than existed, but Ted, Maggie and Jerry argued that there was already too much and that it was, for instance, extraordinarily difficult to make friends outside the group because there was such an immense pressure to socialise within it, friends from outside found it a daunting experience and friendships could not be easily sealed by little intimacies or ceremonies like having a meal together when they were shared with a whole pack of others.

Ted was prominent in every dispute and issue within the commune, and every line of fissure seemed to pass through him. One such line was the children. In the face of them, the adults often presented an almost monolithic unity, in stark contrast to many groups we visited. Jerry remarked that in his view there were two types of communes, those that were built out of idealism and those built out of failure. In his view Red Dawn was the phoenix that sprang from the ashes of Ted and Sue's marriage. But he also claimed that the trend to 'permissiveness' – a word which then one could not avoid – which all communes exemplified was in reality an attempt by many to avoid the responsibilities of parenthood. This, he felt, was certainly true of Ted and Sue (and perhaps himself?). Many of the adults, but particularly Ted, were consistently verbally aggressive towards the boys. Not only that, but the boys were constantly lectured on their antisocial behaviour, and argument after argument was rained down upon their heads in order to push home the point that a particular piece of behaviour was wrong, by adult after adult. The following incidents appeared typical.

Rob had mislaid a recorder and books at school and failed to report the loss there. This emerged in conversation with Maggie, who grilled and criticised him. It was then pursued by Ted and Sue for his stupidity on three counts: losing the things, not reporting the loss and not having adequate reasons for doing either. The scene culminated with Rob on the ground and Ted twisting his arm and asking fiercely, 'Do you see what's getting me annoyed, Rob? You don't want to do anything about it, do you?' Rob was extremely frightened. It was decided that Maggie should go to the school to investigate the following morning. In another incident David went to the swimming pool on his own, which was forbidden. Bill found out and told David off and then told Sue, who herself told David off before telling Ted, who also told David off. This battering repetition was common, and it was rare for a complaint to be dealt with by only one adult. Moreover, it seemed that it was almost impossible for the boys to confide in any of the adults without being betrayed.

Meal-times were punctuated by Ted's sarcastic remarks: 'Have you noticed, Luke, that we do not read at the table?'; 'Acting your age again, Rob?' On one occasion Sue bluntly told Rob, who was not an easy child, that she had tolerated him enough that evening. As the barb penetrated, Ted remarked that the department of home truths was open yet again. All this was considerably at variance with what Ted said he was doing:

Ted: Now the way I treat Luke, and I think the way he is generally treated in the house, is that people really recognise that he is not a child to the extent that he *does* have ideas of his own . . . I don't want him to act on my ideas; I want him to act on his own ideas. Now, when I said things like this to my mum, who's very old-fashioned, she said, 'How ridiculous! He's still only a child. How can you help him unless you make suggestions?' . . . She sees it as a parent's duty thing. Well, I don't.

Jerry: If it was just you, and Sue, and him, that's where you should worry about your suggestions. But he won't, he'll get tons of others. So you have just as much right to suggest things as anyone else. Living like this he is going to hear everybody's ideas, and yours will be just one of them.

Us: Everybody has an equal say in the kids?

Ted: Mm, I think that does work.

Jerry: Yes, it does.

Ted: I think that has a lot to do with Sue's and my attitudes towards them as parents . . . I've not wanted to be emotionally tied to the extent where I couldn't untie myself, or they couldn't untie themselves without a big leaving-home scene. So . . . I have had this attitude towards them of wanting to encourage them to be independent. I don't necessarily go about it the right way . . . I don't think there's anything special about biological relationships. In fact I think you have to play it down to put it into perspective. I think it's so hard to think in a balanced way about a blood relation . . . I feel that

80

the way I behave is from the necessity to play it down, in order to balance this emotional reaction.

I like Luke as a person and sometimes I don't. The same as one does with any person. Someone once said to me, 'Don't you love your children?' It wasn't an accusative thing; it was just an interested question. I couldn't answer it; I couldn't find the relevance of the question. I couldn't understand it . . .

After Ted had left Jerry said:

He's passionate about being dispassionate. The plain fact is that Ted doesn't love his children and neither does Sue, and it's a damn good job we're here. People here don't realise how lucky they are, and I am always trying to get them to realise it. This situation is much better than a normal nuclear family – whatever normal means. This is the only way to live. After all, most people aren't cut out for parenthood, and why should they be? It's a terrible burden for two people to bring up three boys . . . When I first came here the boys were really repressed, really under the thumb. I've tried to make things a bit different. One or two times I've had to tell Ted that I was sick of his constant aggression.

Ted recognised that others might mistake the motives for his behaviour towards his children: 'Perhaps I've got some attitudes and ways of behaving that other people wouldn't . . . underlying that is this feeling – not of dissociation, although I often wonder if that is what it seems like to other people – is that what I am saying is they are nothing to do with me. I hope it doesn't because I don't feel that, but I do feel that, *not* that it's nothing to do with me, but they are not *all* to do with me only.'

Nevertheless there seemed to be iron reluctance to accede to any of the children's demand for affection or attention or to treat them sensitively. The conversations recorded above were not deliberately shielded from the objects they were about, the boys. As a consequence, to the degree that they spent time in the group, the boys were disturbed. The youngest was rarely at home, and he had the sunniest disposition, although his mother believes that to be all surface; the next oldest had very few friends and only one for sure, but the oldest seemed to have no friends at all outside the group, and often had to turn to Bill for comfort when attacked by his father. He had been asked to find more friends. Rob was desperate for affection, but fun was made of him at the dinner table because he wanted to be cuddled by his mother. He was ten years old. Desperately, he had latched on to Peter, who gave him pocket money, and with whom he was going to share a room. However, his mother thought the relationship unhealthy. Rob displayed other symptoms of distress. One was that he wet his bed regularly. On one such occasion he did not wash and change his soiled linen as he was expected to do. Ted discovered this and roared into the attack. Rob pleaded with him not to shout: 'Why do you always shout at me?' The response was immediate: 'Because your wetting the bed is your way of shouting at us', and the unspoken words were not, 'What do you want?' but 'Shut up and be quiet.' When the group broke up and Sue moved out of the house for a short rest with the boys, the bed-wetting stopped, at least for a while.

All the boys, it was believed, indulged in petty theft within the group. One of the causes of this may have been that they were not given a regular sum of pocket money but had to ask for, and justify, each individual thing they wanted, and perhaps they wished to have something not completely on adult terms. This behaviour extended with Rob and Luke into rifling the private belongings of the adults. Duncan, who shared a room with Luke, was annoyed that Luke read all his private correspondence and obviously searched his belongings. He also tended to secrete away, magpie fashion, objects of no particular intrinsic value. He would hide magazines and papers so that they could only be read by himself. He was excessively shy, rarely spoke to strangers or in front of them, had almost no friends and was constantly in danger of being reduced to helpless tears by his father.

The group collapsed when the animosity between Bill and Ted escalated to a point where Ted said at the second anniversary party that he could no longer tolerate living in the same house as Bill, and he must leave. This declaration by Ted was partly prompted by the difficulties with the Council over the mortgage which were due to the presence of those outside Ted's immediate family in the house. Bill refused to go and found that everyone wanted him to stay, except Ted, with Maggie abstaining. Ted thereupon announced that Red Dawn was finished and he was putting the house up for sale. Over the next six months, Peter, Jerry and Duncan quietly moved out and found a flat together, as did Ted and Maggie. Sue was left in a state of shock in the house with the boys, but Ted then moved back in to facilitate the sale of the house, over which Sue was determined to fight tooth and nail. Although initially a reluctant member of Red Dawn, she was now convinced of the rightness of communal living and wanted to start again. Ted asked David and Rob to live with him, but Rob was reluctant to do this, and Sue opposed it. Luke was not asked. Eventually David moved in with his father and Maggie, and the other two boys lived with Sue.

In a sense the destiny of Red Dawn was obvious to us from the moment we entered their world. It may appear ghoulish of us to have stayed in such circumstances, but in our defence it should be made clear that it appeared to us that our visit was wanted by at least some of the group. We cannot be sure of their motives, but we suspect that they felt reassured by the sense of concreteness that being studied gave their fragile experiment. Our attention was interpreted, we hope, as a validation of the seriousness of their enterprise. We do not believe we contributed to their difficulties, although our presence did bring out their differences as attempts were made to ensure that the correct version of their aims and achievements was carried away by the researcher.

We showed an early version of this account to some of the members of Red Dawn in an effort to ensure that what we had said was factually correct and that our interpretation of events was not completely misplaced. There was a general agreement that someone like us could come to describe their life in the way we have, but whilst there was some disagreement over matters of fact there was unanimity that we had missed much. We were told that the boys were very fond of the young baby and that they did receive more warmth and affection from the adults than we saw. However, what emerged above all from our discussions with members of the group over the adequacy of our account was that they clearly felt, despite all the stresses and strains, that they had through thick and thin really and persistently attempted to treat each other as human beings. It speaks volumes that Sue, who was our first contact in these negotiations, still knew where many of the group were. Luke has left school and now works at an adventure playground where John is the leader. Sue copied our bleak account and sent it out to some of the others involved. The group's replies flowed back to us, and to each other, and they did not hide their reactions to what we had said from us or from each other. They were honest to a degree which is very rare. One can only wonder how a human group committed to such frankness could survive for as long in our society and at the enormous costs which must have been involved, which for a time they were willingly prepared to pay.

Findhorn

Findhorn is probably the best-known of British communal projects. It is widely thought of as the most successful, and both in the writings produced by its own members and in such accounts of it as that offered by Andrew Rigby (1974b) its apparent success in realising many of the hopes of communes is attributed to the fact that it combines a commitment to loving relationships among its members with the discipline of religious belief and leadership. Certainly Findhorn is something more than a family commune; it has some of the properties of a utopian community, and for a time it seemed to be taking on the

83

character of both a quasi-commune and a purposive commune. Its success, whether measured by wealth or size or longevity, is impressive; its enthusiasm for publicity and its openness to visitors have made it an appreciable influence in the commune movement as a whole; over the years it has become something of a school for communal living. But the principle it asserts is that communal projects can succeed only if friendship and shared work are reinforced by disciplined submission to the supernatural.

The cornerstone of the Findhorn community is belief in a world of spirits who communicate their wisdom and their wishes to mortals who are 'attuned' to them. By cooperating strenuously with the spirits, mortals can realise on earth a life of harmony and abundance. The spirit world itself abounds with spirits containing, insofar as it has revealed itself at Findhorn, a Supreme Being, the Beloved, St Germain, the Master of the Seventh Ray, a variety of Nature Spirits under the leadership of the god Pan, and the Devas and Elementals whose knowledge is the immediate basis for releasing the natural abundance of the physical world – exemplified in the Findhorn gardens, the triumphant cultivation of the Moray Firth sand dunes. These beings communicate regularly and variously to the core members of the community, who in turn devote themselves to ensuring that the 'guidance' they have received is vigorously enacted by the community as a whole and to leading the other members towards an ever deeper condition of attunement. The counterpart of attunement is 'manifestation'. Manifestation is presented as an explicitly miraculous process through which those who are attuned to the spirit world receive what they need. Pride is taken in the fact that Findhorn has become a prosperous and comfortable settlement, and its well-being is seen as an outcome of the 'laws of manifestation' in action. Thus, the success of the garden is not just the result of organic horticulture and back-breaking work, but of the collaboration of the gardeners with factor 'x', the fact that they were working in harmony with the spirit world on the basis of the guidance received by those who are attuned to it. The manifesting of the harvest is thus also a manifestation of the reality of attunement. Powerful forces are acknowledged to be at work directing and controlling the life of Findhorn, but the power is held to be incorporeal, inaccessible, merely flowing through particular members of the group who are sensitive to it and being mediated by them. The fact that manifestation occurs, that large sums of money or skilled workers or consumer durables appear when they are needed, provides material validation for the eclectic, complex system of belief in a spirit world with which Findhorn is in tune that constitutes the distinctive moral and intellectual milieu of the community. Great emphasis is placed by the core members of the community on the fact that what is manifested is just what

84

is needed and that it appears just when it is needed – whether it is a matter of £12,000 or a twelve-string guitar, a plumber or a piano:

MANIFESTATION OF A PIANO

Ever since the Sanctuary was erected we had been promised that the right piano would come to us at the right time . . . We made our need known in the Sanctuary and asked the community to visualize a baby grand piano there. We realized that it would be very expensive to transport a piano from London or even Edinburgh and the chances of finding one in the North of Scotland appeared negligible, but with God the seemingly impossible becomes possible, for the following week there appeared an advertisement in the local paper for a baby grand piano! It had been stored at Forres only three miles away! It was in beautiful condition and after trying it out we made an offer. We needed it in the Sanctuary in time for the performance of the choir at Jenny and Tony's wedding which was to take place in two days' time. I phoned the removal firm and was told that for various reasons delivery in time for the wedding would be impossible. I remarked that I didn't recognize the word 'impossible' and that I expected the piano that afternoon. It was in fact delivered then and was tuned just in time for the wedding. (*Findhorn News*, Aug. 1971: 42)

Stressing the miraculous quality of these demonstrations establishes the vital importance of intimate harmony between Findhorn and the spirits who guide it. Conversely, access to the spirit world through guidance becomes an unassailable source of authority and leadership within the community. The connection between guidance and manifestation is at once close and obscure. Almost invariably guidance takes the form of indicating that what is needed must be determinedly worked for. 'Work is love made manifest' is a fundamental Findhorn principle and there is no question of abundance being manifested to those who merely wait passively for it. Sometimes a cynic might suspect the spirits of a surprisingly canny opportunism – would the guitar have been manifested if the need for it had been expressed at any time other than during the two-day visit of a former pop musician who was abandoning his career to become a Sufi teacher? More frequently the guidance that is received has a hard-headed realism which clearly grasps the material conditions for the community's survival. Faced with an influx of new members anxious to establish craft industries at Findhorn in the spring of 1970, the following guidance was received:

It must be made very clear to those who come to join you to help create and establish these various industries that . . . you cannot carry them financially nor accommodate them . . . All must contribute something financially to the whole. How this is done is up to each one individually. I have told you that you are not to carry any more. The load is getting top-heavy. It is very important that those who come to join you, whoever they are, do not come under false promises or illusions. I tell you [Findhorn] is not to carry any more people financially. If this means that some have to have part-time jobs, it will all work out. What they do about accommodation is up to them. (*Findhorn News*, Feb. 1971: 26-7)

At the same time the idea of manifestation nullifies the idea of the self as powerless in a universe of accidents. The accidental is seen now as the very link that ties one meaningfully into a purposeful order. Perhaps this is one reason Findhorn appeals so powerfully to the very young and the very old, to people in whose lives accident is especially present and especially troubling.

Findhorn is the creation of Peter and Eileen Caddy and their friend Dorothy Maclean. Eileen and Dorothy both receive guidance. Peter does not, and he can be wryly humorous about the fact that he is merely the executive member of the team; it is he who, on the basis of not recognising the word impossible, ensures that everything that can be done to realise the others' guidance is done. He is the driving force of mortal collaboration with the wishes of the supernatural. These three moved to a caravan in the Findhorn Bay caravan site in 1962, having been guided to do so after Peter had lost his job as manager of a nearby hotel. A series of disasters ended with Peter's having his unemployment benefit cut off, and at that point, almost destitute, they were guided to attempt to cultivate the rubbish tip at the caravan site to grow their own food. With no practical knowledge but with complete confidence and energy, they set about creating the Findhorn garden. From 1962 until 1968 they lived in virtual isolation in the caravan, publishing literature from time to time about their beliefs and about the success of their garden. As their activities came to the notice of others interested in esoteric religions, as articles about them appeared in the *Science of Thought Review* and other journals concerned with spiritual manifestations, as news of them spread through the 'underground' press to people interested either in organic gardening or in communal living (and at that time the two were closely related as the magazine *Gandalf's Garden* testified), and as they attracted the interest of members of the Soil association, they became caught up in the wide-ranging network of spiritist groups propagating religions of the New Age, and they began to receive letters of support, donations and visitors. Some of the visitors wanted to stay, and Eileen received guidance that all who wanted to join them should be made welcome. Newcomers were encouraged to renounce the world, sell their possessions and settle at Findhorn, and by the summer of 1969 a group of some sixteen people had joined them, mostly middle-aged and middle-class like themselves. Further caravans were added, but they also began to build wooden bungalows and a community centre and a Sanctuary. The beliefs and aspirations of the new members at that time were close to those of Peter and Eileen Caddy, and it seemed that a small stable community very much under their leadership and devoted to a sort of transcendental horticulture might be consolidated.

But over the next three years Findhorn experienced a series of invasions –and crises. While continuing to recruit elderly and relatively moneyed people, especially women, through the networks of spiritist belief, Findhorn was, in effect, discovered by the commune movement. It became almost a centre of pilgrimage for the wandering young, for would-be communards, spiritual leaders and teachers of every description, vegans and vegetarians, craft workers and Americans. The community seemed to flourish in the face of all this. It grew dramatically, claiming 45 members in 1970 and 120 in 1971 in addition to an unnumbered tide of visitors. Its buildings expanded and its activities diversified. It became a registered charitable trust and used the funds that flowed into it to develop or buy new buildings, including the former home of the landlord of the caravan site. They established craft studios for weaving, pottery and painting, recording and printing workshops, a nursery and a supermarket; they launched musical and theatrical projects, set up the Findhorn College and consolidated the whole range of these activities under the auspices of the Findhorn Foundation. In all of this they were of course led by the constant guidance received by the core members of the group; as Peter Caddy wrote early in 1971, 'With each new phase of the work at Findhorn Elixir [Eileen's spiritual name] has been given a vision and I have been responsible for the manifestation of it (*Findhorn News*, Feb. 1971: 46).

In practice, to wring success from the experience of these years was a matter of hard and often ruthless leadership. Profound conflicts of interest had to be resolved. Procedures for selecting suitable new members and for excluding difficult existing members had to be devised. The increasingly diverse energies within the community had to be harnessed and focussed. And perhaps most difficult of all but most essential for the morale of the community, all this had to be done in a way that encouraged and recognised the ability of all members to receive guidance while still maintaining the over-arching authority of the guidance received by the core members. Not surprisingly, the growth and continued cohesion of Findhorn in these years left a trail of considerable personal bitterness among those who lost out in the battle for the community's identity. We visited Findhorn three times between 1971 and 1973, and on each occasion behind the warmth and enthusiasm with which we ourselves were received that battle was raging. Just after our first visit, about a dozen of the younger members left following a series of wrangling disputes with Peter about the purpose and nature of Findhorn. Just before our last visit, about forty others, mainly members associated with the craft workshops, left after they too had been talked into seeing that Findhorn was not for them. These departures were quite directly end-products of the invasions that had sustained Findhorn's growth. It had been decided that Findhorn was not to be a quasi-communal haven for the transient young, nor was it to be a purposive commune devoted to the manufacture and marketing of craft products.

A more successful invasion was that of the Americans led by David Spangler and Myrtle Glines. In trying to understand why these newcomers became such a central part of Findhorn so quickly, we found it helpful to see their arrival against the background of the problem raised for the community by some of its other would-be members. The first to appear were the hippies. Initially Peter Caddy had taken a tough line with the young, impecunious and long-haired, but by the summer of 1969 they were turning up at Findhorn in increasing numbers, and influential friends and patrons of the community such as Sir George Trevelyan came to appreciate that insofar as the young were 'questing for a deeper meaning to life' they were 'completely ripe for accepting the spiritual picture of man and the universe'. Eileen was guided that all were to be received equally into the life of the New Age (Findhorn 1969a: 10): 'there is so much youth can learn from the older generation and vice versa . . . let there be a blending together of the two', and it was decided that the doors should be opened to them. With some trepidation, the attempt to blend the original Findhorn membership and the hippies was undertaken. Peter Caddy has described the initial uneasiness very openly:

> Last summer a hippy couple with a four year old daughter arrived out of the blue. Their appearance, with their long hair, off-beat clothes and dirt struck an odd note in this corner of Scotland. Living together was a test and needed tolerance and understanding on both sides. It was apparent from the start that we all had many lessons to learn from this visit. For example, on our part we had to learn tolerance and understanding and an appreciation of the childlike loving simplicity of the 'flower people'; they on the other hand had to learn that dirty, torn and slovenly clothes and being unwashed and unshaven was not acceptable at Findhorn, particularly in Sanctuary. Some of us were particularly concerned because we were expecting a retired naval captain and his wife to join us for a while. Elixir sought guidance on this and was assured

88

that all was well and to leave the mixing of people in God's hands. (Findhorn 1969a: 3)

In general terms the experiment was not a success. Eileen's guidance in the months that followed contained a curious mixture of emphasis on tolerance on the one hand and on obedience and discipline on the other; 'Youth is looking for the answer; the answer lies deep within each one. The answer is so simple, they are afraid to accept it. The answer is to listen to My still small voice and OBEY it. Obedience is essential.' And again (in a manner curiously reminiscent of Family Farm): 'Work is love in action. It is useless talking about love, live it.' And 'Far too many of the young today lack discipline and have lost their way because of it. . . . Therefore they have the greatest difficulty in accepting and acknowledging My authority' (Findhorn 1969a: 11). Some of the young people who arrived between 1969 and 1970 did respond to such guidance, but the presence of a large number, who did not – 'the dregs of Findhorn' as they were described to us by one of the more mature members – was very unsettling. Their mere presence proposed the possibility of a type of communalism quite unlike that envisaged by the older members of Findhorn. And to this challenge the core of the community seemed to be able to find no answer other than discipline, work and the increasing institutionalisation of the community's life. A daily timetable was worked out, 'so that all who come here may know what is expected of them', with three long work sessions and two periods of guidance in the Sanctuary. Eileen provided guidance every day. Peter poured his energy into organising both work and play. But the sense of uneasy authority was plain to discern, whether in Peter's instruction: 'For the efficient running of the community, punctuality is essential', or in Eileen's guidance: 'If anyone is in doubt as to what needs to be done, he can always find out from Peter' (Findhorn 1971: 3–4). The wrangles developed, and Peter was driven to expel the most obdurate of the hippies.

Meanwhile, another invasion had been building up, less obviously threatening and at first easier to accommodate. This was the influx of craft workers, many of them disenchanted teachers who saw in Findhorn a chance to practise what elsewhere they had only been able to preach. So long as they could support themselves these people were welcomed eagerly; indeed, they were seen as a manifestation of the need for skilled workers to develop the artistic side of the community. From the first, however, some of these newcomers were sceptical about the spiritual ascendancy of the Caddys, pressed for greater autonomy in managing their own work and dreamed of developing Findhorn into an essentially secular centre of craft production. Even before the issues of communal identity posed by the hippies had been resolved, new and potentially much more challenging issues were being raised. The com-

89

munity was growing in a spectacular way, but it was acquiring a diversity which was increasingly difficult to contain. 'Unity in Diversity' became at this time its most strongly emphasised slogan. It was into this situation that David Spangler walked when he first arrived at Findhorn in June 1970.

David Spangler and Myrtle Glines had spent several years lecturing and counselling in the United States as teachers of the New Age before learning of Findhorn. They had dreamed of progressing from mere teaching to the practical building of a New Age community and, impressed by the sense of immediate accomplishment in the Caddys' accounts of the Findhorn garden, they visited the group in the summer of 1970 and immediately recognised it as what they had been looking for. The Caddys for their part, struggling with the problem of maintaining the identity of the community in the face of diverse demands, found in David Spangler a vital source of definition and decision, a powerfully guided voice to strengthen and deepen the spiritual commitment of the community. He was hailed as embodying 'the very Spirit of the New Age', and Eileen received a vision of him as 'a happy, joyous troubadour leading a great multitude of people singing and dancing into the new heaven and the new earth'. He and Myrtle were admitted directly to the core of the community, and pending their permanent arrival Eileen received guidance that Findhorn should now restrict visitors to a minimum. The open-door policy was suspended.

The guidance offered through or by David Spangler is of a very much more elaborated and theologically inflated order than that received by either Eileen Caddy or Dorothy Maclean. With his arrival, a complex, elusive and frequently opaque body of rather generalised guidance was added to the relatively direct, pragmatic and often quite naive messages which had previously sustained Findhorn. The mystical celebration of Findhorn as a 'centre of light' was intensified and institutionalised in a corpus of lectures, pamphlets and tape recordings. The old style of guidance, so largely a matter of 'orders of the day', as one member described it, was not superseded, but it fell into place as part of a larger and much more complex and impenetrable account of the community. The idea of Findhorn as the missionary centre of a movement of revitalisation was lifted to a new plane of sophistication and boldly albeit ambiguously asserted: 'It is important that the proper perspective be gained of the role and value of Findhorn and its work in assisting world transformation. . . . This is a planetary movement of consciousness, inspiring a universal outlook both horizontally in promoting the realisation of the brotherhood and oneness of all humanity, and vertically in proving that spiritual consciousness is . . . an indication of man's next leap of evolution into a level of thought and aware-

ness filled with the power and creativity of the wholeness of life.'
Increasing attention was now devoted to problems of 'consciousness'
and 'awareness' and to the notion of Findhorn as having a specific
teaching function. The idea of the Findhorn College materialised, and
its development became the special task of David and Myrtle –
although it seems to have been largely through Peter's efforts that the
building for it was manifested. By the autumn of 1971, a colony of
Americans had come to Findhorn, many of them young, many with
training in the arts, dancing, acting and music, and quite a number of
them recruited on the basis of earlier contact with David Spangler or
Myrtle Glines. The presence of this group caused some problems of
communication for some of the older members – we heard people mut-
tering about the 'mindless devotion' of the Americans – but their overall contribution was both invigorating and strongly supportive of the
new 'cultural' direction of the community. The performing arts became
a very important part of the life of Findhorn both in sustaining constant internal entertainment in the form of concerts, revues or more
informal 'fun nights', and in staging plays and musical entertainments
to publicise the community outside – 'bridges of creativity'.

The issue of 'Unity in Diversity' was progressively resolved during
the two following years by a combination of spiritual pluralism and
material rationalisation. On the one hand, Eileen received guidance
that she and Peter should play a less dominant role in the community's
spiritual life; others, too, were to be encouraged to receive and trans-
mit guidance. Although Peter remained the 'custodian' of the community and Eileen was still to be the 'ultimate' source of policy and arbi-
tration when guidance received by others was questioned, Findhorn
publications from this period referred to 'Peter, Eileen, David and
Myrtle as overall co-ordinators' of the community. On the other hand,
a much tighter control of the membership was established: members
now had to provide their own accommodation and cover their own
living expenses; a minimum charge of £2 a day was introduced
(accompanied by the guidance 'this is not a hippie commune and
nothing should be taken for granted'), together with a rule that there
should be a probationary period of three months for prospective members 'during which time they have the opportunity to integrate with
the whole'. At the same time the various activities of the community
became more formally organised into 'departments' and an increasingly
defined sense of the relative priority of different activities and of the
proper relationship of activities to one another within the broad purposes of Findhorn was achieved. This development culminated in the
idea that Findhorn was to evolve into a 'University of Light'; teaching,
publishing and cultural activities closely linked to diffusing the ideas of

91

the New Age were accordingly given primary importance; independent craft production, especially if conceived of as an economically self-sustaining and morally self-justifying activity, and communal living merely on the level of personal relationships were proportionately deprecated. Beneath the surface this movement stirred deep and intractable tensions which led eventually, during a period when Peter Caddy was in hospital, to David Spangler's taking a decision to close down the craft studios entirely and calling on those concerned to ask themselves sincerely whether Findhorn was really the right place for them. Subsequently, after a large number of the craft workers had left, the studios were reopened, but now much more firmly and explicitly subordinated to the theological purposes of the community.

The process which led up to the departure of unsuitable people in such situations seems to have been one in which fundamental questions about the nature of Findhorn became quite overt. Typically, David, Myrtle, Peter and Eileen would discuss with such people the problems raised by their presence, and in these discussions contrasting images of the community would be frankly identified. In one such session that was described to us the troublesome members were first told that they had been channelling evil forces into the community and then urged to sacrifice their individuality for the sake of the whole. For two hours they put forward their case for developing Findhorn as a 'democratic community' centred on communication between individuals rather than wholeness, and for two hours they were patiently, persistently told that that was not what Findhorn was about. In this case at least, the members in question ended by drawing the conclusion that they were being thrown out and by the end of the session had come to see Findhorn's pretensions to be a community as they understood community as a pious fraud. The conflict of purpose had come into the open. They had been disenchanted, and they left. Many of the people who had been through such processes of disenchantment and extrusion, ex-members of Findhorn whom we met, ended feeling both disillusioned and baffled about what had happened to them. Their bitterness about the core members of the community in particular seemed to be as deep as their original hopes must have been: 'They've got each other conned and together they con everyone else' was the best account one such ex-member could give us. Findhorn had perhaps become an all-or-nothing undertaking – either one participated wholly or one found it wholly oppressive. At the time of our last visit Findhorn had reconstituted itself with a high degree of solidarity, but it had done so at the cost of excluding many communal aspirations from its own range of possibilities. From being a model for the commune movement, Findhorn has become the antithesis of what many members of the movement are looking for. Perhaps it always was.

4. Self-seeking

'With what then do you charge me?' asked Hollingsworth, aghast and greatly disturbed by this attack. 'Show me one selfish end in all I have ever aimed at, and you may cut it out of my bosom with a knife!'

'It is all self!' answered Zenobia, with still intenser bitterness. 'Nothing else; nothing but self, self, self! You have embodied yourself in a project. You are a better masquerader than the witches and gipsies yonder, for your disguise is a self-deception.'

Hawthorne, *The Blithedale Romance*

Much of what has been written about communes and communities is concerned with the problem of social solidarity. Rosabeth Kanter's study (1972) of American communes opens out into a wide-ranging, powerful treatment of the nature and conditions of social commitment in general. In his writings on kibbutzim (1963 and 1965) Melford Spiro similarly emphasises processes of social bonding and attachment. Indeed, it is largely their relevance for Durkheim's old questions about the moral base on which societies can hold together that has made communes analytically interesting to sociologists. But this very interest can easily blur the fact that most individual members of most communes are, quite simply but in a profound way, in it for themselves. The impulse to communal living springs from a sense of personal estrangement, from feelings of threatened or frustrated individuality. The other side of the question of social solidarity in communes is thus unavoidably a question of individual identity. And among the communes we studied the latter side of the coin was normally uppermost.

> How did I join a commune? Through meeting a group with whom I immediately felt a strong connection and who were working towards communal living. Realising that we shared ideals that were impossible to realise within the system. All this happening at a point of change for me when I no longer had a clear direction and was really looking at what I had and where I was heading . . . a realisation that communal living could supply some answers. (Q.261)

Communes have become settings in which the heirs of a culture of possessive individualism attempt to possess a self. In the extreme case communality may express a triumph of self-seeking. But Hawthorne's heroine was wrong or at least naive in equating this fundamental self-seeking with selfishness; for Hawthorne, Hollingsworth is a creative and a tragic figure as well as a destructive one – even when those around him experience his self-seeking as selfishness. In emphasising the central importance of self in contemporary communes we are not trying to debunk communes but to stress a peculiar cruelty of our sort of society: the fact that individuality is a *collective* representation. To the extent that one is sensitive to the most distinctive cultural themes of such a society, one is exposed to extraordinarily powerful pressures to grasp a unique identity. Only thus can one be fully 'of' the society. Communes are, for reasons we shall discuss later on, recruited from people whose situation makes them especially vulnerable to that ambiguous requirement.

The problem of selfishness in communes is an effect of the prestige which the society to which commune members are seeking an alternative has invested in the idea of the self. The completeness of that investment itself drives some sensitive or conscientious people to escape from the routine processes by which selves are constructed in the orthodox system of that society. But insofar as their escape is collective, the completeness of the same investment also undermines their struggle for authenticity. It is a matter of social bad faith. A socially created demand for individuality produces members of communes whose demand for individuality then wrecks communes as societies. When we went to Long Lea, a commune in the least culti-vated stretches of West Yorkshire, we found brambles grown over the path, a gate off its hinges, a deserted farmhouse and, painted on a mounting-block by the door, Brecht's message 'He who laughs – has not heard the terrible news.' Some news is none the less terrible for being familiar, indeed only becomes terrible when it has been lived personally – such as the news of the artificial antithesis of the self and the social which is the heart of the culture of western capitalism. Capi-talist civilisation presents the responsive individual with a problem of personal authenticity. It does not give us adequate ways of grading the success or failure, let alone the moral worth, of different solutions to that problem. Communal projects are fragile and contradictory but not absurd for being rooted in self-seeking.

It is after all only through carefully and mutually negotiated self-seeking that a commune as a collective identity expressing its members authentically can be brought into being. The alternatives, to which endless communes succumb, are splitting up or the more or less overt restoration of someone's domination.

In our view collective self-seeking is the primary reality of com-

94

munes and must be understood before anything useful can be said about the significance of communes as model societies. From this point of view what matters is not the persistence or morale of a group but the opportunity for individuals to grasp a more or less enduring personal reality.

> I just *had* to find out who I was and where I was at. I wanted to break down stereotyped ideas of how one has to live or ought to live. I wanted to avoid hating, disliking, being indifferent, competing, ignoring. I wanted to try to live by love, not manipulation. There's no relief in 'I' separate from relations with others.
> (Q.161)

Of course if we took what some members of the commune movement say about communes very seriously, we should expect the achievement of personal identity to coincide with the cohesion of the commune. That is just what getting together is all about. But the fact that this ideal is very rarely achieved does not mean that many communes may not be serving other purposes very well indeed. Ross Speck (1972: 156) goes so far as to suggest that the constant disintegration of communes, their very failure as societies, is itself evidence of their success as settings for the conquest of personal identity. For him, communes are temporary refuges from society in which the individual can piece together a sufficiently integrated self to allow him to reenter society and make his way with reasonable competence in it. The value of communes is thus related directly to the transience of their membership, to their contribution to what Speck calls the 'phoenix phenomenon'. This interpretation is normally put forward as a way of saying something positive about communes, and we shall take it seriously as such in this chapter. But such accounts also tend to deny what is explicit in most communal projects, the possibility of overcoming the basic separation of the self and the social given in our culture. They discover a valuable latent function for communes, but in doing so they devalue the most cherished of the overt purposes for which communes are constructed. For Speck, communes are a type of 'detour from reality'. The communal claim to be rather what Rigby (1974a) calls an 'alternative reality' is rejected out of hand. While recognising self-seeking as the major source of energy in the commune movement, we should like to leave the question of the reality or unreality of what that energy achieves unanswered at this stage – if only because the *form* taken by self-seeking in communes, the communal intention, commands a certain respect.

Many people join communes to find or realise their selves. People are embarking on such ventures all the time, of course. What is peculiar to the people who turn to communes for that end is that they have at once rejected socially given recipes for self-construction and understood that selves are constructed socially. They turn *to* social relations at the same time that they turn away from society. Although we found a great deal of criticism of self-centredness in communes, and perhaps too many people spending too much time eyeing one another uneasily for signs of self-centredness, we hardly found anyone who subscribed to the naive religion that sees self-realisation as a matter of doing-your-own-thing. Rather, there was as the prevailing mood in most communes an acute, sometimes inhibiting, awareness of the connectedness of personal autonomy with reciprocity in social relations. It was this very awareness that put so many members of communes anxiously on their guard against what one of them described as 'possessive assertiveness as people battle to grab shapes for their own identities from the glamour of this movement' – an anxiety which in its turn easily and frequently becomes a new obstacle to reciprocity. But whatever its practical difficulties the common sense of the problem of self-realisation in communes is a thoroughly social one, involving a firm conception of autonomy as a quality discovered through and in reciprocity of relationship. The point of a commune is, through living with others, to make one's way to a satisfactory account of oneself, an account realised and expressed in terms of one's relations with those others. The importance of communes may be said to be the understanding they embody that personal autonomy is concomitant with interpersonal reciprocity, together with their claim that the normal social relations of modern Britain *therefore* make personal autonomy unattainable for most people. Whether they succeed or fail as societies, they confront us with a significant moral challenge. Whether they succeed or fail, their existence as a form of social deviance is a serious comment on the moral capacities of our normal society. The values and ideals which our culture has carefully set up as peculiarly worth building into one's personal identity have become, communes imply, to the degree that they are really valued, sources of a counter-culture, reasons for separating the self from society.

Patterns of self-concern

I want to get out. I want to live. But how? Because I must pay a high rent, or make compulsory insurance contributions, or dress in seemly fashion, I must work my hours away at tasks in which I do not believe and must be grateful for a little leisure in which to ponder the meaninglessness of it all. I am not work-shy. But I do need to believe in what I am doing – to see it as self-justifying or as a reasonable price to pay for the rest of time – time to look and love and meditate and be creative or be still. I want to live in the now, not in the future. I want to harm no one, to help a few, to

96

love and be loved, to eat a little and sleep a little and laugh a lot. Is that so very wicked? Yet how to do it? (*Communes*, 33: 18)

In trying to interpret the meaning of self-seeking in the communes we studied, we were particularly struck by four patterns in which self-seeking seemed to work itself out: there was a pattern woven around the themes of love and work; a pattern of concern with self and society; a pattern of solemnity and playfulness; and a pattern of openness and closure in relation to the possibilities of individual action.

It is said that once when he was asked for a formula for human well-being, Freud answered simply, 'to love and to work'. We shall never know whether he meant merely marriage and a job with the trick of socialisation worked so that in both one was adjusted to society or whether in some more utopian sense he meant loving and working lived and experienced in such a way as to balance, actively and creatively, the qualities of autonomy and reciprocity in each. But probability favours the latter. It is certainly in the latter sense that many communes see themselves as utopian projects. Almost without exception, commune members treat the relationships of love and of work as equally important centres of value. If we were to abstract a theory of communes from our observations, its main principle might be that it is above all through the right sort of working and loving that communal identities, identities fusing the self and the social, will be created. People in communes spend a great deal of time talking to each other about each other – indeed, a not uncommon source of strain is for some of the older members to find the endless soul-searching so exhausting and its returns of insight so diminished that they withdraw from the talking in search of some moments of privacy, a withdrawal which newer members then see as a major falling-off from proper standards of mutuality. Two of the topics most talked about are the conduct and state of members' personal relationships (and the meaning for those relationships of countless scraps of action), and the problem of meaningful work.

But in both cases the talk, and everything one can observe as well, reveals a curious ambivalence from the point of view of Freud's ideal. Some stable and mature relationships are achieved and talked about, if at all, in a rather off-hand, taken-for-granted way. But for the most part the search for love seems to be experienced and discussed in a strangely wary and conditional manner. An odd combination of fascination and scepticism, enthusiasm and hesitation is revealed: 'love is when two people's selfishness pulls the same way'. Frequently it seemed as though a calculus of giving and receiving was at work putting all relationships, but especially prospective ones, constantly in the balance, so that we observed wild swings to and fro between the principle of 'loving everyone' and the ruthless appraisal of the emotional costs and benefits a particular newcomer might involve for all existing members of a group. 'Love' is at best an obscure and tendentious word. Its use with such strong reference to both personal identity and group solidarity in communal contexts makes it especially difficult to interpret. There are certainly new recruits to communes who when they speak of 'loving all men' seem to envisage a state of permanent euphoria, and there are old hands who use the word as a synonym for being patient and tolerant. Perhaps the nearest one could come to an agreed meaning would be something quite close to the suggestion made by David Cooper in *The Death of the Family*:

> I think that the minimum condition for a relationship to be a love relationship is the experience after a great deal of relationship work, of tenderness, which is the positive residue after all negativity, resentment, hostility, envy and jealousy have been dissolved away frequently enough and deeply enough. If one tightens one's definition of love considerably the feeling amounts to trust. (Cooper 1971: 48)

And again:

> The positive centre of the experience of the community, however, resides in the guarantee that some other will always accompany one on one's journey into and through one's self. This guarantee . . . implies an implicit promise made by one or several people to other people. (p. 60)

Most serious communes are groups trying to hammer out such implicit promises within their everyday relationships. But to do so involves the slow, hard taming of the rampant self-awareness and self-seeking that brought the individuals concerned together in the first place. It is this that gives the daily story of the vicissitudes of love in many communes its peculiarly frantic quality. The problem is both recorded and well understood in most accounts of the break-up of communes:

> We didn't place enough importance on a person's need to be able to express his confusion and his fears in his own way without others getting uptight about the way he did it. Everyone was so fiercely independent, even if that independence was expressed in terms of non-committal, non-involvement in whatever particular conflict had been brought to a head at any time. It was after all the first time most of us had the chance to work out what we were and what we believed in out of the way of state institutions – school, paid work, university, family, etc. (*Communes*, 40: 9)

In the communes we came to know best, most personal relationships were of a shifting, exploratory, open-ended nature, at once intense and guarded – and minutely observed both by the participants and by everyone else around. Several times we were offered the comparison

98

between this world and a series of shipboard romances, life lived at a high emotional pitch and always changing – a situation in which individuals could be both tentative and deadly serious, both involved and irresponsible. We have suggested before that the structure of a relatively stable commune is likely to consist of a core of fairly long-standing members and a fringe of transients. On the whole we found that the active and explicit interest in experimenting with love as a dimension of self-realisation – 'I want to love and be loved' – was a characteristic of the fringe rather than of the core groups. The latter tended to be relatively cool about love; perhaps because their particular relationships had over a longish period taken root in the everyday practical life of the commune. When members of the core of a commune allow themselves to become caught up in the hectic shipboard life of the fringe, it can have explosively disruptive effects for the commune as a whole. On the other hand, it is the comings and goings of members of the fringe that sustain the awareness of love as a basic communal value calling for active attention. The overall effect is that on the one hand the capacity to love and be loved, and therefore involvement in loving relationships, is treated as a fundamental personal value and component of identity ('communities are built of lovers . . . the first step is to get together with people you love'), but on the other hand the effective test of the authenticity of love seems to be not so much commitment as choice.

A comparable and complementary ambivalence appears in communal attitudes to work. There is an almost universal rejection of conventional occupations, of nine-to-five, of wages and salaries, of alienated labour in all its routine organised forms. Hand in hand with this rejection goes a demand for work that realises and expresses the self directly, work which like love serves to bind and sustain the group, thus providing the second essential basis for the integration of the self and the social. But the actual picture is always more complicated than this. And almost always it includes a number of people whose involvement with work is noticeably tentative, fluctuating and uncertain. Even in communes where a well-defined central economic project has emerged, such as Family Farm with its shop and workshop, a number of members at any time will be engaged in independent projects, or paying their way on the basis of occasional chores and odd jobs or by cash contributions derived from more or less unrelated 'outside' work: 'three people here work full-time at present, three part-time and the four others have various means of support and are around the place most of the time'. At Fern Hill, where something like a village of independent craftsmen is developing, there are still members who make an essential financial contribution to the project as a whole on the basis of commuting to office or professional jobs in nearby towns. But it is not just that the pressure for funds to keep going until the subsistence farming reaches subsistence level or the craft products find a market forces compromises on many commune members. There is also a pervasive uncertainty among many as to what sort of work they really want and in consequence a great deal of uneasy shopping around, of trying this and that, of having periods of not working at all in order to try to sort things out, of intensive bursts of work on the commune, building, gardening, plumbing, child-minding, alternating with spells of purely calculating employment outside, teaching or emptying dustbins or programming computers to earn some necessary cash.

These uncertainties are especially common, again, on the communal fringe, but even core members of long standing have periods of questioning the value of their work, of worrying about its compatibility with other values of the commune. There are endless echoes of Sombart's dilemma: 'Either economic interests in the broadest sense, *or* love interests form the central point of all life's importance. One lives either to work or else to love.' The greater the independent self-consciousness of members of the commune as individuals, the more acutely these dilemmas are likely to be felt. The communes which are most successful in drawing a commitment to work from their members (and normally a pretty heavy work-load, too) are the religious–mystical ones such as Beshara and Findhorn – where the importance of a submissive acceptance of work is explicitly related to the promise of eventual personal transformation. Sombart's problem has been solved by making work the expression of love which is in turn the condition for rebirth. In many psychedelic communes, on the other hand, although there is a good deal of talk about the value of working together and a good deal of sporadic casting around for suitably unalienated projects, very little actually seems to get done. Even basic household chores tend to devolve on to one or two dedicated members rather than being the work of the group as a whole. But it is in fairly large, fairly stable secular communes that the problem is most acute. For all their claims to be willing to work, many new members resist the notion that the work that really expresses their identity is washing up. Lacking the elaborate doctrines available in the religious communes to relate work to identity, the fringe members of these communes have to make their own way to a conviction that the work that has got to be done is the work that they want to do. Conversely, those who have managed to find a way of working that expresses implicitly their personal creativity and unites them as a group, as some of the people at Family Farm seem to have done, tend to be impatient, even resentful, of what they see as the weakness or irresponsibility of others who fail to pull their weight. Such people often seem to suggest that attention to the work side of the pattern of love and work may be a

100

surer way of realising communal identities than too much attention to love:

> How a person ticks psychologically takes a very long time to learn, and several of us find it satisfying discovering this level of people in a working-together situation rather than just getting together for 'love' . . . These levels do come into relationships, of course, but development cannot be forced faster than the natural pace an individual will give. (*Communes*, 41: 6)

The natural pace, it is suggested, is the pace required by the momentum of communal work. In communes of this type, failure to work can lead to what is in effect expulsion: 'She had to go, really; we expect people to do what needs to be done; her idea was to do what you feel able to do.' But for many of those on the fringe the issue of work does not present itself in this way at all. Rather, as the letter quoted at the start of this section suggests, it is a question of a choice between self-justifying work, whatever that might prove to be – and it certainly does not mean being hustled into work that someone else *says* is self-justifying – and work that, however unjustifiable in itself, does provide the means to satisfying non-work. Over and above their rejection of the rat race these people have made no commitments about work. They are indeed 'not work-shy', but their principal requirement is that in finding themselves they should be free to explore as many options in work as in love.

If the pattern of work and love is marked by a certain cool withholding of commitment in practice that is in sharp contrast to an overt dedication to love and work in principle, the pattern of self and society in communes seems to reveal a similar but perhaps less surprising ambivalence and tension. Self is defined in terms of a withdrawal from society and entry into the counter-society of the commune. But the withdrawal and rejection are never quite complete. Not only is the commune itself a society built on values the larger society professes but cannot practise, but the commune is more often than not seen as a vantage point from which society as a whole may be spoken to, reentered, transformed. In an important sense, the commune is seen as not of society precisely because it exists for society, is the vanguard of a necessary process of social development and change. For those communes and individuals formally associated with the Commune Movement this idea of a network of communes as an instrument of general social change is quite explicit. But in other communes too, while constant efforts are made to break off those connections with society that are seen as threatening the communal pursuit of an alternative identity (to, for example, 'reduce our dependence on the consumer society as much as possible'), the normal and prevailing mood is one that combines an often bleakly pessimistic image of society as a whole as way-

101

ward, stultifying and corrupt with a curiously positive, albeit quite passive, determination to maintain at least some contact with it, 'whatever the hassles'. Thus, the sending of children to local schools as an alternative to attempting to educate them within the commune was often justified to us on the ground that 'we don't want them to be cut off from the rest of the world' (Q.141). If self-realisation requires a measure of withdrawal from society, it also seems to require a measure of openness to it. Communes must, after all, be socially visible if they are to demonstrate the viability of their alternative to straight society. The perception on the part of outsiders that communes are an alternative is by the same token an important way of validating the process of self-seeking as something for the commune member. Of course complete withdrawal is impossible anyway: 'What are you going to do with your ideas of total self-sufficiency when the rate-collector comes round?' But there are stronger reasons than that. As Geoff Crowther puts it in his long account of the commune in which he was involved:

> We didn't want to pretend that we weren't part of a larger society – that way we'd have had no contact with it and we felt we needed it. There'd always be something to learn from them and something to teach them. Isolation was suicide and none of us was suicidal. We only existed in relation to other people and quite a few of those people were our friends. (*Communes*, 40: 13)

This sense of a quiet but polarised contact with society rather than a complete break from it is particularly marked among members of the core groups of fairly stable communes. Thus, one of the founding members of the Family Farm commune firmly rejected the idea of economic self-sufficiency and independence: 'It is not possible; no one here has the skills to achieve our standard of living independently . . . it is in any case a silly aim which people can only cheat themselves into thinking is possible; it is more sensible to maintain and accept mutuality with the rest of the world and look for ways to improve the lot' (R.004). Those on the fringe, more actively engaged in an open-ended exploration of possibilities, often moving through many communes as part of their movement away from society, tend to emphasise simply the aspect of withdrawal. There is, however, something of a progression here, as commune members stabilise their own lives and identities, towards the feeling for contact and confrontation. This movement is indeed the basis for the claims made by people like Cooper and Speck for the therapeutic functions of communes. But there is no need for it to result in the restoration of a 'healed' individual to society. Rather, it may lead, and this is what most communes themselves hope for, to the long-term attachment of the individual to the collective work of social transformation *within* the commune. The development is described on the basis of an engineering metaphor in one article in *Communes* as a matter of negative feedback:

When an individual becomes disenchanted with society he tends to become a floater, society waste, as he no longer contributes: he drops out. This dropping out allows a period of quiet, a first taste of freedom – from the duties imposed from without. Duties from parents, teachers, employers and society-in-the-mass. This kind of freedom is enjoyed for a while until further disenchantment occurs, being a limited freedom and realisation of this brings about discontent.

To enter into society once again in such a sensitive state would be self-ruinous . . . The alternative is to form your own closed circuit of life-sustaining activity, to have a creative aim. This can be done most effectively in a group and naturally a group entertaining a similar search would be the ideal. A community. (*Communes*, 34: 2)

From this point the author seems to envisage some people reentering society but others remaining permanently within the circle of creative activity of the commune, acting *on* society from outside.

But commune members experience their selves in relation to two societies; there is the society of the commune as well as the society outside. The sense of rejection of the latter is of course one important source of attachment to the former, a necessary condition for believing in the value and possibility of creating a collective identity in the commune. But again the problem of the core and the fringe presents itself. For relatively new, transient or provisional members, for the apprentice explorers of communes who far outnumber the core groups, the commune is not something they are creating on equal terms with everyone else. In some degree it is already there when they arrive, a social artefact not so very different from school, parents, employers in its separation from their selves. So there is tension here too while one decides whether the commune is 'our' project or merely 'theirs'. The irreducible and primary importance of self-seeking makes this unavoidable. Only the most firmly entrenched members of the core of a commune do not at some time or other experience this tension between their selves and the commune. And precisely because they do not, everyone else does. We might, since Hawthorne spotted it so clearly, call this the Hollingsworth problem. Just because the commune has become the collective identity of a few, it cannot be an automatic basis of identification for others; the selves of the few are projected as an alien and demanding fantasy on the many. The problem is encountered in the insistent demand for work at Family Farm, where Valerie's willingness to bake bread was not enough to offset her unreliability in

103

turning up to help in the shop. It was experienced by one member of one commune as a feeling that the commune could never be 'ours' because Barry had made it so emphatically 'his':

> Much of the trouble stemmed from the fact that the commune existed as an ideal, a fantasy, in his head and he was forever trying to perceive it as though the fantasy were in fact the reality . . . From this platform he frequently attacked others in a condescending and dismissive manner when they expressed opinions in dissent of his own . . . He seemed to have an intolerance which prevented him being able to see that everyone saw things in essentially a unique way . . . as I saw it I had to provide some psychological balance to his stake in the community so that those less vociferous or introverted would have more say. (*Communes*, 40: 11)

Sometimes an inequality of identities of this sort is rooted crudely in ownership or other differences in material contributions to the commune. Thus the break-up of Red Dawn seems to have turned on the fact that whenever Ted's psychological dominance, the truth of his account of what the commune was about, was challenged, he tended to remind everyone else that he owned the house. Whether or not the point is made as brutally as this, a commune is bound to embody some individualities more fully than others – only very long stretches of very sensitive relationship work can produce a different result – and to that extent most members will feel their selves in tension with the commune as well as with society most of the time.

It is difficult not to write about communes in a way which emphasises, indeed dwells excessively upon, the seriousness of communal life. In taking communes seriously, one's language slides alarmingly towards that of Mr. Pecksniff. So it is worth noting that alongside the extraordinary solemnity devoted to the most trivial matters in communes, there is a counter-current of cheerful irresponsibility by which even the most solemn matters are likely to be touched. After all, one of the points of a commune is to have fun. And people in communes do spend a good deal of time in high spirits enjoying themselves – not least in putting on visiting journalists or sociologists: 'Do tell me about the extended family'; 'We were busted last year – Dave has moved to a commune in Brixton.' In many communes there is a constant ferment of play; picnics, jam sessions, paper chases, swimming parties, cook-ins or simple larking around; whatever else communes achieve or fail to achieve, they certainly offer adults far greater opportunities for play than they are likely to find elsewhere. This playfulness is of course essential to making the egocentric solemnity of most communal life bearable. It takes the threat out of many potentially disruptive situations and preserves the individual's vital exploratory, provisionally

104

committed, relationship to the serious involvements of collective identity, or love. To be able to carry off 'I'd like to sleep with you tonight' as though it were 'How about ping-pong?' and to be able to count on having the one invitation received as though it were identical to the other (whether the answer is 'of course' or 'no thanks') is vital to the preservation of personal integrity as one journeys towards a communal commitment. For it to be possible, presupposes a taken-for-granted playfulness in the background of every social encounter. Conversely, when playfulness lapses, the solemnity with which the least things are treated can destroy whole groups:

> Well, we never got on top of the problem of individual ego-trips. These hassles go deeper than the surface issues. I think when people live together there's this fantastic suppression of the ego, and then it breaks out in petty hassles. We had this terrific bust-up the other day because Graham insisted on knowing who had eaten his peanut butter. When someone starts something like that what they really want to know is who am I? Where do I stand? But Emma and Harry couldn't take it; they left. (R.092)

The movement from one mood to another can be amazingly rapid and disconcerting to an outsider. Gradually one realises that communes are neither essentially solemn nor essentially playful but that they survive on a tightrope between the two; that each is part of the necessary setting for the other. The playful withholding of self from serious situations is one of the distinctive modes in which the pursuit of collective identity is managed. One of its best effects is perhaps the way experienced members of communes learn to express even their anger with an undercurrent of self-mockery. One of its worst effects seems to be the remarkable irresponsibility with which people will abandon chores, such as looking after a child, when they have ceased to be fun. The contrary pull of seriousness and playfulness is felt in every commune. But taken as a whole, the pattern is, again, not evenly balanced between the two. The strategic importance of keeping playfulness alive, whether in the form of 'having some laughs' or simply as keeping cool, is widely understood. And yet the investment and the vulnerability of self in all communal situations, the prevailing uncertainty as to the boundaries of self in the collectivity and the unforgettable seriousness of self, mean that, in all probability, the next time someone's peanut butter disappears it will again be treated not playfully, but very, very seriously.

The final dimension of communal self-seeking that we want to emphasise concerns the sense of the possible. Almost without exception, members of communes appear to believe in the possibility of revolution: revolution anchored within the self, to be sure, but revolution that will end by transforming the world. A sense of the intransigence of

105

the organised social world combines here with a sense of the openness of the context in which one is acting within the commune. A lot of writing about communes', for example, 'A Federal Society Based on the Free Commune' (Commune Movement 1970: 1), many articles in *Communes* and the concluding passages of Rigby's *Alternative Realities* (1974a), have an unashamed visionary tone. The remarkable thing to us is that this belief in the practicality of transformation is echoed, perhaps in less inflated terms, in many actual communes – communes that have experienced cold, poverty, mud, poor food, the police, intransigent landlords, near-disintegration in the face of violent rows and personal possessiveness. Many of those whose communes have been smashed by economic strain or personal ego-trips turn to industrial cooperatives or intentional villages or a different type of commune. There is a persistent belief not only that the world needs to be changed but that it can be changed; that a new type of person expressing an authentic fusion of the self and the social can be created through the love and work of communal life, and that once such people have been created they will serve as compelling examples for others to imitate. Hence 'now is the time to take each of our lives and to mould them into a new beginning'. Again, there is a continuum of shades of emphasis and enthusiasm in terms of which one could distinguish the core members of communes from the fringe, but even the most experienced and hardened, although they may be very cautious about the possibility of communes' changing the world, continue to be convinced that communes can change people and that therefore at least in a small compass 'you can make the world you want'. Therapeutic communes and religious communities such as Beshara are of course explicitly committed to a belief in the possibility of total personal transformation; so too are the mind-sharing psychedelic communes which seek to do with drugs what the former seek to achieve with magic. But what is really striking is that the same ideas are found in otherwise highly pragmatic secular communes as well. There are few that would not subscribe to the spirit of the Findhorn song:

> Together we were thought of
> Together we belong
> Together we will change the world
> Together we are strong.

Despite all the communes that have folded, despite all the stories of disaster in *Communes*, the belief persists, and is said to be securely grounded in communal experience, that people can be changed, that the world will learn. And if people in general can be changed, then of course particular individuals can be changed. It is to be changed that people bring their selves to communes. Unfortunately, though, the feeling for change does not usually take any particular direction in any

106

particular commune. More or less at one in their account of what needs to be changed and in their belief in the possibility of change, members differ dramatically and deeply in their sense of what they are moving towards. Typically there is a diffuse sense of movement and improvability, not a clearly defined common goal – a fact which contributes both life and instability to communes. Perhaps Blithedale was not so very different:

> On the whole it was a society such as has seldom met together, nor, perhaps could it reasonably be expected to hold together long. Persons of marked individuality – crooked sticks, as some of us might be called – are not exactly the easiest to bind up into a fagot. But, so long as our union should subsist a man of intellect and feeling, with a free nature in him, might have sought far and near without finding so many points of attraction as would allure him hitherward. We were of all creeds and opinions and generally tolerant of all, on every imaginable subject. Our bond it seems to me was not positive but negative. We had individually found one thing or another to quarrel with in our past life and were pretty well agreed as to the inexpediency of lumbering along with the old system any further. As to what should be substituted, there was much less unanimity . . . My hope was that between theory and practice, a true and available mode of life might be struck out. (Hawthorne 1962: 89)

Clearly in turning a negative appetite for change into a positive sense of direction, religious and other ideologically well-defined communes have a great advantage – as the many people who move from secular to religious communities testify. But perhaps in the business of striking out 'a true and available mode of life', the harder, because open-ended, struggle to make something of the common feeling for change that goes on in the secular communes comes nearer to realising Hawthorne's hope.

Communes, identity and youth

> I am eighteen now, and I do not intend to settle down for several years, yet I hope during this time I can become easier to live with and learn how to find other people easier to live with as well. (Q.074)

The patterns that strike us as providing the main strands of the process of self-seeking in communes, the ambivalent patterns of love and work, of self and society, of playfulness and solemnity and of possibility, have an obvious and immediate meaning as typifying a world of youth. This is not a matter of biological age, of course – although the average age of the members of most communes is in the twenties, and com-

107

munes could be thought of as youth groups in that sense. Rather, it is a question of youth as a social and psychological condition, a particular moment in a socially ordered life-cycle. The modes in which the issues of identity are met and managed in communes suggest that communes are also youth groups in this more interesting sense. Their revival at a particular historical time, the kinds of people involved in them, the forms of collective identity they seek to realise and the distinctive problems they experience in doing so can all be usefully understood in this way.

In *Youth and Dissent*, where he urges the recognition of youth as a special stage of life in capitalist societies, a stage distinct from both adolescence and young adulthood, Kenneth Keniston has pointed to a number of themes which may be considered crucial to youth. He identifies these characteristic dimensions of the special world of youth as follows: refusal of socialisation; ambivalence towards both self and society; a sense of tension between the self and society; alternating estrangement and omnipotentiality; an experimental style of action which he calls 'the wary probe'; the placing of enormous value on movement, change, development and transformation; the emergence of youth-specific identities; and associated with that a process of banding together in youthful counter-cultures (Keniston 1971: 3–26). Such a characterisation is so obviously also an account of the distinctive features of communes that perhaps no more needs to be said; it is certainly remarkable that Keniston himself does not include communes in the range of phenomena of youth which he goes on to discuss. There can be few other settings in which the whole of life is constituted so emphatically and exclusively in terms of the themes of youth. Keniston's notion of the wary probe, for example, describes perfectly the skirmishing explorations of self and others, the experimenting with work and love, the playful or angry testing of commitments that make up so much of the routine everyday experience of communal life. Refusal of socialisation ('living in an unreal world', 'dormant and stagnating under the lethal gases of society'), estrangement ('My reason for wanting to join some community is because I want to reject conventional society which has rejected me'; 'There must be somewhere I can fit in'), and even omnipotentiality, which Keniston sees as 'the feeling of living in a world of pure possibilities' ('Our aim is to create the Kingdom of God on earth'), are all closely related, reflecting the objective dissociation and openness of the situation of youth, and all are immediately manifest in almost all communes. There is of course a significant difference so far as omnipotentiality is concerned: in an important sense communal life starts from the recognition that one has no power in the face of the larger world – omnipotentiality is confined to the circle of the commune.

However, the forming of youth-specific identities which is perhaps the heart of Keniston's argument calls for a little more attention. It is clear that communes are used by their members as sources of identity, that forming a commune is a process of negotiating a collective identity and that through ideas and images of the commune older members seek to impose their identities on newer members. But in what sense are communal identities *specific* to youth? Keniston's own account (1971:9-10) is not very helpful; he says of such identities that they

Contrast both with the more ephemeral enthusiasms of the adolescent and with the more established commitments of the adult. They may last for months, years or a decade and they inspire deep commitment in those who adopt them. Yet they are inherently temporary and specific to youth; today's youthful hippies, radicals and seekers recognise full well that, however reluctantly, they will eventually become older; and that aging itself will change their status.

Some such youth-specific identities may provide the foundation for later commitments; but others must be viewed in retrospect as experiments that failed or as probes of the existing society that achieved their purpose, which was to permit the individual to move on in other directions.

Now although the majority of people who live in communes are in fact transients, very few commune members see their communes in that way. An important part of their refusal of socialisation, perhaps, is the rejection of the relevance for them of social definitions of the life cycle and of socially imposed changes of status of the kind Keniston has in mind. A significant number of people do indeed live out the greater part of their adult lives in communes. Can we seriously suggest that their identities are specific to youth? What are these youth-specific identities anyway? Keniston offers us a better clue in a later passage when he is talking about the distinctive psychological and social transformations associated with youth as a stage of life. Youth is now seen as that phase of the life-cycle in which what Jung called 'individuation' is first securely achieved – that is to say, in which the individual works his way successfully towards an account of both himself and society in which 'the autonomous reality, relatedness yet separateness of both is firmly established'. There is obviously no biological reason why individuation in this sense must be achieved at any particular age (although there are biological conditions which make the achievement more or less possible at different ages). That it is normally the achievement of youth in the sense of a certain span of years and that it can be spoken of as a phenomenon of youth in the sense of being a critical moment of personal development, a synthesis as well as a point of departure, is evidently an effect of social organisation. And at this point we can begin to see why individuation is an achievement which for some people in some societies can be accomplished, perhaps can only be accomplished, in communes. The concomitant of individuation at the level of relationships Keniston sees as a shift from various adult styles of relationship towards 'mutuality', a style in which closeness to others is based on the recognition of the uniqueness of others. That is of course precisely what the core groups of the more stable secular communes see as the basis and value of their existence.

In all this there are quite audible echoes of Erik Erikson's account in *Childhood and Society* and in *Identity: Youth and Crisis* of late adolescence and young adulthood as normally involving a movement from 'identification-with' to 'identity'. One serious disadvantage of Erikson's masterly schematic presentation of the life-cycle of identity is, as he was the first to point out, the extreme rigidity and philistinism with which his model of successive stages and crises of identity can be applied to the interpretation of people's lives by writers less subtle or less cautious than Erikson himself. Despite that warning it does seem to us that much of the experience of the commune movement can be usefully understood as a drive towards individuation and that as such it is centred on the resolution of two of Erikson's crises, those of 'identity versus role diffusion' and of 'intimacy versus isolation'; and that a third issue for identity, that of 'industry versus inferiority', is often an active consideration in the background, too.

Summarised very crudely, Erikson's argument is that the early stages of development equip the child with certain raw materials of identity, which he refers to as balances of trust and mistrust, of autonomy and self-doubt, of initiative and guilt, and, as a result of his or her experience of the world of social techniques and skills at school, of industry and inferiority. Thus equipped, for better or worse, the individual is pitched into the universe of adolescence and youth in which he or she is required to integrate all those previously acquired elements of personality into an identity rooted in definite social commitments, an occupational commitment and a commitment to serious intimate personal relationships, an identity experienced as a sense of 'the sameness and continuity of the self and of one's meaning for others'. It is precisely in the forming of intimate relationships and in the mastering or acceptance of occupational roles that the quality of one's identity, in particular its degree of integration or diffusion, is realised and tested. This task of identity-formation, although normally carried out bearably well, is presented by Erikson as one of great difficulty and delicacy – especially so in societies such as pluralistic capitalist societies where the range of possible choices facing the young individual is, Erikson believes, very wide, and the moral authority of all particular choices is in question. The greater the structural and moral diversity,

110

the greater the risk is that the product of this phase of life will be identity-confusion rather than identity, a dissipation of personal integrity over a diffuse spread of conflicting and alternative roles making itself felt disruptively in subsequent attempts to form intimate relationships and impelling a retreat from intimacy to isolation.

To enable the individual to navigate these dangerous waters Erikson suggests that a period of socially approved irresponsibility, which he calls a 'psycho-social moratorium' is institutionalised in which the individual, being in some important ways out of society, can safely try out various choices without any mistakes he might make carrying their normal social costs.

> A moratorium is a period of delay granted to somebody who is not ready to meet an obligation or forced on somebody who should give himself time. By psycho-social moratorium, then, we mean a delay of adult commitments, and yet it is not only a delay. It is a period characterised by a selective permissiveness on the part of society and of provocative playfulness on the part of youth, and yet it also leads to deep if often transitory commitment on the part of youth. (Erikson 1968: 157)

The moratorium, in other words, is a socially sanctioned space in the life-cycle in which 'the young adult through free role experimentation may find a niche in some section of his society, a niche which is firmly defined and yet seems to be uniquely made for him'. Much of Erikson's further treatment of the psycho-social moratorium is in terms of its specifically psychological, intra-psychic dimensions. However, he also discusses some social processes which he considers essential to it; chief among these are the processes of play, apprenticeship, ideological commitment and social recognition. Again, the functional power and relevance of communes in all these respects is not hard to see. Not only do communes provide settings for the moratorium which are actually out of society to a significant degree, but they offer a peculiarly clear ideological point of reference for the individual in terms of which self and society can both be positively and negatively related, and they explicitly put personal and work relationships on an experimental basis. As a member of a commune, one at once asserts a demand for recognition from society and *secures* recognition from the immediate group of one's peers in a way which makes sense of and makes up for the fact that the larger society has not recognised one. As a member of a commune, one can at once take the exploration of possible work roles and possible relationships very seriously and yet be in a position to declare, if things go badly wrong, that one was only playing, that the integrity of one's self-conception is not badly damaged by the disaster. If the passage from using relationships in what Erikson calls an 'identity-hungry' way as a means of self-seeking to genuine intimacy is the centre of the course youth steers towards individuation, communes may be said to ease the passage in a way few if any other social arrangements can. They permit one to experiment with intimacy even while the process of identity-formation is going on and without pre-judging its outcome. Erikson suggests that the individual cannot really cope with true intimacy until identity-formation is 'well on its way'. Hence the sequential ordering of the two in his scheme. Communes, however, do allow one to collapse the separateness of these two stages of development precisely by permitting playful–serious experiments with intimate relationships in a socially unreal, but socially significant, environment. The great advantage of this simultaneous encounter with the issues of identity and intimacy is of course that one can hope to incorporate a much richer and more varied experience of and capacity for intimacy into one's still-emerging identity. Falling in love with one person in the conventional manner involves the individual in great costs in terms of both commitment and isolation. The inner openness of communes, their *collective* intimacy as it were, enables the individual to explore many types of intimacy without incurring these costs to anything like the same degree – and to that extent without having to face, to anything like the degree envisaged by Erikson, the crisis of intimacy versus isolation if any particular relationship fails. Those adults for whom communes have really worked in this sense, in whose lives identity and intimacy were mastered together, could with some honesty take to themselves Erikson's formula, 'We are what we love.'

The advantages of communes from the point of view of identity-formation are not in themselves enough to explain the existence of communes or the whole of their special contemporary character, however. Here a curious moment of unreality must be noted in Erikson's analysis. Having argued that a psycho-social moratorium is in all societies necessary to enable youth to complete the process of individuation, he then goes on to write as though in all societies all young people did in fact find an appropriate moratorium more or less readily available to them. But this is quite plainly not the case. Even if we allow that one can experience a moratorium without experiencing it consciously, it is clear that there are many young people in a society such as contemporary Britain who have identities forced upon them in a quite inflexible way before they are well into adolescence. Even without reference to the now well-documented meaning of educational selection, streaming, competitive examinations and all our other apparatus of pre-adult social classification, the realities of restricted opportunity are visible enough. The sort of 'free role experimentation' in fundamental relationships which is said to be the essence of the psycho-social moratorium is simply not a serious possibility for them.

Normally in societies where the assignment of young people to adult roles is highly pre-determined within a relatively undifferentiated culture, the moratorium offered youth is brief and stylised – a single ritual or ceremonial event may suffice. What is needed for the formation of identity is not free role experimentation but simply a correct and enthusiastic anticipation in fantasy of what adulthood is bound to be like. For this purpose the exotic and highly determined rite of passage serves well enough. Complex societies with a culture centred on values of individual self-determination need longer and more genuinely experimental, if not open-ended, moratoria – if only so that the most culturally alert of the young can acquire some reason in their own experience for attaching themselves to the values of self-determination. But in such societies there is in practice a contradiction between what is actually offered and the idea of free role experimentation (which might not matter had not moralists from John Stuart Mill to Erik Erikson sensitised us so thoroughly to the importance of self-determination). The extent and force of the contradiction varies from one social group of the young to another but may be felt by all. The 'selective permissiveness' of society in dealing with the young tends for all of them to be highly selective and not very permissive. Whatever one's background or achievements, whatever one's socially assessed balance of industry and inferiority, the world of occupations and of personal relationships stands before one as a strictly limited number of serious (that is, socially recognised) possibilities. So that if one wants a true moratorium, a real and felt delay of commitments, an authentic choice of experiments, one will not find it given to one by society. You have to go out and make it.

The issue of recognition is important, perhaps decisive. For both Erikson and Keniston the transformations of youth are profoundly and directly affected by youth's social audience. Identity and individuation are both concepts which involve a relationship of recognition between the individual and society. The point, which has become something of a commonplace, is neatly made by R. D. Laing (1961: 25): 'We cannot give an undistorted account of "a person" without giving an account of his relation with others . . . All identities require an other; some other in and through a relationship with whom self-identity is actualised.' Martin Buber's version of this sentiment is a little more challenging and certainly points more sharply to the situation of youth: 'a society may be said to be human in the measure to which its members confirm one another'. It is taken for granted by both Keniston and Erikson, as by most other writers of Freudian inspiration, that the achievement of identity involves some broad act of recognition of the individual by society as a whole or some effective representative of it. Thus Erikson (1968: 159-60):

Identity formation . . . is dependent on the process by which a

113

society (often through subsocieties) identifies the young individual, recognising him as somebody who had to become the way he is and who, being the way he is, is taken for granted. The community . . . gives such recognition with a display of surprise and pleasure in making the acquaintance of a newly emerging individual. For the community in turn feels 'recognised' by the individual who cares to ask for recognition; it can by the same token feel deeply – and vengefully – rejected by the individual who does not seem to care.

Such a passage at once makes the element of social confirmation absolutely indispensable to the achievement of a defined identity and in a remarkably strong implication quite ignores the extent to which society *dictates* the terms on which a welcome is in fact available to the emerging individual. And yet of course a pluralistic society valuing self-determination cannot properly behave like that. So it is fortunate that what matters for successful individuation is not recognition by society but only social recognition by some others. The confidence, wholeness and so forth that constitute identity call for affirmation by a community but not necessarily by the community. It is on this basis that identities are sought, and can be found in communes. Society's values can be affirmed –indeed, given the real closing-off of options in the psycho-social moratorium available to most people, can only be affirmed – in societies outside society.

But we are still not close enough to the specific content of self-seeking in communes. There is at least one important theme of the commune movement which is missing from Keniston's analysis of individuation and from Erikson's treatment of identity-formation. Indeed, from a historical point of view it is perhaps the most important communal theme. For all their concern with love and work, communes are about the family in a way that 'normal' identity-formation is not. As we argue in the next chapter, the interest in communes is not just an interest in making a freer moratorium than is offered by society; it is specifically an interest in making a moratorium in which one can experiment with better versions of the family. The extraordinary influx of people to the commune movement since the mid-1960s needs some explanation in terms of this particular concern. In turn this calls for some consideration, however brief and polemical, of the family, and of family-based conceptions of love, in the British version of modern capitalist society. In adolescence, as distinct from youth, one's account of the world is perforce dominated by thoughts of the nature and value of the family. It is, after all, in relation to that world that one has at that stage to identify one's self. It is in our view initially from a concern with that world, and only in the second place from a concern with the problems of adult intimacy, that the compulsive interest in love and especially,

114

in the most hackneyed slogan of the commune movement, in 'love and peace', draws its vital importance.

The justification for the power systems of family life in modern capitalist societies is love. Whether or not we are persuaded by the arguments of Parsons and others as to the functional value for the occupational requirements of emerging capitalism of a kinship system consisting of small conjugal units held together by love, there can be little doubt that for about two centuries now a central theme in the history of the family has been the struggle of young adults to emancipate themselves in small conjugal units on the basis of appeals to the rights of love. Nor that as a form of solidarity the other face of the rights of love then became the debts of love. Nor that the love-nexus as an instrument of attachment is typically extended from the relationship between spouses to the relationship between parents and children as well. The first thing a child learns, almost, is to substitute a need for love for its crude initial need for pleasure. With that accomplished, the giving and withholding of love, a moral economy of love, becomes the compelling medium of family relationships for all concerned. Small wonder that in adolescence, when the individual is moving towards a definition of self, his thoughts are centred on the problem of defining a self in terms of love and in counterpoint, often, to the sort of love that has been experienced in the family: love has been so powerfully the measure of personal worth and the family is still so centrally the source of all the individual has in the way of identity. What more sensible, if one has been hypnotised by the idea of love as the pivot of identity but has experienced love in actual family relationships as a kind of currency (to say nothing of the possibility with which Cooper and Laing are so concerned of experiencing it as a kind of violence), than to begin one's move towards self-definition with an attempt to love authentically in an alternative family? 'I'm not asking for much, just for love without all the wrangling and recriminations; love and peace without the bickerings of the nuclear family' (Q. 233). The whole point about communes, Clem Gorman, the author of *Making Communes*, has argued, is that they 'put love on the agenda' (*Communes*, 40: 31). Where but in a commune could one take love so seriously, while at the same time treating love so socially, so much a matter of *variety* of relationships as it is in the family, without living in a family, without love's being an instrument of status?

This concern to take love seriously, the sense that love is born free but everywhere is in chains, is a theme of adolescence, not of youth (at least in the Freudian account we have been following), and we must understand communes accordingly. To do so strengthens our view of communes as settings for deliberately made psycho-social moratoria for those who, having been led to expect that sort of freedom, find that it

115

is not in fact available. It is after carrying around with one for some time the issue of where one stands in relation to love, and after discovering that the opportunities held out for self-definition in youth culture, or work or academic life, are illusory in this respect, that one begins to consider the serious step of making or joining a commune. Keniston suggests that the concern with the family as a decisive point of reference for conceptions of the self is a characteristic of adolescence as distinct from youth. We would agree with this, and it follows that the predicaments of adolescence must be seen as a particularly important source of people and energy for the commune movement in its present form. Two cases are indicative of the pattern:

> Eighteen, troubled with approved schools and borstal, gentle, unsettled, beginning to wonder what was 'wrong' with him that he didn't feel at home in this so beautiful world, and get a good job as he had been so often told to do. One of so many, yes. . . . The point about Ken is that there is nothing for him, or the people in the same state of mind, to relate to. They have enough wit and sheer self-preservation to see that the structures of their home environment are destructive and life-negating. . . . They can see there is something not clicking but can't grasp quite what it is, and don't find any alternative. (*Communes*, 34: 1-2)

And again:

> I have been searching for a long time for an alternative. . . . In which I could use all my talents for the good of others, and not have a great deal of pressure put upon me, especially by people in authority, to actively participate in a way of life that is totally opposed to all the good things in people and which does not allow me to reach my true potential as a human being. My earnest desire in life, and which provides the key to my whole personality growth, is to be given the full opportunity to love and be loved, and if communal life gives me this opportunity I will be eternally grateful. (*Communes*, 37: 25)

But having recruited many people who are experiencing the world in this way, communes are not merely playgrounds, not just do-it-yourself psycho-social moratoria. The seriousness with which communal experiments are undertaken and the spread of types of people who make up any given commune make communes genuine forcing-houses of identity. One of the things that happen in communes is a movement from adolescence to youth.

The longer a commune has existed or the more communal experience an individual has behind him, the more, generally speaking, the extreme emphasis on love and the alternative family fades, the more the concern for self-transcendence and rebirth diminishes. And the more clearly individuation is achieved. Often this can happen very

116

rapidly – which is why we think of communes as forcing-houses of identity rather than as mere alternative universities. The pace and intensity of communal social relations permit one to travel at great speed from an oceanic appetite for a universe radiant with love, through a good deal of intricate relationship work, to a quite firm realisation of who one is and what matters to one. As one commune member we talked to put it, the unique thing that living in a commune has to offer is 'accelerated experience'. Of course this acceleration may be in some senses quite negative, too – thus the social audience provided by a commune can advance the disintegration of the relationship of an unhappily married couple quite amazingly. It is remarkable to see how quickly a gap opens between the language of those who have newly entered communes or are still looking for them and those who are well embarked on communal life. The first enthusiasm for the totality of the commune — 'It's such a zap as so much love floods in and around' – gives way to a noticeably guarded ambivalence, a sense of wanting to rescue oneself from the flood:

> Committedness: this word much used by some, doesn't please me; it's too much like marriage. But to join a commune is a sort of marriage, with an intention of on-goingness, some sense of mutual responsibility. Why do people marry? Why do some 'decide' to live together, as if some special step is being taken? But there is *some* meaning. The inhabitants have their work to do and their relationships to build and explore, and a flow of temporary people coming to find out about communes . . . is rather like being offered a succession of temporary lovers while one is building one's marriage. . . . The idea is to better life for all who are involved. So it seems to me that at least some needs of one's own must be satisfied, or why stay? (*Communes*, 37: 8)

The pace of movement from identity-hunger to identity can be bewildering: 'Living like this has helped me to be more myself but to get to this I have been very confused and I felt I lost myself completely.' One can travel in just a few months from entering a commune as a 'reaction against the isolated nuclear family', to marriage and the rejection of communes as a 'tiny little world as crazy as the world outside had seemed; anarchic, hedonistic, middle-class, confused, chaotic'; and in the case of this particular ex-commune member, to a feeling of overriding 'responsibility to my family'. Or one can move to a rather strenuous attachment to the commune which is at the same time on guard against the commune:

> When all else seems to be going wrong we can rely on the love around us and the security offered by it; however, the more you lean on and sink into this security the less useful it becomes since it is the security of the group and a home, not within yourself and

117

you can remain trapped by it, unable to translate into personal terms. Then the commune can become, or we allow it to become, an institution, a shelter restricting our personal development . . . We need to use our liberation, not remain stuck in the security which is a residue of it. (R.022)

Or one can arrive at a considered commitment of the self to the commune as a permanent object. In the case of any of these outcomes a significant accretion of identity has occurred.

It follows, indeed it was implicit in our suggestion that the structure of communes consists of a core and a fringe, that communes are built around two kinds of people, each engaged in a significantly different kind of self-seeking. There are those who, not having been offered an effective moratorium in which to evolve a youthful identity in society as a whole, turn to communes as a setting for 'deep relationships . . . self-discovery, a situation in which one can experiment and develop', who hope that one way or another communal experience will resolve the ambivalence and tension they feel about both their selves and others, perhaps through a fusion of self with others, perhaps in a firmer differentiation of self from others. And there are those who, having *achieved* a youthful identity, whether in a commune or not, find that society has little or no use for that identity, does not 'recognise' it in Erikson's sense; and who, instead of surrendering the identity they have created to society in the manner Keniston seems to think normal, choose instead to protect it from society, establishing it as a permanent commitment by winning recognition for it within a commune. For some people a commune is a place where they can *seize* a youthful identity unconstrained by the pressures with which society surrounds normal adolescence. For others it is a place where they can *freeze* a youthful identity into an identity for life. Both live naturally among the patterns of self-seeking we described earlier in this chapter. For both, communal identity is youth-specific. But they are not the same. The difference between them is the difference between Zenobia and Hollingsworth in Hawthorne's novel. It is a difference which is probably bound to produce many conflicts and schisms. However delicate the relationship work in a commune, the Zenobias must win their own identities, which for most will mean sooner or later a struggle to escape from identification with the Hollingsworths to a more substantial autonomy. However noble and generous the communal projects of the Hollingsworths, there will be points at which they are experienced by others as intransigent just because they are in a fundamental way expressions of someone else's formed identity. In such situations each type experiences the other as unreasonably demanding, as tending 'to lose sight of people as individuals', as liable to engulf other people's selves in fact. The difficulty, and the unavoidability, of this two-sidedness of communes was well understood by almost all the people we talked to who had had experience of commune living:

> Communal situations seem to attract emotionally insecure individuals and to attract stronger, domineering individuals with a tendency to impose themselves on others; from this you get a lack of respect for people's emotions and tension in members which can come to destructive, hurtful expressions of negative emotion. (R.071)

Naturally enough, the two different types of commune members, while both aware of the problem, tended to see it each from their own point of view; thus, many people in fringe situations complained of the way authoritarian leaders trampled on the spirit of sharing, while members of core groups tended to speak of the fine balance of giving and giving-in: 'It is some curious blend of bending and accommodating differences while not finally being converted or seduced into other values and not in the end caring so much about being reproached as about doing what we meant to do' (R.119). The difficulty, of course, is that the vitality and value of a commune depend quite largely on the presence of both types within it.

We said at the start of this chapter that it was important not to make Zenobia's mistake of confusing self-seeking, the paramount source of communal energy, with selfishness. From this point of view it is important to understand, but not to go along with, the sorts of criticisms commune members tend to make of each other. Of course there are those who see communes as little more than a system of cheap lodging or baby-sitting. But the striking thing about members of the commune movement, both on the fringe and at the core, is the degree to which their self-seeking is altruistic, oriented towards others. On its own, a dominant concern with self-definition is not enough to distinguish the commune movement from other worlds of youth. What does distinguish it is the prominence within it of a concern for a type of self-definition centred on the idea of the *mutuality* of self and others. Sometimes this concern was expressed in naive or grandiose ways as a matter, for example, of being able to 'give "oneself" to One Self'; and sometimes much more pragmatically as a matter of, say, securing that 'good feedback which stops the ego over-amplifying itself'. But however it was put it came through as the ubiquitous mood of the movement, its peculiar style of self-seeking. It is this which justifies the suggestion that the patterns of self-concern observed within the commune movement should be understood as aspects of a struggle for individuation in Jung's sense rather than as a mere chaos of egocentricity. The widespread interest within the movement not only in the writings of Jung but in the whole range of contemplative religions, especially in Taoism and Buddhism, is quite deliberate and meaningful in this

119

respect. As a member of one eminently down-to-earth commune put it, the really important quality in communal life is 'to be in the frame of mind to be able to like people – I identify this frame of mind with Buddhism since both require a certain selflessness' (Q.083). In some cases, as for example at Fern Hill, an intellectual discovery of meaning along these lines has been quite explicit and is seen as central to the development of the commune and the successful passage of its emotional crises. More generally, the seeming inconsistencies of communal relationships, the endless worrying about spontaneity and constraint, are often best understood in terms of such an underlying sense that, in the process of becoming a whole person, acquiring and giving, winning and surrendering are inseparable if not identical; that, indeed, the whole point is to abolish the polarities of meaning and morality which western culture has built up out of these categories. As Jung himself has it (1959: 231):

> This means open conflict and open collaboration at once. That, evidently, is the way human life should be. It is the old game of hammer and anvil; between them the patient iron is forged into an indestructible whole, an individual. This, roughly, is what I mean by the individuation process.

Whether the communal worlds that result are, in the sense in which Zenobia accused Hollingsworth, self-deceptions, is not a question that can be answered simply or in principle at a psychological level. 'You have embodied yourself in a project' is a true charge. But whether the project is experienced as 'yours' or 'ours' is a matter of good faith and of the degree of mutuality with which the everyday relationships of men, women and children in communes can be worked out.

5. Men, women and children

The communal type of relationship is, according to the usual interpretations of its subjective meaning, the most radical antithesis of conflict. This should not be allowed, however, to obscure the fact that coercion of all sorts is a very common thing in even the most intimate of such communal relationships.

Weber, *Economy and Society*

When we started the research on which this book is based we had been led to believe by the existing literature on modern communes, including the writings of many active advocates and practitioners of

120

communal living, that the commune movement involved a serious, open-ended attempt to achieve a radical alternative to the nuclear family. In the last chapter we suggested that the family relationships typical of our society, especially as they impinge on adolescents, may be seen as explaining much of the demand for communes and many of the expectations people in communes have of one another. But are communes also involved self-consciously and explicitly in trying to construct alternatives to the family? And if so, how far do they succeed?

In the light of what we had read we certainly expected the answer to the first of these questions to be yes. We expected, that is, to find a variety of more or less deliberate efforts to restructure the relationships of men and women and of adults and children in such a way that at least the business of building and protecting the emotional commitments of adults and of carrying out the early socialisation of children was performed in patterns of association which avoided the more painful costs to the individual commonly blamed on normal domestic arrangements. We were interested in particular in what could be done in communes to redress conventional inequalities between the sexes, and in what could be done to make the life of children more spontaneously loving or secure. In both respects our aim was to assess as carefully as possible the ways in which different communal projects could be said to be conducive, as social structures, to the achievement of an alternative family system. Two questions concerned us, therefore: what did the structure of communes *permit* people to do in the way of making new types of personal relationships, and what did it *require* them to do? We took the idea of an alternative in this context to imply relationships that were functionally equivalent to those of the family but took a significantly different structural form and had significantly different effects in terms of the moral and emotional climate in which individuals moved and related to one another.

So far as the conscious involvement of communes in overt attempts to build alternatives to the family was concerned, we were not disappointed. The antithesis between communes and a conventional stereotype of the nuclear family is cited endlessly as a major element in the case for communal living. Among people trying to start or join communes the positive qualities of communes are seen with overwhelming frequency as being set in opposition to the negative qualities of the nuclear family: 'To me a commune-type set-up seems to answer many of the problems of the conventional isolated family structure and to be a means of being independent of a society which is headed for collapse' (Q.053). For some, this sense of the need to redesign family relationships was evidently their strongest single feeling: 'We have no uniting ethic apart from a belief in communal life as a possible happier alternative to the normal family unit', as two writers in *Communes*

121

(37: 17) put it. For some, feelings about straight family life were obviously strong and painful: 'My whole life so far has been fucked-up by my family; there's got to be an alternative' (Q.111). For many others a reconstruction of the family – to substitute openness, spontaneity and growth for domination, possession and violence – was at least a prominent part of a larger imagery of the alternative society associated with communes. In a diffuse but surprisingly consistent way advocates of communes revealed themselves as sharing the views of ordinary family life developed by sociologists such as Bronfenbrenner (1963) and Green (1946), by anthropologists such as Leach (1968) and by psychologists such as Cooper (1971) and Laing (1971). Green's account of the processes of personality absorption finds constant echoes in the commonsense talk of members of the commune movement. The echoes of Edmund Leach's Reith Lecture are even stronger: 'Today the domestic household is isolated. The family looks inward upon itself; there is an intensification of emotional stress between husband and wife, parents and children. The strain is greater than most of us can bear. Far from being the basis of the good society, the family with all its tawdry secrets and narrow privacy is the source of all discontents.' The familiar quotation is worth quoting again because both its emotionalism and its tendency to psychological rather than sociological analysis turned out to be symptomatic of what is happening in communes and a clue to explaining the general inability of communes, in our view, to achieve a sufficient solution to the problems their members sense so keenly.

The formal critique of the conventional family which comes closest to expressing the pattern of sentiment we found in the commune movement is thus not surprisingly that offered in the work of Cooper and Laing to which we have already referred; conversely, those which are least realised in the rhetoric of the commune movement are those which treat the inner life of the family as an aspect of a larger political economy, whether in the manner of Parsons (1949) or of Engels (1951b). This emphasis springs directly, of course, from the primary concern of the commune movement with the self. Cooper's search, after all, is above everything else a search for 'the spontaneous assertion of full personal autonomy'. It is in this context, for him, that the family destroys people, turning the possibility of mutual affirmation into the reality of systematic mutual invalidation. Cooper and Laing are not interested in any close way in why the ethos and economy of love, the love-nexus, as we have called it, have been introduced so totally into the domestic relationships of capitalist societies. They would not necessarily disagree with such arguments as those of Parsons and Firestone (1971) which suggest a direct and causal connection between these inter-personal developments and critical structural features of capitalist

122

economies. But their concern is emphatically with the micro-dramas resulting from the love-nexus, the binding of individuals into universes of bad faith legitimated by the supposed debts of love, and not with the social explanation of the general patterns of inequality in the setting of which those dramas are staged and acted out. Thus Cooper presents the family as legitimating the perpetration of four evasions of autonomy: (1) the manufacturing of self–other dependencies – the 'family', to fill out the incompleteness of the individual, permitting the latter to live stiltedly through others rather than self-sufficiently; (2) the locking of the individual into the specified roles required by the 'family' as an alternative to 'laying down the conditions for the free assumption of identity'; (3) teaching the child to accept the social order as naturally given at the expense of its own integrity; and (4) specifically, equipping both mother and child with a 'need for love' which is then used not as the basis for a growth of spontaneity and tenderness but to justify repression, violence and guilt. The use of the term 'family' is taken from Laing (1971) to refer to the family as an internalised coercive fantasy, 'an introjected set of relations'. In general, Laing's treatment of these matters is both subtler and more sociological than Cooper's; but Cooper seems to be the more resonant author for the commune movement, and it is perhaps not unimportant that for Cooper at least the family appears to be seen as a microcosm of all conventional social institutions, so that the rejection of the family is by implication a rejection of the whole social order. Although the adult woman as wife and mother is at the centre of this system of personal invalidation, the analysis is not pursued at the level of the 'woman question', as a matter of the class and status position of women generally. Instead, like the idea of the 'family' it has a curiously self-contained, socially isolated quality. What is presented is the way in which the hopes of love are turned into the debts of love; motherliness generating childishness; romance generating a stale and ritual togetherness; spontaneity generating compulsion.

There is another tradition of criticism of the family which finds expression within the commune movement and which revolves around Freud's discovery that civilisation is bought through the repression of sexuality. Freud did not think this price too high, but Roheim, Fromm, Reich and other Freudians have concluded that we have paid too dearly: 'The primitive, despite the obvious hardships he faced, had solved the problem of communal life in a much more satisfactory manner than his civilised brother. Modern civilisation with its insane methods of education, its repression of sexuality and its sphincter morality had made men sick' (Robinson 1973: 111). The work of Marcuse and Reich combines this critique with a variety of Marxism. Reich thus formulates a powerful attack on the family, and in particular the lower-middle-class family, as the basis of fascism, describing the 'patriarchal' family supplemented by monogamous marriage as the prime means of ensuring the survival of exploitation and class domination. Marcuse similarly sees the almost total elimination of sensual and sexual life accomplished by the family as intrinsic to the continuance of western culture, considering 'bodily repression one of the most important attributes of the exploitative social order' and developing a critique of western dualism that 'emphasised not only the economic but also the sexual misery perpetuated and rationalised by dualistic metaphysics' (Robinson 1973: 143). Marcuse also argues that one function of the concentration of sexual feeling and expression in genital sexuality is to permit the rest of the body to be treated purely as an instrument of labour. We would suggest that the emergence of the concept of the self as the repository of essential individuality has a similar function. The restriction and concentration of personal being in the self can mean that, whatever the indignities inflicted on us by social relations beyond our control, there is always a most precious and most 'real' aspect of us that we can disengage from the situation, persuading ourselves that it at least has remained pure and unaffected. Bettelheim among others has argued that this capacity is indeed an essential survival mechanism in the more extreme situations of modern society.

Some parts of our research indicated strongly that, in this sense of breaking the love-nexus, building an alternative to the family was really what the commune movement was about. This was particularly true of the results of our questionnaire study of members of the Commune Movement. The appeal of communes was explained by those who answered the questionnaire broadly in terms of the stock discontents and broken promises of industrial society – 'materialism', the 'rat race', 'Heinz duo-cans', the 'technological society' – but specifically and with striking emphasis in terms of the particular discontents of family life. The most often recurring and most precisely expressed single aspect of the whole broad pattern of estrangement which we encountered was 'disillusionment with the nuclear family', the 'farce of the semi-detached existence'. It was within and around revulsion from the family, in connection with the perception of the family as the specific cause and context of alienation, that platitudes and clichés about the rat race gave way to more directly felt and sharply expressed reasons for innovation: 'They say "I love you", but they mean "I own you" – that's what I'm against' (Q.119). Insofar as a motive for communes adequate on the level of meaning emerged from the research, it lay in the perceived idiocy of normal domesticity: 'the realisation that the nuclear family and suburban living are too often isolated, narrow-minded, egotistical, lacking in concern for others' (Q.093). However dimly the larger society might have been seen, the family as a setting

124

for inhumanity had been seen in plain relief: people spoke of their 'deep unhappiness with the nuclear family, from my own experience and observation of other families' (Q.227), and of the ways in which the family tends to 'restrict human potential, freeze relationships, stunt the exploratory and innovating side to our consciousness and cause manifold frustration' (Q.040). Some accounts spoke mainly of the material world of the family: 'Present methods of family living put great stress on even happily married couples with adequate finance; if you are unhappy or a single parent or faced with illness the stresses are often intolerable and result in breakdowns for adults and disturbed children and poverty' (Q.261). Others, and these were the majority, spoke very much in Cooper's terms of its psychic world, of 'disliking the limitations of existing male–female roles – both for any particular couple and especially for the mother and child forced to learn only from each other and often not able to get any relief from each other ... our first ideas were of trying to find a way of living that would begin in the right direction, towards un-hung-up, loving, fully-realised children' (Q.125).

All this, together with other bits of superficial evidence such as the names chosen by many communes, Shrubb Family, Miller Family Commune, Family Embryo, and the very large numbers of unattached mothers among those looking for or trying to start communes, tended to confirm our first impression of the meaning of the contemporary commune movement. In a way which, so far as one can tell, was not true in the past, the family has indeed now become one of the main problems communes are designed to solve — the relevant point of attack for changing the world. Insofar as there is a social demand for communes today, one of the things that distinguish it from the long-standing tradition of interest in communal living documented by, for example, Armytage (1961) is its emphasis on the commune as an alternative family: 'communes offer an excellent, workable alternative to the monogamous single household' (Q.204). The concerns with property and work and with mystical communion and education that emerge so prominently as the central meaning of communes in earlier periods have been joined and to some degree pushed aside by a distinctly modern imperative – the desire not just for an escape from the family but for a new setting for familism, which, while performing essential family functions, will sustain for the individual those self-discovering and self-fulfilling relationships which our folklore leads us to expect of the family but which our experience teaches us the family can seldom support and often denies. The family as a setting for intimate relationships is seen as a threat to the free development of the individual. It is not clear whether what is needed to combine intimacy with personal autonomy is no family at all or a different sort of family.

Communes have assumed the latter. Their general position is a romantic-interactionist one — that the self is created through processes of social confirmation but only insofar as those processes are genuinely open-ended and exploratory – not, in other words, governed by prescribed roles, especially by the prescribed roles of the family: husband, wife, father, mother, child. Whether or not a particular commune is aware of itself as an alternative family system, this commitment to open-ended interaction as a formula for both love and self-realisation makes every commune immediately relevant as a possible model of new modes of domesticity.

As a result, it came as no surprise to arrive at one of the communes we had decided to study closely and find two women busy putting a new roof on the barn while one of the men cooked dinner indoors. More generally what we found was an elaborate and varied array of arrangements designed to disperse conventional male–female divisions of labour. Some of these were formally defined, involving rotas of housework, the creation of limited companies as a means of pooling ownership and commitment, provision for overt collective decision-making, explicit policies of treating children as children of the commune rather than of particular parents. But most were informal, a matter of continuous and fairly elaborate relationship work, an open-ended and pragmatic struggle to preserve the viability of relationships in which gender had simply ceased to be a conceivable basis of inequality. There was of course plenty of falling-off: 'Hey, look what *your* kid has done to *my* trousers . . .', as it were. And there were plenty of communes which turned out to be little more than ego-trips for dominant males, or dominant females, obscured in part by rich and complicated ideologies of togetherness. We found many different types of commune, many with core projects which played down or obliterated altogether the issue of a possible reconstruction of the family; groups for whom mystical or religious exploration, drugs or farming, politics or voluntary social services or craft production of various kinds dominated the issue of personal relationships. Conversely, we found groups for whom private sexual and parental life of a more or less experimental kind was an overwhelming concern. In general, and not surprisingly since we were dealing with intentional self-selecting groups for whom a crucial element of any particular group's reasons for being was a will to abolish sexual divisions, we found that communes could indeed do just that. And here, too, whether or not the nature of domestic relationships was felt to be an important part of the communal project, almost all of these communes were inescapably *relevant* to any consideration of the possibility of any reconstruction of domestic life.

For the more important finding to which we were driven, and which is our main concern in this chapter, was that although communes *could* do away with sexual divisions there was no sense in which they *had* to do so. Communes, that is, do not provide a social structure in which a reworking of gender relationships along more egalitarian lines is in any way unavoidable, a component of the structure. The most they provide is a precarious area of freedom in which people who are sufficiently determined to rework gender relationships can, under certain conditions, do so. These conditions in turn are closely linked to the relationships developed between any given commune and the outside world. And looked at in this way, it will be seen that communes are not really all that different from ordinary families. The important differences seems to be that unscrambling a 'commune' (an introjected set of relations based on recent, conditional choice and a strong sense of equality including sexual equality) is a little easier than unscrambling a 'family'.

Familism without the family: communes as anti-structure

Communes are made by teachers, psychologists and students, by unattached mothers, potters, silversmiths and architects; by, as one commune member put it, 'the sons and daughters of the middle class'. Recruited from the rump of the free craft occupations and the fringes of the minor professions, they can be characterised more precisely than that. They are in Poulantzas' (1973) sense a phenomenon of the petty bourgeoisie. We adopt the term 'petty bourgeois' as, simply, the best available analytical category; readers must convince themselves that the normal derogatory connotations are *not* intended. In any event, the term must be broadly construed. At one commune we visited, we found ourselves sharing a meal with graduates of Eton, Marlborough and Benenden and discussing the hazards of going to school with royalty. In a repertoire of petty-bourgeois protest – anarchism, freethinking, nudism, civil liberties and the whole gamut of 'spiritual-healing' projects – communes are the specific response to an ambivalent discontent with the specific experience of the petty-bourgeois family. In almost all its forms, therefore, the commune movement is an attempt to maximise values while minimising structure. It is what happens given the sorts of people who are making the most serious efforts to live communally in this country just now. 'The value of our place is the lack of formal structure' (Commune Movement 1970: 23). At both a personal and organisational level, there are many connections between the commune movement and anarchism. We shall take up this issue in more detail in chapter 7.

The values in question are themselves both distinctively petty bourgeois and peculiarly problematic. What is sought is *both* freedom (self-realisation) and security (togetherness), both a sense of autonomy and a sense of attachment. Merely to admit that one finds these values difficult to reconcile is, arguably, to admit that one is oneself difficult to live with. But if one then goes on to repudiate the possibility of drawing on externalised, 'structural', arrangements as a source of reconciliation, the whole burden of solving the problem is thrown on the daily *ad hoc* practice of relationships. Among other things this makes the life of a commune highly unpredictable. Again and again communes we had judged stable and successful a few weeks earlier turned out on a second visit to be in crisis or to have broken up completely. The story was almost always the same. 'The emotions involved were very strong and eventually the whole thing collapsed.' Here is an example (Commune Movement 1970: 22):

> Our nucleus is now seven or eight adults and three or four kids, our ages about two to forty. Usually there are also transient members and visiting friends. The adults share chores without sex distinction and all pay the same weekly sum, finding cash however they can (writing, painting, occasional jobs). We accept people according to how they behave, not according to age, politics or hair length.
>
> Because we are open about each other there is a constant liveliness, and we don't accumulate emotional hangups. Visitors usually find a stay healing. We have no formal aims or policy. We don't consider ourselves part of any movement, including the commune one. We think that the way to heal this society is by healing ourselves. By trying to live full and interesting lives we automatically work some change on the people we meet. Life is pretty good here, and we've hardly begun.

So one group described themselves in the autumn of 1970. By the autumn of 1971 their project had collapsed; the commune had vanished. The pages of *Communes*, like our own research files, are replete with such records. Police harassment and financial insecurity compound the difficulties of many groups, but the common problem is that in the absence of structure it is impossible to separate the fleeting difficulty from the life-and-death issue; the question why there is never any toilet paper in the loo turns out to be a matter involving the basic lack of commitment of some members to the group. More often than not, when we were able to unravel the reasons for the breakdown of a commune what we found was a familiar domestic crisis, a crisis of emotional possessiveness with all its usual reduction of people to commodities; having put her life's savings into getting the commune going, Anne was simply not willing to share 'her' Paul with Margaret; Paul's insistence that his simultaneous relationship with both women was part and parcel of the commune's commitment to self-expression deflected Anne's rage, denying her the normal legitimate grievances, but did

128

nothing to pacify it; the other members of the commune were dragged into a tide of complaint and recrimination which eventually so soured the atmosphere that the group broke up.

Experiences such as this are a common feature of the world of communes. But in commenting on such experiences, members of the commune movement reveal again their extraordinary ambivalence about any sort of social structure. The recognition of any ground-rules for the relationships in question would have pointed to a solution of the crisis short of disintegration; the more sanctioned such rules were, the more they would have done so, but only at the price of binding members into something rather like the 'family' and of restricting self-expression, above all the expression of love. So the favoured interpretations of such difficulties turn either on statements about personal qualities ('Anne was too hung-up'), or on the possibility of achieving values without structures through sheer hard relationship work ('We should have given Anne more help'). We would stress again that under certain conditions, with the right combination of people, this can be done. The 'small community influenced by D. H. Lawrence' which Armytage (1961: 417) discovered in Cornwall in the 1940s still exists and has grown into something like a small intentional village based on a mixture of farming, craft production and some slight involvement in professional careers 'outside'. At various times in their thirty-year history, they have deliberately torn up the sets of rules they had previously evolved as the basis for their life in order to confront a new problem freely. Then they have slowly, under the guise of developing new beliefs, evolved new rules, new social relations. Significant endowments of capital (a gift of several thousand pounds towards the cost of the farm) and of skills which could be pursued without involvement in socially organised work have allowed this group to repudiate the dominant social relation of the outside world, wage-labour. Once that has been done and a suitably closed environment created, there is little difficulty about reconstructing other relations. When husband and wife are both poets or potters and can afford to work only at what they find fulfilling, the sexual divisions built into normal marriages are at least much less compelling. Here, and in a few other exceptional communes, something like a society of free craftsmen (and craftswomen) has been created. The question is, is this any sort of model for a larger reconstruction of social relations? Here the issue of just how far the repudiation of social relations is to go becomes crucial.

The ideology of petty-bourgeois protest seeks to detach the bourgeois ideal of complete personal freedom from the unfree realities of bourgeois society. It seeks in a variety of fantastic ways to withdraw the individual from the social. The formally stated object of the Commune Movement, reprinted as such in every issue of *Communes*, is immediately of this kind, seriously engulfing the reality of social relations in the kind of sentiment that only makes sense if one has wished-away society: 'Everyone shall be free to do whatever he wishes provided only that he doesn't transgress the freedom of another.' The initial publication of the Movement, the Commune Manifesto as it were, not only proclaims this contradiction as its ideal but sets it firmly in an almost ideally petty-bourgeois account of the bourgeois world:

> We are beset with troubles which we have neglected for far too long and which could be brought to an end in an ideal community. We feel we want to do something of real value but there is nothing we can do; hands without power-tools on the end of them have become almost redundant and whatever we would like to be active in we find the ground already covered by a whole army of experts with supporting administrative and executive teams. We can read the paper but cannot write to it effectively; we can listen to the wireless but cannot speak to it; we can read a thousand books but cannot write one unless we have special ability. We feel utterly inferior and impotent in the face of this social monolith.
> (Commune Movement 1970: 4)

There is a true distress here, but it is expressed flailingly without location in any specific sense of what has gone wrong. Capitalism is indicted, but only vaguely; industrialism in the form of large-scale organised work is a more sharply felt evil – specifically as it obliterates the individual:

> We have, sadly, reached the stage of evolution, where few individuals are valued in themselves in such a way that they cannot be readily replaced. It is too expensive to be unique. In the time it takes a craftsman to create an object which is a thing of beauty as well as utility, a machine will produce a thousand, stamped out with unerring precision and monotony and fed on the vast conveyor belts which are the life-blood of this regimented society to the stereotyped minds that lie like doomed prisoners in the gloomy shades of bodies tied to an endless round of work, sleep and play.
> (Commune Movement 1970: 3)

'Stereotyped minds' is a revealing phrase and is taken up elsewhere in references to mediocrity, to 'civilisation in the mass' as 'basically a dictatorship', to mass ridicule and the 'smooth stagnation of the secure and glorious muddle of the present'. The prospect of the proletariat is as horrific as the prospect of capital. Not, of course, that the language of class is used. The analysis is at the level of the individual – masses of individuals but merely individuals:

> What has life to offer for these millions of beings who provide the main part of the productive labour upon which the monolith rests? The average man with only average intelligence and average par-

130

ents gets little encouragement or incentive to strive for higher things. He enters school in a soulless industrial town and consciously or otherwise competes fiercely for what education is available only to discover that his average abilities afford him only average opportunities and therefore approximately half of average pay. He is doomed to a life of poverty or endless overtime or both sapping his energies both physically and culturally. He has a wife and usually two children to support, and can offer them nothing better than to keep their heads above water in the same endless rut; he can offer them no capital sum; he will not win the football pools and he could offer them nothing in any way spectacular in their genetic makeup. He can only admit to his children that in the mad rat-race they have been born to be losers. His relaxation is conditioned by his lack of drive, lack of education. He turns to drink . . . he smokes . . . he sacrifices what remains of his life in mute supplication to the idiot's lantern until his thoughts are those of the tinsel God and his millions of degenerate addicts and lastly, in his mad frenzy, he drives his HP car in insatiable fury to the horizon – any horizon – to escape the drab monotony that was his death sentence at the moment of his birth. (Commune Movement 1970: 4)

The task then is not to confront but to escape ('indeed why should we not escape?'), but not to escape alone. Members of the commune movement depart in this from the pure-craft, surrealist, or art-for-art's-sake versions of the petty-bourgeois rejections of the social. Theirs is, as it were, the flight of the *average* petty bourgeois. Lacking a secure art or other 'ideal' proficiency in the technical cultivation of which the realities of the world can be denied, they discover themselves simply as individuals – 'Nobody but our small family really values us' – with nothing but their selves to gain or lose. And it is as selves that they protest: 'Isolation is probably our greatest burden . . . our greatest asset is each other: let's get together.' Theirs is a movement to create not beautiful art but beautiful people. And since people are created through being valued by others, it becomes, in its asocial way, a social movement.

This is the paradox: the social stifles the self; but the self can only realise itself in a society. The only known society is a monstrous offence; a new society must be created, but the only account of it that can be given is that it should be not society – that is, not the society that is known. The most that can be said is that it will be an opposite: 'We must create a sub-culture in which we, the deviationists, are the normals.' Love, freedom, equality, self-expression, or for the less ambitious, companionship, mutual help, convenience, are to be won, but all with a startling lack of awareness of the way in which any of these

131

values must, to be realised, be embedded in specific social relations (as distinct from gatherings of like-minded individuals). Members of the commune movement commonly recognise two kinds of problem which they must overcome if their ideals are to be made good: 'emotional and mental problems' and 'problems of sheer practicability'. The former is the way in which, given the denial of specific social relations, the relationships within communes are experienced. The latter involve mainly the relationships between communes and the outside world. What emerges from our study of communes is that notwithstanding the essentially fantastic nature of communalism as a project, a fair number of communes have in fact found ways of solving these problems at least to their own satisfaction. What happens of course is that social structure is smuggled back in – often in the form of a religion. The question which then arises is, if one has made one's own chains is one a slave or free?

We must look at these problems and their solutions more carefully. But first it is worth insisting again that the creation of communes as a denial of social relations is, within limits, really possible. Thus, systematic sexual divisions can be abolished voluntarily within communes because they are a derived type of division. Once the involvement of personal relationships in a wage-labour economy has been broken, sexual inequality at the level of personal relationships is neither plausible nor necessary. Communes can for long periods of time insist quite convincingly that even the most inescapable variations between individuals – man, woman, adult, infant – are insignificant for them as bases of differential treatment. When they become significant, when a woman finds she is after all being treated 'like a woman', the failure will be explained either as a result of an 'emotional and mental problem' or as a consequence of some unavoidable practical difficulty. We must see what this means.

Beyond the notion of getting together and overcoming emotional, mental, and practical difficulties, the ideology of communes offers no coherent or detailed account at the level of social structure of how the self-denying properties of the larger world are to be transcended. All we can do, therefore, is to consider what happens in practice when the attempt to get together is made.

Practical difficulties

Some problems are solved by a process of self-selection that occurs at the outset. Grammar school and university (started if not finished) provide the educational experience of the overwhelming majority of members of the commune movement. Their chosen fields of work are those in which a direct relation between producer and product rooted

132

in personal technique persists: poetry at best, architecture acceptably, teaching at worst. The profession most consistently represented amongst commune members is that of primary or secondary school teacher. The shift envisaged by most is towards still more directly expressive modes of work, uncontaminated by the needs of capitalism. Since they come from this sort of background with such intentions, it is both desirable and to a degree possible to attenuate significantly at least the perceived involvement of most communes with the economy around them. The financial basis of many communes is something few members of the commune movement are keen to study closely. A surprising number are launched on the basis of inherited capital or large gifts; in some cases the frankly middle-class character of members' occupations has induced a 'friendly bank manager' to produce substantial loans; whatever common ownership or income-sharing arrangements may be made once a commune exists, a disconcerting proportion of the more stable communes we have discovered came into being on the basis of successful private transactions within a capitalist market. The effective terms of reference for communal experiments were more than hinted at in some passages of the manifesto of 1970: 'Setting up a community in a rural environment can be quite cheap . . . we think £30,000 is an average figure to keep in mind for a good beginning' (Commune Movement 1970: 12). In today's property market that presumably means £60,000 – which is not everyone's idea of being quite cheap. Mobilising this kind of sum is of course more than a problem of mere practicability. Those who can do it, however, may well be able to treat personal social relations as alterable at will.

The nature of the remaining relationship between communes and the economy around them is embarrassing quite apart from questions about where the initial capital came from. There is a transparency about the image of economic life in communes which cannot bear much scrutiny. In the absence of an ability to insist on and demonstrate a mastery of genuinely esoteric skills, the image of craft work is curiously unconvincing:

—— Commune has the usual Commune aims. We want to make pots, posters, clothes, carpets, bags, beads, etc., grow our own food, become a family, an arts lab, a health food restaurant, folk club and country retreat. We are a happy bunch of artists, farmers, etc., who love the simple life, peace, quiet, meditating. (Commune Movement 1970: 20)

Making candles may be unalienated labour at a purely phenomenal level for the first few weeks. But it is hard to shield oneself from the real relationships with the larger economy which this quality of craft work implies for very long. Talk of the intrinsic value of the craft product becomes hopelessly mixed up with the most blatant forms of com-

133

modity fetish when what one is really doing is making a living making bric-à-brac for tourists. Members of the commune movement come frequently to recognise, often with a brutal honesty, the contradiction at the root of their typical escape from the market. But what is left is only either subsistence farming – which calls for an organised and systematic division of labour, structured social relations, of which only those communes which have accepted the discipline of a religion or managed to recruit trained farmers seem capable – or a return, perhaps part-time, to professional work, or odd jobs, on other people's terms outside. In either case the limitations placed on communes as an anti-structure project become rather evident. There are exceptions, of course. The farm and health-food-shop type of project can be made to work – given sufficient initial capital and so long as the health-food fad lasts among stereotyped minds.

So far as their material conditions of existence are concerned, then, communes have been able to achieve only a restricted and partial freedom. Within that area of freedom, however, so long as the pots and belts sell, the illusion of a suspension of economic relationships can be sufficiently maintained. In this sense it is necessary to qualify Rowbotham's (1972) argument about the conditions governing the liberation of women. 'The woman at home', she writes, 'is thus a victim of the reflected alienation of the man's work situation and also an alienation of her own. Only significant structural changes can radically affect this. The production relations of the man would have to change, the woman would have to be paid directly by the community and the social division of labour would have to be transformed.' What this underestimates is the capacity of our society to sustain pockets of life within which alienation is wilfully redefined as freedom – within which, although the economic connection is not really broken, it is sufficiently attenuated for people to behave in their personal lives *as though* significant structural change had occurred. Even with the high degree of official control of land, buildings and accommodation which exists in this country, communes and particularly the Commune Movement are slowly finding ways in which at least fairly small-scale common ownership and common residence projects can be set up and in which both men and women can withdraw from the labour market, if not from the commodity market, far enough to live as equals if they choose. Given appropriate recruitment, the alienation of the man's work situation can be seriously eased or at least made less obtrusive. Similarly, the entailed typing of domestic relations can be significantly relaxed so that the woman at least does not *have* to experience the 'alienation of her own'. Of course this may involve a good deal of fudging of economic realities, but the point again is that with good will it can be done. An account from one of the few communes (R.006)

134

which we are agreed in thinking has proved itself a success shows how:

> The cash was put up by five people. Three of them had inheritances and for the other two it was savings from hard work and economical living. One lump of capital is in the form of a loan over ten years. The whole thing is set up as a limited company, since basically this is a ready-made democratic structure in which all participants in the community can be shareholders. We were seeking to avoid the ownership principle, but because we have not got all the details of the shareholders agreement yet sorted out, the people who put in the money are still technically the owners.

> The trouble is that it isn't that easy to have a place non-owned unless the capital holders who bought the place actually divest themselves of their money and give it to the company. But they still may need that money to use again, especially those persons who put in all their savings and have nothing much coming in as income. So we have chosen to accept the risk that the place might get sold up if certain people are not satisfied, or cannot carry out their plans due to circumstances beyond their control. But it took a long time for many of us to understand the complications and implications of this.

Having watched this particular group live their way through this particular problem is to be more than half convinced that at least some of the practical problems of communes can be solved *in practice*: 'We create our own problems that other people wouldn't dream of having; still, that's our fun in life, and that's how we like to be.' (*Communes*, 40: 10)

But at this point another kind of practical difficulty presents itself. At the level of domestic relations very few men or women are actually qualified to live as equals; they lack the technical skills to effect the structural changes that would have to take place *within* the domestic group. The point is made constantly in accounts of communes that have broken up. The experience of communes that survive for any length of time is normally one of continual selection and reselection of individuals until a viable mix of talents – for cooking and cleaning as much as for teaching or loving – is found. This is a persistent theme of articles in *Communes*; it was for example particularly stressed by one of the secretaries of the Commune Movement in summing up her first year in office: 'If you are interested in joining or starting a community sometime, I would suggest that in the meantime you get yourself as skilled as possible in things like electricals, plumbing, gardening, animal keeping, driving, sewing, cooking, cleaning, building and carpentry' (Eno 1972a: 4). If domestic tasks are not to be attached to types of people, it is not enough to free domestic relationships from the

135

external–internal division of labour and the sweeping dominance of outside work relations: in addition, domestic skills and a belief in their intrinsic validity (for the self) must be dispersed. The crucial difficulty in this respect, and not just for communes, appears to be that of dispersing mothering. But at this point 'practical' difficulties begin to blur into 'emotional' and 'mental' difficulties.

Insofar as a systematic reconstruction of domestic relations is blocked by the practical problems of communes, then, communes tend to solve these problems by partially re-entering the 'plastic society' or drawing on its resources just enough to maintain economic viability without enforcing a conventional allocation of domestic roles. This delicate balance can be struck at the occupational margins of an industrial economy, but only at the cost of a degree of involvement with 'supermarket culture' to which many members of the commune movement cannot take kindly. Communal groups are in this respect little different from newly married couples from the same sorts of social circles as those from which communes are largely recruited. Enjoying maximum disposable income and minimum responsibilities, they can very considerably arrange their lives to suit themselves. But as most women in such situations know perfectly well, their relative freedom and equality have been bought, briefly, at the cost of not being 'really women' – not having children, that is. In winning their freedom they proclaim their unfreedom. The freedom of communes to recast domestic relations is equally conditional upon the rejection of other kinds of relations – a rejection which is in the last resort spurious (the owner of the commune always might sell up if he is sufficiently thwarted: sooner or later factory production will produce better candles, cheaper), and not realistically available to most people.

Emotional and mental difficulties

The same incapacity of communes to master the issue of personal domestic relationships in principle (as distinct from settling it satisfactorily for particularly carefully selected groups *ad hoc*) is revealed in their distinctive ways of dealing with 'emotional and mental' problems. The largest single source of such problems is probably also the largest and most socially challenging source of·the demand for communes – young mothers unattached to men. These women have simple but irreducible demands to make of communes, for companionship, for social recognition of the value of their labour as mothers – or as non-mothers in the form of substitute mothering so that they can work at other things – and for an opportunity for new intimate adult relationships. It might well seem that if communes have a recipe better than that of the nuclear family for an unalienated, meaningful life for the

136

individual, it would be revealed especially in their ability to accommodate the unattached mother in these respects. In a sense her demands do not amount to very much — mainly to the idea that there should be an opening up of domestic relationships sufficient to prevent the obliteration of her life in that of her child. As a principle, this is a notion widely supported in the commune movement. In the actual life of communes, however, it is experienced as a problem – one much discussed in the pages of *Communes* and in most of the communes we visited. The problem is presented in a language of giving and taking, a language remarkably similar to that one might expect from the nuclear family. Communes, it is argued, are not cheap hotels but fragile social experiments; the question to be asked is what a potential newcomer could contribute to that experiment in return for what she (or he) would undoubtedly impose on it in the form of new strains:

> Another frequent request is for communes that are willing to take drug-addicts, so-called social deviants, young mothers and babies and so on. Now I know ideally that probably communes would suit many of these people, but please bear with us that life in a commune is not easy anyway and much as we would like to take people who have difficult problems, unless they can help the commune as well, it is not likely to be a success. Perhaps some day when the community scene is much more together, and more common, we can all share the burdens and help people less able than ourselves. I'm sure that most communal places would like to help but they often have a lot of problems already. (Eno 1972b: 20)

So writes a secretary of the Commune Movement in what is of course effectively the emotional equivalent of the demand for access to £60,000. The practised sentiment – 'we're terribly sorry, but you can't join us' – contrasts starkly with the ideal statements about communes made to us by so many members of the movement for whom the case for communes turned on their ability to 'extend the strong and protect the weak'. The general ideological stance of the commune movement stresses open relationships both within communes and between communes and the outside world. In principle, doors are open to visitors, observers, every sort of would-be member. In practice, with one or two exceptions such as the Anarchist Commune in Sheffield, all actual communes move towards some degree of closure in the interests of the cohesion of the existing group: 'We are choosy about new members after lots of bad experiences with "beautiful people" who expect a community to be a family (mums and dads, brothers and sisters, just to look after them)', or 'Others assume too much about our willingness to give; we see many needs in others but do not propose to sacrifice ourselves to all of them, only certain sorts on some conditions.' After a few

137

months of experiencing the costs of openness, communes can become pretty tough-minded and explicit about their real terms of entry:

> One important rule should I think be pinned to the entrance of every commune, NO ROMANTICS WANTED. (*Communes*, 39: 12)

> Communal living is more stressful than single or paired set-ups. It tends to divide well paired people. To smooth over frictions à la love-and-peace brigade is to reduce viability frequently below survival level. To apply criteria of practical effectiveness and to be firmly realistic is too heavy for many a communal aspirant. (R.035)

> Our experiences have led us to become very selective in who we accept on a visiting trial basis, as some go to a commune seeking the mother that will feed shelter and love them, but they are unable to help the commune in any way. (Eno 1972a: 8)

It is of course perfectly 'realistic' to sidestep problems by excluding them from one's sphere of responsibility, but in this case it does rather diminish the plausibility of the claim that communes constitute a setting *within which* such problems can be solved. No doubt the life of ordinary families could also be made much freer and more fulfilling if excessively dependent members could be excluded at will.

Yet essentially the same procedure that is applied to the vetting of newcomers is adopted by most communes in handling mental and emotional problems which arise within a group once it has been constituted. If the difficulty becomes acute, the group splits. The conditional nature of membership is in fact an all-important condition for the fullness, equality and autonomy of members' relations with one another. As one writer in *Communes* (42: 12) put it after arguing that communes had, contrary to the opinions of some other members of the movement, to have rules 'or the chickens would not be fed', these are rules of a special sort: 'Of course no punishment or fines follow if rules are not kept. The individual concerned would leave.' That is indeed just what tends to happen. When the struggle for consensus becomes too wearing it is normally solved not by one party's accepting the domination of another, as perhaps in the family, but by one or other party going away:

> I eventually left to live with Hilary . . . after feeling that I couldn't continue to live in a house in which I wasn't an equal psychological shareholder. I was going off Barry's trip. I had begun to resent . . . the general idea of being 'one of his household'. (Crowther 1972: 11)

> So this guy plonks himself in the commune and after a while bad vibes start to infuse the building. Maybe some of the group like him, and some don't. Little arguments take place behind closed

138

doors. Eventually either he goes or the commune splits and he stays with the new group. (*Communes*, 38: 15)

So what are communal objectives and priorities and what happens when it has been agreed by everyone to do something and then half the people change their minds? It seems that with the split into two groups no balance or compromise was possible, so one group left, taking four adults and five children. (Eno 1972a: 3)

It would seem that in one respect communes really are an alternative to the family; members retain their right to decamp; the active prospect of dissolution is the condition for equality. To an outsider it might well seem that communes are coping with the problems of family life by deliberately not coping. This is in fact unfair. A lot of strenuous work is put into making relationships within communes succeed – most successfully, it seems to us, by diverting members' attention away from the problem of relationships as such and towards either practical matters (getting the garden organised) or transcendent matters (understanding God's will). As a result there are many ways in which communes prove highly supportive of their members in situations where the family is often unavoidably quite inadequate. The situations in which we were most impressed by this capacity of communes to sustain the individual were not in fact situations of courtship and emotional pairing but rather situations of loss; in particular, situations of old age and bereavement. The more extended and varied intimate environment of a commune means, as we saw for ourselves on some occasions and were frequently told, that such predicaments are not experienced as acute problems of loneliness; the individual who has lost a husband or a child or has been retired from work is immediately re-engaged in a social world in which his or her own presence has a positive and unquestioned meaning. Within the communal division of labour, age does not entail redundancy; within the emotional world of a commune the loss of a loved person does not mean that one is hurled into an emotional vacuum.

This softening of intimate personal loss through shared mourning and renewed relationships is most marked when the bereaved remains within the group and the loved one has either died or gone away. It is less pronounced when both remain within the group after one has withdrawn his or her love from the other. Such situations are difficult to manage, because for most people in communes love is seen as an undifferentiated mode of relating. There is an effort to deny the idea of degrees of love with sexual romantic love as a qualitatively unique highest form, a tendency to insist that love is love and its forms are interchangeable. Nevertheless, relationships expressed as romantic love are both formed and broken within communes, and the problem of sus-

139

taining love once romantic love has been withdrawn is thus both common and profound. We do not doubt that it can be done and have indeed seen such situations successfully resolved on the basis of much tender relationship work by all concerned. On a number of occasions we were told that a dénouement of this kind was possible in communes because the shared ethos of the commune freed members from the corrosive experience of guilt. We were not entirely convinced by such arguments, however. To withdraw romantic love from another is unavoidably to diminish the individuality of the other – very acutely so when the setting of the relationship is one that emphasises the unique worth of individuality as communes do. To be the victim of a diminution of that kind certainly induced resentment, the communal ethos notwithstanding, in many of the cases we learned about. It is hard to believe that to have been the perpetrator of it could have failed to induce guilt. What communes do is perhaps not so much to eliminate resentment and guilt as to constitute worlds in which resentment and guilt cannot be directly expressed, worlds in which one must live, often quite desperately, with sentiments one may not enact. Indeed, many communes seemed almost masochistically to court this predicament, recklessly pursuing the joys of romantic love while superficially ignoring the hazards of its transience. Moreover communes are quite often founded on the attempt to create new romantic relationships without facing up to the pain of destroying earlier ones. Without going so far as to agree with the disenchanted member of one commune who asserted that most communes are the result of failed marriages, we are inclined to conclude that the whole life of some communes and substantial parts of many others can be understood as objectifications of guilt, deriving their original impetus and their existence from a concern to manage humanely the consequences of a romantic sexual hedonism which stops short of total selfishness because of the high value placed on mutual respect and affection. One of the more remarkable achievements of those fairly long-standing communes in which the bonds between couples are relatively fluid is the balance that is struck between the almost continuous manufacture of suppressed guilt and resentment on the one hand and the maintenance of an environment of friendship on the other.

Nevertheless, the seriousness with which the voluntaristic or intentional element in the commune movement is invoked to give individual members the right to decide whether or not they will stand for 'bad vibes', for the costs of domestic relationships, can but make communes in the last resort a fantasy solution to the problems of domestic life — *someone* is going to get stuck with the addicts, deviants and mothers with babies. The position towards which most communes tend to move in facing the issue of emotional problems is not very different from the unashamedly hard line taken by Postlip Housing Association on practical problems:

> We are looking for a stable young couple to come and live in one of our cottages. They will need enough income to be able to find about £25 a month for rent and for Association dues; and they will also have to find or borrow £500. . . . We know that this, sadly, lets a lot of people out straight away, and we're sorry about it; we can help with advice and encouragement, but they will have to come up regularly with dirty pound notes, or it will all fall down. The hard fact is that you do need some money if you want to live the way you want; if you want to live our way, it's essential. (*Communes*, 40: 15)

The emotional equivalent of this is of course to build communes around the strong, around just those people who in any case would find the problems of domestic relationships least problematic.

Interpretation: communes as fantasy

> The less the development of labour and the more limited its volume of production and, therefore, the wealth of society, the more preponderatingly does the social order appear to be dominated by ties of sex. (Engels, *The Origins of the Family, Private Property and the State*)

We have chosen to regard the commune movement as a species of petty-bourgeois protest. There are quite compelling reasons for members of that class to take to protest of this kind in contemporary Britain. It is not so much that the traditional predicament of the petty bourgeoisie has changed – although of course the steady decline in status and income differentials between middle- and working-class occupations and especially the withdrawal of esteem from many traditional craft-like occupations have greatly increased the transparency of that predicament; the notion of the special standing of these occupations becomes manifestly more illusory in the face of the inability of modern capitalism to maintain their special rewards. Nor has the traditional ideology of this class been significantly modified. For example, their critique of the economy of which they are victim still fails to move beyond the idea of capitalism as a way of life; the issue of emancipation remains essentially an issue of the emancipation of the individual – that is, emancipation *from* social relations rather than *through* social relations. There is a minor innovation here, associated, it would seem, with the popularisation of certain kinds of anthropological and psychological work in which the creation of personal autonomy is seen as a task accomplished in the setting of intimate personal relationships. But even

141

here the point of concern turns out, when put to the test, to be the individual, not the relationships.

Within this fairly stable structural and ideological setting, certain new things have happened, however. To begin with, the tumultuous experiences of a previous era from the fall of Eden to the fall of Nixon have served to exhaust and discredit, or, perhaps more important, to block off, previously conventional channels of political protest for the petty bourgeoisie. After a few years of apparent freedom, politics have as it were been recaptured by capital and labour, now locked again in a series of relations from which the petty bourgeoisie are excluded – the eating up of the Campaign for Nuclear Disarmament by the Labour Party was clearly an especially poignant symbolic moment for many of the older people we met in the course of the research. At the same time the diminishing functional relevance of the nuclear family as a component of capitalism has permitted the champions of individualism to wage a relatively successful war against traditional domestic structures ('The chain of capitalism breaks at the weakest link' perhaps?). The withdrawal from politics was thus followed by a quick reconstruction of the problem of individual liberty as a problem of the family. And in this campaign, as we hope to have shown, limited victories were possible; unlike the state, the family turned out to be unsupported by other powers. The world of the family looked as though it might be the one world which the petty bourgeois, deeply committed to individualism and thus impelled to eschew large-scale solidaristic action, could after all conquer. At the very least he could effect a real escape from *its* constraints, however helpless he might be in the face of the larger movements of history.

But our point is that the rescue operation only appears to succeed. It is in fact undermined by the very individualism which leads to the selection of communes as a solution in the first place. We hope to have demonstrated this in an illustrative way already. Now we should like to approach the same conclusion by way of an explicit discussion of the experience of women in communes in the context of some of the arguments to have emerged from the Women's Liberation Movement. By far the most useful concept thrown up in recent discussion of the position of women is, in our view, the notion of 'social secondariness' suggested by Rowbotham (1972). The value of this idea is that it recognises the degree to which the inequality of which women are victims is mediated by, among other things, personal relationships rather than springing directly from economic or political oppression. It directs attention to the practice of social relationships between men and women, to the constructed facticity of the women's world. It raises the Durkheimian issue of the extent to which we create our own constraints – and could therefore hope by our own action to free ourselves: 'the peculiar characteristic of social constraint is that it is due not to the rigidity of certain molecular arrangements but to the prestige with which certain representations are invested'.

Freeman (1972) has suggested a number of ways in which the secondariness of women is mediated, the 'core concepts of sexist thought', in her own terms. Firstly, 'men do the important work in the world and the work done by men is what is important'; secondly, 'women are here for the pleasure and assistance of men'; thirdly, 'women's identities are defined by their relationship to men and their social value by that of the men they are related to'. In each of these respects a woman sees the world through one end of a male telescope and is herself seen, suitably diminished, through the other end of it. In each of these respects, however, one might think that the situation of women would be drastically altered in communes. To begin with, the home becomes in principle the primary scene of value and action for men and women alike. 'What is important' is deliberately not what is done outside but what is done in and for the home. Again, among the social relations that communes seek to repudiate, those involving recognition of structured differences between men and women are prominent. Their intention would be to rewrite Freeman's second proposition as 'people are here for the pleasure and assistance of each other'. Although few communes are consciously concerned with women's liberation as an issue, their unconcern is meant to have egalitarian implications. Similarly, their commitment to the openness of relationships, to the freedom of men and women to make and break relationships on their own terms, is tied directly to a rejection of the idea that any partner to a relationship is 'defined' by the relationship.

Now whatever the differences between the theory and practice of communes might be, communes clearly do involve something more than a mere transplanting of the conjugal family into a collective setting. To the extent that the conjugal family is a cornerstone of the exploitation of women, communes should therefore offer at least a serious potential for change – even allowing for the fact that the location and status of conjugal and quasi-conjugal units within communes is one of the main sources of communes' emotional problems. If, that is, the secondariness of women is felt to be embedded in the conjugal family, communes might be expected to provide settings in which women could innovate in social relationships at least to the point of lifting the veil of secondariness and sharing on equal terms the alienation of men. And yet quite plainly this does not normally happen. Any attempt by women in communes to assert themselves as women is more likely to lead to the departure of the man than anything else. What does happen is that men in communes concede a certain enlargement of the significance of domestic relationships for them but in a

143

context still strongly dominated by effective, albeit potential, inequalities of freedom and economic competence 'outside'. Thus what commonly occurs is that women in communes broadly go along with everything that femininity, motherhood and the like ordinarily connote and seek to alleviate the burdens of their role through essentially passive cooperative female action; for instance, a rota of mothers feed the children. In many communes one sees what is tantamount to a conspiracy to enlarge the value and meaningfulness of conventional women's roles on the basis of more or less elaborate symbolic concessions to participation by men and the guarantee that women's work will be in the end performed by women. The understanding that this is the real state of affairs – not perhaps hard to grasp when one hears commune men talking casually of the need to 'find more chicks' – probably inhibits many women from snatching up even the few crumbs of freedom that the communal situation does offer. The root of the problem seems to be the very uneven way in which the elementary structures of the nuclear family are dismantled in communes. Of the three links that compose the basic family unit, wife–husband, father–child, mother–child, the first two are often seriously opened up in communes, but the third is hardly touched; motherhood remains an all-demanding and totally female role. The notion that communal relationships are intentional and sustained only on the condition that both parties find the necessary relationship work gratifying breaks down in the face of child-rearing.

There seem to be two main reasons for the general failure of women to seize even the limited opportunities for liberation which are available in communes. Firstly, the aim of communes to create situations in which people can be 'more themselves' is in practice susceptible to exploitation, mainly, but not exclusively, by men to their own advantage. Given that the terms of reference of male–female relationships have not changed all that much, many kinds of 'emotional problems' can be made systematically less burdensome by the values of communes – in effect, the male can exploit the female with a lighter conscience in a situation in which she poses as his equal without the strength of real equality to defend herself and in which he can maintain in the face of emotional havoc that 'she wants it that way'. Femininity was, after all, some protection against this sort of treatment; ironically, the initial effect of abandoning it as a mode of personal relationships seem to be to make the weaker sex still weaker. For all the extra housework contributed by men in communes – and it is not always all that much – the woman, especially the woman with a child, is not appreciably freed from dependence by the communal commitment to equality in male–female relationships. Her secondariness can be too easily recreated by some man. The second reason has to do directly with the enormous pressure that continues to be applied from

144

without for children to have 'normal parents' and to know who they are. This pressure is of course especially strong if the children are at school. Because the man is able to assert his freedom within the commune, these pressures tend again to be met by the mother's succumbing to the demand that a social role be filled. She meets outside society half way by accepting that traditional status which in turn gives the child the fixed point essential for its well-being and self-respect in the world at large. Here again the element of fantasy in the communal withdrawal from social relations becomes transparent. The basic problem is of course not very different from that which Mitchell (1971) and others have attributed to the ordinary family:

> The belief that the family provides an impregnable enclave of intimacy and security in an atomised and chaotic cosmos assumes the absurd – that the family can be isolated from the community and that its internal relationships will not reproduce in their own terms the external relationships which dominate the society.

The odd thing about communes in this context is that while many of their members would wholeheartedly agree with this comment as applied to the family, they largely fail to see that there is no reason why it should not apply equally to communes.

Communes, then, represent a reconstitution of familism on the basis of a marginal relaxation of the facticity in which the ordinary family is engulfed. What happens when the constraints of legally enforced monogamy and the wage-work–housework division of roles are removed is not the creation of an alternative system of personal relationships but rather a making plain of the deeper obstacles to equality through which men and women in this society struggle to relate. Voluntarism, and a commitment to self-realisation, far from being a way of transcending these obstacles, turn out to be a way of realising them more acutely. The commonest worry of women in communes, so far as we could tell, was still 'What shall I do if he leaves me?' The commune provided some insulation against the worst and most painful dénouements of such predicaments; it did not provide a setting in which women could count on not having to experience such predicaments.

In this context something should be said specifically about Findhorn. The majority of communes, insofar as they pursue the idea of an alternative family, think in terms of a dismantling or at least a serious relaxation of the conventional structures of family relationships. Various necessities of the communal situation drive them towards a more or less explicit restoration of familism. Findhorn is quite different in this respect. The family is seen as one of the essential building-blocks of the New Age; the external form of the family unit is to be preserved and cherished, the object being to construct a community of families

145

based on strong and spiritual attachments between mates and between parents and children. A marriage, such as that of John and Joy which took place during one of our visits, is an important moment of community solidarity. This ideology of Findhorn, combined with the residential organisation and the sheer size of the commune, transforms the meaning and viability of domestic relationships. What Findhorn is seeking is not to disperse familism throughout a commune but to build a commune out of families; there is a constant and emphatic assertion of the value of conjugal attachment and fidelity. The immediate presence of the ideology of the New Age as an authoritative moral yardstick in all difficult situations makes conjugal ties the most powerfully and positively supported relationships within the commune as a whole. Indeed it is only through these ties that the realisation of the larger objectives of Findhorn is envisaged. This ideological translation of conjugal love into a moral force of cosmic significance does give family relationships at Findhorn the standing of social facts; facts, however, which are experienced by the individuals involved as achievements, not as constraints. Through its special religion Findhorn comes much closer than most communes to the actual creation of alternative families. And at a quite mundane level the sheer size of Findhorn supports the ideological transformation. Although most of the cooking and cleaning is still done by women, it is at least distributed and organised on the basis of communally determined rotas and assignments which at once bound such work and significantly reduce its meaning as something that goes with being married. Here again the ideology comes into play. Not only is the meaning of domestic work withdrawn from its normal entanglement with domestic relationships, it is transformed, through the idea that perfection in all tasks including 'kitchen awareness' is the vital expression of the individual's oneness with the commune, into a social attachment. A small but significant move has been made in such communities towards, as Engels put it, turning private housekeeping into a social industry.

Children

If few if any British communes have evolved a structure which frees the adult woman from her normal state of secondariness, giving her socially sanctioned resources to use as a member of the commune in asserting her equality with men, what can we expect in the case of children? The all-important step in transforming the world of the child must of course be the creation of an alternative system of education. Despite a number of experiments with Free Schools, communes as a whole have failed to withdraw their children from school. In a few cases, communes with suitably qualified adult members have made

146

arrangements to take over the education of their children up to the age of eleven. But even in some of these cases the resulting wrangles with the Local Education Authority about the adequacy of communal premises and facilities have led to the abandoning of the effort. The more common situation is for the commune to send its children to the local school and to see that as a positive move towards closer contact with the local community rather than as an offering of hostages to the system – in fact, of course, it is both. This willingness to accept the established system of education not only has the effect we have already mentioned of facing commune members with a very powerful demand, mediated by the children, for the establishment of 'normal' family relationships and responsibilities, it is also indicative of the real situation of children in communes as something less than full members.

On the whole, members of the commune movement have positive attitudes about children and believe that the business of bringing up children is likely to be easier in communes than in ordinary families. Of those who answered our questionnaire, for example, nine-tenths of the people not living in communes and seven-tenths of those living in communes thought in this way. Many of those who did not think it would be easier nevertheless thought that it would be 'harder but better'. In the communes we studied closely, our attention was often drawn in an obviously deliberate way to the merits of communal child-rearing: 'You can see what a good place this is for kids.' But what we tended to see actually was a remarkable gap between the promise and the practice. There was, to begin with, an impressive consensus about what communes have to offer children: freedom from over-dependence on one or two adults; a wide range of others, both adults and peers, with whom to relate and from whom to learn; a broad-based, non-possessive security – all this adding up to a much greater and more positive opportunity for the child to form a personality of its own. Variety, vitality, stimulation – all these were often mentioned. But as one would expect in the light of the general image of the ordinary family that prevails in the commune movement, it was the possibility of freeing the child from the hazards of personality absorption rooted in the conventional domestic love nexus that was most emphasised when the question of children in communes was discussed: 'Children can relate to more people, reducing the hideous friction of the nuclear family prison' (Q.202); 'Excessive dependence on the mother and with it the liability of fixation is diminished in a commune' (Q.177); 'The effect of any one adult and therefore the damage any one adult can do a child is much less' (Q.157); 'In a commune kids benefit from the vibes of *all* the other people; they are likely to be more open-minded than if brought up in a bi-parental system' (Q.212); 'Children can relate to several different adults on a deep

147

level, but with less smothering emotional involvement' (Q.181). This spreading of relationships was seriously attempted in many of the communes we studied, and often successfully realised – up to a point. But like everything else about British communes, the experience of children in communes is powerfully affected by constraints and contradictions which communes on their own cannot overcome. The critical problem in this instance is the child's need for a certain stability of attachment – and the inability of the commune to find any regular and effective substitute for the child's mother for that purpose. That mothering can be separated from motherhood has been demonstrated by the kibbutzim. But the conditions of adult life in British communes do not make it a realistic possibility here.

Alongside the advantages of freedom which communes are seen as offering children, there are also thought to be advantages of a rather different kind of freedom for parents. What is envisaged at this level is quite simply a reduction of 'the terrible responsibility of parenthood' (Q.129); 'Tasks are shared and the responsibility can be got rid of easily for a short time' (Q.121); 'There is always or nearly always someone to cover you . . . the pressures are so much less all round' (Q.111); 'A commune takes the strain off the mother and allows her to lead a life of her own' (Q.103). Clearly the pursuit of this kind of freedom, if it is to be coupled with the more positive freedom envisaged for children, calls for delicate, elaborate and self-conscious organisation of the relationships between children and adults in the commune as a whole. It is this sort of organisation which the constant turnover of membership of most communes and the ideological objection of many commune members to anything resembling deliberate social organisation make extraordinarily difficult. What tends to happen in practice is that, since the self-determination of the adults is after all the main reason for the existence of the commune, and since adults are, as in ordinary families, rather more powerful than children, a balance is struck between the respective freedoms of the child and the adult in which in most cases the parent, especially the male parent, does manage to 'spread the load' of responsibility somewhat, while quite often the life of the child is haphazard at best and manifestly insecure at worst. Whatever one may conclude about the secondariness of women in communes, it became clear to us that children, although usually taken seriously by adults, tend to be kept in a firmly secondary condition. The heart of the wrangle about the children's food at Family Farm which we described in chapter 3 was not, so far as we could judge, the question of what the children wanted to eat but the question of what they should be required to eat. Again, we were told of parents' 'keeping a child's hair long because it looks nice despite seeing the child fretfully pushing hair out of its eyes', and more generally

148

encountered situations in which 'the children run wild but no one seems to consider very much what the children themselves might offer on decisions' (R.004; Q.117). The experience of a four-year-old girl, Amy, at one of the communes we visited is only a particular version of the type of situation in which many commune children find themselves: when we first stayed there she had five other children to play with and seemed wholly caught up in a world of children; on our next visit all the other children had gone, following a major break among the commune's adult members; Amy was devoting enormous energy to making a father of Robin, a young man who had just joined the group; however, Robin's willingness to play this role was fluctuating: often completely generous and whole-hearted, it could vanish suddenly when more pressing adult concerns claimed his attention; one night when her mother was away Amy cried desperately for hours before Robin got round to remembering her. The typical, inevitable response to difficulties of this sort is for mothers to go back to mothering. In extreme cases – and often this seems to happen in relatively stable and successful secular communes once a woman willing to accept a mothering role has been found – she tends to end up as the effective mother of the whole commune.

Again, however, the contrast between most of our secular family communes and Findhorn must be noted. Of the communes we studied closely, only Findhorn runs a nursery on a regular basis with the tasks of child care assigned as communal work to particular members. At one stage two members of the commune also taught in the local school; relationships with the school remain good, and the fact that Findhorn is in any case built around normal family relationships eliminates the kind of pressure felt through their children by more experimental groups. Here, too, size and ideology have combined in a peculiarly happy way for Findhorn; within the commune, adult women are freed from the ascribed chores of mothering, pursuing instead this or that type of achieved work, which might be mothering or might be bookbinding, but which, whatever it is, has the positive value of being integral to the working of the commune. At the same time the moral and emotional standing of the mother–child relationship is not diminished but enhanced by the belief system of the New Age. No less important and perhaps more directly an effect of size and insulation than of ideology is the ability of Findhorn really to disperse much of the socialisation of children among a wide range of adults simply because a wide range of adults is consistently there. One of the noticeable things about Findhorn was the assurances we were given, which our observations confirmed, that fatherless children there really could and did make new fathers for themselves. This possibility of course depended not only on there being a large supply of unattached men at

149

Findhorn but also on their being caught up in an ideology which gives them a strong belief in family attachments. To echo Engels, once again, in communes of this type a small but significant step can also be made towards making the care and education of the children a public matter.

In general, then, communes provide children with a life that is neither systematically better nor systematically worse, so far as we could tell, than the life of children in most families. The larger and more stable communes such as Fern Hill, where thirty-five children have grown up, do offer something more than the family in the range of generally affectionate others, children and adults, with whom each child can relate. While none of the Fern Hill children have chosen to make their own adult lives on that commune, they do 'go home' a great deal for weekends and holidays, and it is clear that strong and positive relationships between the generations have been built, although the firmest ties are possibly within generations rather than between them. Comparing communal life with the life of what have been called symmetrical or dual-career middle-class families, it would seem that on balance the world of the communal child is richer in human content and that, if only the commune can break certain barriers of size and stability, children in communes can develop a very remarkable capacity for extensive social relationships without being in any way incapable of intensive relationships as well. Unfortunately of course, very few communes in Britain can cross these barriers at the present time for reasons we have discussed. Were they able to do so, it seems that the advantages in terms of introducing an alternative mode of child-rearing might be very considerable for both children and adults.

Afterword

The attempt of communes to do the basic work of the family better than it is done by the family is not, then, commonly very successful. Typically, pair relationships between adults both threaten and are threatened by the commune as a whole; the more stable they become, the more this is the case. Typically, children find themselves at sea in the flux of adult relationships; whether the sea is calm or tempestuous is beyond their control, and often beyond that of the adults, too. Having freed personal relationships from the constricting possessiveness that can develop within the conventional home, how does one institutionalise attachment? Possessiveness is of course one of the prices individuals can charge as a return for their collaboration in a social institution which constricts them. But how, if one rejects that sort of Durkheimian trade-off, does one establish a commune as a social fact for its members? How does one give communal relationships the solidity of a social institution without allowing that solidity to become a power that others can use against one? There are some ways in which this can be done, and we shall discuss some of them in a later chapter. But for the most part they are not available to secular communes in a modern capitalist society. Their distance and dissociation from that society means that communes cannot achieve the status of an institution of society; their dependence on and contamination by that society mean that they cannot emerge as institutions of an alternative society. Unable to establish institutionalised relationships, their life is dominated by personal relations.

This is a bleak if not a despairing view, much at odds with the largely optimistic tone of many other studies of communes. We suspect, however, that this difference is not a consequence of any difference in methods or assumptions or even observations between us and other writers. It is simply that we have been interested in an aspect of communal relationships which previous studies have largely ignored. One can be interested in communes as a laboratory for investigating the basic principles of social solidarity in the manner of Kanter, or as an expression of the issue of identity created by our existing social organisation of generations in the manner of Speck, or from many other points of view. Only if one looks at them as alternative families, taking their claim in that respect as seriously as it is made, is one likely to reach the conclusions to which we have been forced. Much of the research and analysis and writing for this book was completed before the publication of Andrew Rigby's admirable studies of British communes (1974a and 1974b). We have to a considerable extent trod in his footsteps so far as field research is concerned, visiting many of the same communes and being told much the same things by the same people. However, our interpretations differ widely; where Rigby tends to be humanistic and hopeful about communes and sees them as having a serious revolutionary potential, our view is plainly more sceptical; we would tend to see them, at least in the context of the present chapter, as alternative *unrealities*. And in this respect it is particularly noteworthy that Rigby does not deal directly or in much substance with the issue of gender relationships in communes. Moreover, what he does say about such relationships is at odds with his general interpretation of communes and very much in line, implicitly, with ours. Thus, most of his chapter 'Communes and the Nuclear Family' is devoted to a discussion of what we have termed the 'practical difficulties' of communes, but in a very brief passage on 'sexual relationships' he observed that 'there can be little doubt that this can be, and is, an important area of conflict', and he goes on to quote the experience of one American woman: 'The talk of love is profuse but the quality of relationships is otherwise; the hip man like his straight

151

counterpart is nothing more, nothing less than a predator.' What one makes of communes perhaps depends on what one is looking at. Gender relationships were of passing interest to Rigby and of central concern to us. So far as such relations are concerned, communes in contemporary Britain cannot easily detach themselves from the constraints of a larger moral economy; for that reason these relationships themselves remain a field of coercion.

6. Solidarity, survival and success

> The coercive power that we attribute to it is so far from being the whole of the social fact that it can present the opposite character equally well. Institutions may impose themselves upon us, but we cling to them; they compel us, and we love them; they constrain us and we find our welfare in our adherence to them and in that very constraint . . . There is perhaps no collective behaviour which does not exercise this double action upon us and is contradictory in appearance only.
>
> Durkheim, *The Rules of Sociological Method*

In the last two chapters we have considered communes as settings for the creation of individual personalities and for the conduct of domestic personal relations. We have done so largely by studying the immediately given, phenomenal, level of communal life. But communes are also societies, and in some cases at least societies that constitute viable worlds for their members for quite long periods of time – among those we have studied closely this would be true at any rate of Fern Hill and Findhorn. In this sense communal life is also an experiment with the larger principles of social solidarity. It is an experiment of particular interest just because it is conducted on the basis of a distinctive moral imperative of modern capitalism, the insistent demand for personal autonomy. The problem of assessing the nature and extent of social solidarity in communes raises some peculiar difficulties, however. Not the least of these is the need to see the commune movement in one aspect as a fairly deliberate attempt to deny the ability of social science to understand the sort of social reality represented by communes.

As an alternative to the forcing of experience into dualistic categories, communes assert a possible and actual unity of opposites. In Durkheim's terms they advance a claim that we *can* 'at one and the same time develop ourselves in two opposite senses'; that we can achieve both great individuality and great social solidarity and that this can be done in societies based on 'likenesses', without an extended division of labour. Durkheim's argument is of course that one must choose; the strength of individual personality and the strength of the collective type can in his eyes 'grow only in inverse ratio' to one another in such societies: 'Solidarity which comes from likeness is at its maximum when the collective conscience completely envelops our whole consciousness and coincides in all points with it. But at that moment our individuality is nil. It can be born only if the community takes smaller toll of us' (Durkheim 1933: 130). The important function of the division of labour is to make possible a society in which individuality and solidarity are both enhanced by substituting practical interdependence for an inclusive community of sentiment. In these circumstances, although societies cohere, the common conscience within them is enfeebled – with one exception, of course: 'the individual becomes the object of a sort of religion', and as he puts it later on, 'the only collective sentiments that . . . become more intense are those which have for their object not social affairs, but the individual'. Contemporary communes are plainly phenomena of an advanced society in that respect and their attempt to deny the necessity of Durkheim's alternatives might not be thought important were it not for the endless and often painful reminders we have had of how right Durkheim himself was when he admitted that the normal outcome of the progress of the division of labour is not the 'mellowed dénouement' of organic solidarity for which he hoped but rather a chronically disordered condition of anomie, coercion and other 'abnormal forms' which the state, through regulation, education and discipline, must be called upon to remedy. But in these circumstances other suggestions for combining individuality with solidarity are worth taking seriously. Is there a viable mode of *communal solidarity* which could be regarded as an alternative to both mechanical solidarity and the disordered actuality of organic solidarity in its ability to support *both* strong individual and strong collective sentiment? And if so, under what conditions could it be realised? Insofar as the denial of dualism is more than a matter of faith or assertion, how is communal solidarity given institutional substance?

The problem is fairly easily solved in principle. It is a matter of what Kanter (1972: 65–6) has called commitment: 'a reciprocal relationship in which both what is given to the group and what is received from it are seen by the person as expressing his true nature and as supporting his concept of self'. Her account of the nature of commitment is exceptionally clear and apt as a statement, at an ideal–typical level, of what communal solidarity would have to be like – a situation in which the

153

distinction between self-interest and social interest no longer made sense:

> A person is committed to a group or to a relationship when he himself is fully invested in it, so that the maintenance of his own internal being requires behaviour that supports the social order. . . Commitment thus refers to the willingness of people to do what will help maintain the group because it provides what they need . . . When a person is committed, what he wants to do (through internal feeling) is the same as what he has to do (according to external demands), and thus he gives to the group what it needs to maintain itself at the same time that he gets what he needs to nourish his own sense of self.

As an ideal of social integration this image of fusion and mutuality, of a condition in which people want to do what they have got to do, is of course as old as Plato and in sociology as old as Mead and Cooley. But what has always been at issue is not whether such a condition of full commitment is conceivable, but whether it is possible. Specifically, is it possible in communal situations today, given that on the one hand (as Durkheim puts it) 'no one today contests the obligatory character of the rule which orders us to be more and more of a person' (1933: 405), while on the other hand so many commune members are themselves so keenly aware of the chameleon-like relationship between commitment and coercion ('committedness . . . it's too much like marriage')? It is not just the critics of communes who see that when looked at in process, the building of commitment is often a matter of appropriation and surrender.

In such a context, to postulate the need for absolute commitment as Kanter does – 'the problem of securing total and complete commitment is central' – is in our view unrealistic. If communal solidarity is a possibility, especially for the kind of secular communes in which we are interested, the conditions of realising it must surely be at once more relaxed and more dynamic than that.

For communes that see themselves as enclaves in the world rather than as definite withdrawals from it, the problem of commitment is not so much one of being either committed or not, but rather one of a flow of commitment both within the commune and beyond it. Kanter's whole conception of commitment is perhaps over-influenced by the specifically religious nature of the purposes of the nineteenth-century communities she studied as well as by the long-standing instinct of too many social scientists to treat religious relationships as adequate models of social relationships in general. This is very clear in her characterisation of the main processes of building commitment: sacrifice, investment, renunciation, communion, mortification and transcendence. Investment is clearly the odd man in this list, and it directs attention to

154

what might be called a secular, economic dimension of communal life which Kanter, despite an initial concern for 'how people arrange to do the work the community needs to survive as a group', largely ignores. To ignore the division of labour as a source of solidarity is, to say the least, an odd thing for a sociologist to do. Our research suggests that it is at this level, around the economic dimension of communes and around related essentially secular processes, at least as much as at the level of transcendence, mortification and so forth, that the effective sources of communal solidarity are to be found. Before taking up this theme, however, it is necessary to make clear what we might mean in calling a commune a success.

The problem of success

It is plain from what we have already said and from the record of modern communal life as a whole that very few communes do achieve an enduring solidarity. Before we can properly assess communes as societies, however, we must decide on some appropriate criteria by which to judge their success or failure. These in turn need to be related to both the purposes and the problems with which communes distinctively are faced. A commonsense and often-used measure of success is of course simple survival, the ability of a group to stay together for a given span of years. Thus Kanter treats as successful any commune which persists for twenty-five years or more (1972:178). But will this do? Solidarity has many forms and qualities, and few if any of them can be realised only in groups of long duration. Moreover, the solidarity of a group is rarely a matter of cherishing a single value or purpose indefinitely but rather of creating a setting in which multiple values can be at least partially and fleetingly realised. Simmel made this point well (1955: 21):

> Neither love nor the division of labour, neither the common attitude of two toward a third nor friendship, neither party affiliation nor superordination or subordination is likely by itself alone to produce or sustain an actual group. When this seems so nevertheless, the process which is given one name actually contains several distinguishable forms of relation.

This is plainly true of communes. Not only are they not sustained by single principles of solidarity, they are successful or unsuccessful in relation to many different criteria which may often seem to oppose one another and which are differently valued by different members of the group. In some cases, in the psychedelic groupings, for example, persistence is specifically devalued: the whole point of being together is to create moments of spontaneous experience, an intense now, and therefore to disperse and move on as soon as the quality of the moment,

155

which is bound up in its momentariness, begins to fade. Similarly, the therapeutic communities, whether they are recognised as such or are performing a latent 'phoenix' function of the kind envisaged by Speck, are societies for which impermanence must be a measure of success; not only should individual members be able to complete the detour back to the straight world, but the community as a whole must be able to dissolve rather than assume the introjected rigidity of a system of family relationships. And even for the secular intentional groups with which we are mainly concerned, permanence in itself is an ambiguous value. The object of these communes is of course to stay together for as long as possible; but the freedom to determine what is possible is, on the basis of other more important values, retained by each member. In the course of our research we met many people who had lived previously in communes which they had left or which had broken up; almost without exception these people regarded those periods of their lives as successful, 'good while it lasted', an episode of valid experience part of the validity of which was related to the fact that those involved treated it precisely as an episode. Perhaps it is only for religious communes and communities, where the point of existence is the defence and perpetuation of a faith, that persistence can reasonably be used as an unambiguous measure of communal success.

On the other hand, it is *some* sort of measure; we cannot discard it altogether. From a Durkheimian point of view communes may be thought of as attempts to create new social facts, as attempts, that is, 'to transform morality through association'; one relevant yardstick of the success of such projects has to be the persistence or non-persistence of the association in which the attempt is made. Here the comparison between communes and marriage can perhaps help us.

It seems that sociologists have all but given up their efforts to identify successful marriages. There is still a lurking sense in the textbooks on the family that we ought to be able to find indicators that would make the old aim of measuring relationships in terms of a package of stability, happiness and adjustment viable. But the loudest chorus of scholarly voices is discouraging such efforts. Thus Simpson (1966: 214) finds most of the suggested measures of marital success naive, barbarised and misguided: 'All the factors found associated with marital success and failure are so general and vague and so lacking in depth specificity as to be almost worthless as scientific indicators.' Given the mechanical, spurious or subjective nature of all the possible criteria for talking about the success of intimate relationships, and the inability of most research to enter the backstage area of domestic life, he in effect recommends an end to attempts to be scientific about marital success. Skolnick (1973: 208) takes a similar view, emphasising for example the

156

degree to which stability and happiness, even if they could be measured, may be alternative rather than complementary principles of married life to which one partner's adjustment may be bought at the expense of the other partner's unperceived loss of identity. What is at issue here, of course, is just what is at issue in communes. The more stress one places on marriage as an authentically voluntary relationship, the more one views it as a rational and conditional contract designed to maximise essentially hedonistic values, the more ambiguous the criterion of stability becomes and the more elusively notions of happiness and adjustment retreat into the intra-subjective world of each partner. In the face of such difficulties Skolnick finds it, quite simply, 'impossible to define a successful marriage in an objective way'. In the same vein Ryder (1967: 807) rules: 'There is no descriptively defined entity that can reasonably be called a successful marriage because there is no general agreement as to what marriages should be.'

Nevertheless, as Cuber and Haroff (1965) suggest in their account of 'total marriages', there is a perfectly good sense in which the persistence of a relationship must be one's point of departure in any attempt to talk of its success or failure. We can agree with Skolnick (1973: 231) that 'marital stability does not necessarily indicate marital happiness or satisfaction', and indeed that it may indicate nothing more than collusion in the most ruthless war of attrition, and still take this view. A persistent relationship must be potentially a more successful realisation of whatever values the relationship is mainly about than a transient one in all situations where transience is not itself the central value, as it is in some of the psychedelic quasi-communes. By the same token, persistent relationships may prove to involve worse subversion and corruption of those values than transient ones in all situations where persistence itself is not the central value, which it is not in any communes we know of, even the most religious, although it may be in some marriages. We shall shortly come back to the question of whether one can get away with talking of some values as more central than others in such a crude way. For the moment it is bound to be the case that an enduring relationship involves more relating, more relationship work, is more of a relationship in a qualitative as well as a quantitative sense, than an ephemeral one. What Cuber and Haroff call a total marriage takes time to emerge; it is a matter of a long experience of choosing mutual affirmation as a course of life rather than other, perhaps more adventurous, possibilities. Indeed, the interesting thing about the studies of these authors is that all five of the types of marriage they identify ('conflict-habituated', 'devitalized', 'passive–congenial', 'vital' and 'total') are, just because they are types of social relationship rather than types of personal sentiment, forms which can only come into being on the basis of relatively protracted relating. Each type is an achieved

157

pattern of relating which requires considerable time for its accomplishment.

So we are inclined to accept persistence as one of a set of criteria in terms of which one might talk about the success or failure of marriages or communes. But the important question is, persistence of what? While sharing the reservations of Simpson and Skolnick about the possibility of establishing acceptable general indicators of the quality of domestic relationships, we do not ourselves feel that the qualitative interpretation of such relationships is wholly beyond the social scientist's powers of observation or empathy. In the case of marriages, for example, it is clearly possible, above all if one can break through to the backstage area of the relationship, to discriminate between particular relationships in terms of a host of evaluative criteria. Perhaps the most important of these, since it springs directly from contemporary images of the value of marriage, is attentiveness, the extent to which partners are alert to and generous towards each other's expectations. The quality of attentiveness within a relationship plainly is accessible to observation, and to the extent that the actors in question express the value of the relationship in terms of an ideology of mutual involvement, such observation would be a meaningful and adequate way of talking about the success or failure of the relationship. The connection of a quality such as attentiveness to the formal persistence of a relationship is, moreover, intimate and direct. Properties of relationships such as attentiveness and indifference, or exploitation, *become*. Social relations differ from social action precisely in having a record. It is the accumulated probability of, say, attentiveness that would justify one in speaking of a good marriage as distinct from a pleasant occasion. The creation of a marriage, or a commune, is a matter of setting up a system of probabilities. Observed at any point of time, a relationship can thus be described as having moved some way towards the realisation of some probabilities and some way towards precluding others. This process of definition and filtering — of establishing the capacities of a relationship — takes time. Some degree of duration is required for the possibilities of a social encounter to become defined as the taken-for-granted expectations of a social relationship. How long a duration is required will depend, of course, on the range and complexity of the probabilities the participants in any particular encounter are hoping to realise in moving towards becoming a relationship. In other words, one cannot assign a fixed time-span to a marriage or a commune and say, as Kanter does, that survival for so long constitutes success. And neither can one say that inability to survive for any particular period self-evidently constitutes failure. The principle of good-while-it-lasted is perfectly valid here. If a marriage or a commune breaks up in the face of some new or unmanageable exigency, that is certainly an indication of

158

the limits of possibility of the relationship, but it is not a negation of the value of what was possible. A marriage or a commune that has realised its possibilities cannot be invalidated by ceasing to exist. The appraisal of the significance of the length of time a commune lasts must be made, then, in the context of an appraisal of what the commune existed for and of the contradictions and problems it thereby had to resolve – the appraisal, in other words, of its bases of solidarity. What matters is not the time it lasted but what was made of its possibilities in the course of its existence.

That this is the sensible way of talking about the success or failure of communes, whatever may be the case for marriages, follows from the essentially and explicitly voluntaristic and conditional terms on which they are set up. The intention is to cohere in the absence of legal or financial sanctions enforcing cohesion – specifically, of course, without that facticity of marriage which encompasses relationships in a sanctioned commitment to continuing cohesion as a moral end in itself. In this sense it is quite improper to judge communes as though they were the same sort of project as marriage. By the same token, it is equally inappropriate to compare them to the sorts of communities produced by powerlessness in the labour market (traditional working-class communities) or by the surrender of the individual to a chiliastic belief-system (millennial movements). Communes introduce a new possibility into the theory and practice of social solidarity. They envisage choice as a basis of community. Their success or failure must in our view be judged primarily in terms of that particular possibility.

To maintain the integrity and solidarity of a voluntary group, the group must be regarded by its members as in principle temporary, however long it actually lasts. The tension between the wish to stay together and the wish to maintain the authenticity of individual attachments to the group thus becomes the main problem of solidarity for communes. In extreme cases, as in the psychedelic quasi-communes described by Mills (1973), this leads to situations where the only meaning members can give to the idea of success is to break up. The capacity to separate is, for groups whose members value the group for the spontaneity of relationship it achieves, the ultimate assertion of the value of the group. This argument was put to us not only by members of psychedelic communes but by many who saw the commune movement as part of a larger anarchist tradition, such as the Greenwich Squatters, or who, like the members of a commune we visited in Northumberland, had a highly developed sense of communes as *fundamentally* an alternative to society, quoting to us the words of Marx (1959: 104): 'What is to be avoided above all is the re-establishing of "Society" as an abstraction vis-à-vis the individual. The individual is the social being' (R.015). What this means in the context of a commune is of course that as soon as any members begin to take the solidarity of the group for granted, as soon as they begin to invoke the idea of the commune as a means of solving problems, the time has come to disperse. Nor did the members of our secular family communes see things very differently. Quite consciously the problem of solidarity is first and foremost a problem of self-interest – whether it is a matter of picking an acre of potatoes a day or of coping with the sort of double bind involved in having people tell you to be spontaneous.

One member of the commune we have called Family Farm, a member who was in many ways the anchor of the group as a whole, explained the relationship of self-interest and group interest to us very clearly in this respect (R.104). We had asked her what she thought of the view that a commune can only succeed if its members are willing to put the group before themselves:

> Group before myself! I have done a lot of thinking on this. What keeps a group together? Surely some self-interest? It has recently been brought home to me that all my actions are geared to group interest, but it remains true that I seek to get the group to satisfy my interests as well as theirs. Which means that one has to get the right group – as each member has to review how far his interests are inherently dependent on a group. Self-interest I feel is the ultimate force; but in any life this is contingent on cooperation or will-power to exploit others in some sort of network. So I feel that self-interest is the best motive but I find that my interests are best secured by an acute awareness of the group manoeuvring within the limitations of the material available.

In the context of this sort of account of what communes mean to their members, it has been suggested by Vidich (1974: 333) that 'rationality and a calculation of self-interest may be two of the fundamental foundations for the theory of temporary communities'. Vidich was thinking mainly of groups such as student residences and housing associations and other highly instrumental collectivities, and we would not want to state the issue quite as a matter of calculation in the way he does; one of the distinguishing features of the commune movement, after all, is the attempt to engulf one-sided orientations such as calculation in a practice balanced more evenly between reasoning and feeling. However, we do agree with him that the idea of temporary communities is an interesting possibility of advanced societies – perhaps *the* possibility so far as recapturing community at all is concerned – and that the crux of the problem of solidarity for such communities is the involvement, as distinct from what Kanter calls the commitment, of self. The basic social relationship of such a group is built on an active consideration of self-interest held in play by an equally active consideration of the interests of others, leaving everyone free to decide in the course of

160

each encounter whether the game as a whole is or is not worth
Far from the personality of each member having been immer
that of the group, communes of this kind are only conceivable i
member is equipped with a resilient awareness of self. Success f
a commune would be a matter of staying together on the basis ω. ρ---
erating sufficient attentiveness among the members for each to feel that
his or her self-interest would from moment to moment be best served
by his or her own continuing attentiveness to the interests of all the
others.

This conception of success, though it accords well with both the ideology of the Commune Movement and the dominant pattern of sentiment in the secular communes we studied, is far removed from those
views, expressed for example by Kanter (1972) and Zablocki (1971),
that see communes as faced with a terrible dilemma of freedom versus
community or postulate the need for the selves of individual members
to be transcended and absorbed in the collective identity of the group.
It is a position that takes one kind of communal project seriously, using
the purposes and problems of secular family communes as a decisive
point of reference and thereby necessarily doing less than justice to
other types of communes. These other types, whether psychedelic, religious or political, have their distinctive purposes and problems, and
their success or failure must be judged in terms appropriate to them.
This of course is just what Kanter and Zablocki have done and is why
properties like commitment, persistence, self-transcendence are the
vital dimensions of communal success in their eyes. Zablocki has also
noted, however, that the 'most common, successful and least-studied'
type of commune is precisely the secular family type (Skolnick 1973:
141). But it is from studies of the more exotic types that existing generalisations about commitment and solidarity in communes mainly
derive. Yet the rational and self-centred properties of the family commune make it the all-important type of communal project so far as we
are concerned; it is the possibility of social solidarity on *that* basis that
mainly interests us. So we shall say that a commune is a success insofar
as its members seem able to negotiate their way towards the creation
of a society of equals – and to do so without sacrificing their individuality in the process; without reestablishing 'Society', that is.

Communal solidarity

In the most usual case, the strain of sustaining the delicate balance of
self-interest and mutual attentiveness that is required for the successful
survival of a commune is overwhelming. Accordingly, most communes
move either towards the lesser success of disintegration or towards
persistence on the basis of a reestablishment of 'Society'. The most

161

common form of the latter involves remaking the commune or making a new commune under the auspices of a religion. Although this particular evolution is in an important sense not a solution to the practice of intentional community at all, but rather a change in the terms of reference of group life in the face of a failure to achieve communal solidarity, it is very common; and because it does in a way clarify what communal solidarity is *not*, we shall deal with it first.

For the first twenty years of its existence Fern Hill was a commune with no common religious beliefs; the members made their living from dairy farming and from a few small craft workshops. All major items of property and means of production were owned in common; the commune was open to newcomers, and members worked to minimise the growth of formal structures and rules within it. Decisions were made at weekly meetings; the development of leadership or of any fixed pattern of authority within the group was carefully resisted. The family was not accepted as necessarily valid, but members were left to form whatever stable relationships suited them best. Insofar as there was a common ideological position among the members, it was one with a mild political colouring, a humanistic anarchism expressed among other ways in an enthusiasm for D. H. Lawrence, pacifism and the Bruderhof. By 1960, however, many members had come to feel that these ideas, sufficient as they had been as a response to the world of the late 1930s, were no longer enough to support the sense of purpose and identity of their project. Emotional crises came to be experienced as more turbulent and challenging than they had been in the past. The divisive pull of egocentricity was less easy to contain as members were less sure of the adequacy of their account of what the commune was for. Their response, however, was not in the first place to try to redefine the commune but rather to try to redefine themselves. They were drawn to an interest in Jungian psychology; many members had analysis, and the commune as a whole came for a while under the influence of a powerful Jungian psychotherapist. As we have suggested before, Jung's thought is a uniquely suitable medium in which to tease out essentially self-oriented worries about social solidarity. In this case, however, the experience seems to have heightened rather than modified the self-consciousness of the members of the commune, and in the next few years there was a great deal of varied experimenting at Fern Hill with transformative mystical traditions, including yoga, Zen, individual and group meditation and moving towards a shared and increasingly pronounced interest in the Christian mystical tradition. With the acceptance of Christianity, the difficult task of changing individuals begins to give way to the easier task of reestablishing 'Society': 'One by one over the next two years we were all received into the Roman Catholic Church' (R.016). In the next phase of its history, in the early 1960s, the commune set out to build a monastic type of con-templative institution for men, women and children. A written constitu-tion was adopted; forms of membership were specified; officers were appointed, and leaders were elected. Participation in ritual events, prayer and religious instruction became the new basis of solidarity.

This was not the end of the history of Fern Hill. One of the sources of the vitality of this particular commune is the combination of honesty and adaptiveness with which its members continue to respond to their own experience. The intense religious concentration of the life of the commune just after 1960 has been greatly relaxed now in the face of new relationships within the group. But the episode is instructive. What it involved, quite simply, was an effort to save the commune by reifying it. The religious redefinition of the commune shifted members' attention away from themselves and their immediately experienced relationships and allowed them to contain personal demands within an over-arching, thing-like communal idea. As this occurred all the proce-dures of commitment characteristic of 'Society' in general and of reli-gious societies in particular could be brought into play. The yardstick of intentionality was subordinated to a yardstick of unity in the accom-plishment of an externally set mission. In effect the members of Fern Hill conspired to bring about their own alienation. Sensing a constrain-ing artificiality in their relationships, they had withdrawn a little from the practice of those relationships to try to *think* their way to new rea-sons for solidarity. Out of their introspection they had constructed an abstracted, estranged account of the commune invested with powers and purposes which, once they had invented them, became the means by which they themselves were united and constrained. Religion, as Feuerbach pointed out, is a word derived from *religare*, to bind. Out of their loss of control of their real destinies they created an illusory collective destiny controlled from without. This 'crystallisation of social activity, this consolidation of what we ourselves produce into an objec-tive power above us', is surely the essence of alienation; and 'out of this very contradiction between the interest of the individual and that of the community the latter takes an independent form . . . divorced from the real interests of the individual and community and at the same time an illusory communal life' (Marx & Engels 1939: 58). The members of Fern Hill themselves described their monastic episode as a period of loss of self. What they did not see was that because it involved a loss of self it also involved a loss of community. The strug-gle to relate to people is arduous and endlessly beset with bad faith; the easiest way to withdraw from it is to relate through the mediation of things, man-made abstractions, the collusive acceptance of social facts, by making the commune a higher reality presupposing a certain surrender of self. As Marx observed, 'religion is the illusory sun which

163

revolves round man as long as he does not revolve around himself . . .
the self-feeling of man who either has not yet found himself or has
already lost himself again' (Marx 1975: 81). The commune survived its
crisis because the direct human relationships which were its basis were
by mutual consent mystified and engulfed for a time in a more abstract
communalism.

Religious projects, whether in the form of purposive communes such
as Fern Hill became for a time or in the form of utopian communities
such as Findhorn, are at once a symbolic statement of collective human
values, giving them a heightened clarity and force, *and* a dehumanisation of collective life in which a symbolic order is intruded between
individuals as an object of relationship in its own right. Thus Beshara
described itself as 'a focus of discovery, a matrix for self-transformation,
an opportunity to discover the One by seeing Him in everything
we do and to carry this vision back into the relative world' – the relative world being the world of mundane, direct human relationships.
The development of Beshara is described in one of its publications as a
journey through 'the valley of non-attachment' to 'the valley of unity', a
journey involving 'offering up all that we think, all that we do, all that
we are'. The externality and independence of the symbolic world is
powerfully stressed: in the devotion of energy to the design and building of a temple; in the idea that 'Beshara itself is the teacher' (rather
than any individual members of it); in the distinctive commands of the
deity 'love me, love me alone: love yourself in me, in me alone'. Such
projects attempt and often effect a total reconstruction of the person
and in so doing create strong social orders. But it was our impression
that this strength, this capacity to remake individuals so totally, was
not unrelated to a tendency of purposive communes, whether religious
or therapeutic, to draw to themselves individuals whose secular identity had previously collapsed or become profoundly confused. Others
have also commented on the apparent relationship between an initial
smashing of personality – whether by drugs or personal disaster – and
the subsequent remaking of the individual which seems to occur in
such enterprises (Daner 1975; Richardson et al. 1972; Wallace 1956;
Sugarman 1975). Both the way in which members are made available
for these societies and the way in which the societies then make over
their members on the basis of religious or therapeutic fundamentalism,
discipline and attachment are dramatic and extreme to a point which
makes it necessary to see them as fundamentally unlike secular communes.

The religious solution to problems of cohesion and commitment in
communes is then of little direct interest from the point of view of a
concern with communal solidarity as a form of social attachment based
on intentionality, voluntarism, human social relationships and an

164

actively considered self-interest. It is just such a humanistic social practice that the secular family communes in which we are mainly interested envisage. What such communes have to learn from the achievement of solidarity in religious communes is therefore what to avoid rather than what to imitate. Zablocki (1971: 287) is right to conclude that the particular reconciliation of freedom and community accomplished by groups like the Bruderhof is only available within the setting of mystical belief – and specifically, as he put it, of a certain 'death of the self'. What is not so clear is that this is the *only* way in which freedom and community can be reconciled. It is possible, of course, to define community in such a way that it must involve self-immolation so that, to quote Zablocki again, 'the idea of an intentional community is almost a contradiction in terms' (1971: 64). But if we resist the temptation to do this the puzzle that remains is not a conceptual one (about what words like 'freedom' and 'community' mean) but an empirical one (about what people can do to secure themselves a sense of freedom and community). And one thing they must plainly do is to refuse to surrender the experience of freedom to the idea of community.

The history of communes suggests that this is difficult but not impossible. The trouble is that communal solidarity, especially in the case of the secular intentional commune, occupies an uneasy middle ground between community as a socially bonded form and what Schmalenbach (1961) calls communion. Its precarious situation in this respect means that, without a great deal of attention and good luck, communal solidarity easily dissolves or hardens into one or other of these alternative types. The more resistant the members of a commune are to one, the more likely they are to find themselves unintentionally establishing the other. For Schmalenbach the difference between communion and community lies mainly in the degree of consciousness of emotional attachment displayed in each. Communion is essentially a matter of actively felt connections; the feeling of attachment is itself the direct basis of attachment. In the case of community, attachment is based rather on a lived interdependence; feelings of fondness and solidarity are a product of the working of community, but the community is constituted unconsciously – perhaps by a socially organised division of labour. Community is a taken-for-granted social reality; communion is a created relationship. Zablocki (1971: 65) argues that the construction of an intentional communal system is likely, empirically, to involve a passage from an initial state of communion to a more or less achieved condition of community. In the first instance members come together on the basis of enthusiastic feelings for one another. Whether or not they stay together is a matter of how far they succeed in transforming communion into the 'organic and natural coalescence' of community.

165

But for the group valuing intentionality, the problem is to move in this direction without setting up the idea of the community as an encompassing social fact, without reaching the point where the taken-for-granted qualities of community are experienced as constraints on the feelings of individual members. The object is for intentionality to remain an active element in communal life, for the individual to continuously choose what are in effect the taken-for-granted conditions of existence of the group, for both sides of Durkheim's paradox of constraint and choice which we quoted at the beginning of this chapter to be equally actively and simultaneously present in communal experience. To do this the move towards community has to be counteracted by constant reference back to the condition of communion. An intentional communal system, to the extent that it is unwilling to succumb to religion or to other reifications, has therefore to strike a constantly moving balance between preserving communion and constituting community. This balance is what we understand by communal solidarity as a special form of association.

Our research suggests that such a balance can be struck quite successfully on the basis of a number of quite mundane social arrangements. We would be inclined to characterise these arrangements as primarily economic or ecological and as having to do with the management of self-interest. What is above all involved in the successful accomplishment of such arrangements is the very opposite of a loss of self. Rather, as we were told with great emphasis by one member of Family Farm: 'The theory and aim of this place is about consensus decision-making. In practice this relies heavily on each individual's ability to stand alone' (R.007). This standing alone is, however, largely a matter of knowing *where* one stands within a mutually approved division of labour. Successful secular communes are in this sense very exact embodiments of the *idea* of organic solidarity – the realisation of individuality through interdependence and of interdependence through individuality. In that respect the contrast between communes of this type and mystical, religious and psychedelic communities could not be greater – it is precisely in the latter that writers such as Zablocki have found an example of something approaching a condition of pure mechanical solidarity. Places like Fern Hill in its contemporary form (compared to say, Findhorn, or Fern Hill as it was in 1960) satisfy their members because they provide settings in which the weaver, the electronics research specialist, the architect, the farmer can each devote himself to his own particular work wholeheartedly and in the way that suits him best, because the group as a whole protects each of them from the coercive and anomic forces flowing within the abnormal division of labour that prevails in the larger social market. His protection is never complete, of course. But in the successful cases at least, a

166

significant degree of insulation is achieved. And this is without doubt one of the most compelling ways in which self-interest is woven into communal solidarity. As Parsons has pointed out, it is easy to exaggerate the difficulties of fusing self-interest and social solidarity (1971: 12-13), given the moral philosophies that tend to prevail in western thought: 'Individualistic social theory has persistently exaggerated the significance of individual self-interest in a psychological sense as an obstacle to the integration of social systems. The self-interested motives of individuals are, on the whole, effectively channeled into the social system through a variety of memberships and loyalties to collectivities.' However, the special feature of communal solidarity which does make self-interest something of an obstacle is the demand that the mutuality of self-interest and social integration should be actively and consciously felt for at least most of the time; within the commune it is precisely the *immersion* of self-interest in collective memberships that is unacceptable.

Practical arrangements for sharing work and space and for sustaining a comfortable and convenient setting for personal activity provide the ground-plan on which communal solidarity is built. As Brecht has it: 'Erst kommt das Fressen, dann kommt die Moral': without wanting to demystify communes totally, we must say that a successful commune tends to have a shrewd instinct for putting first things first. And whether we see it as a basis for exploitation, as did Marx, or as a basis for morality, as did Durkheim, the division of labour does seem to come first. There is no one right formula for the division of labour in communes, so far as we could judge. What matters is that whatever division of labour exists is felt to have been mutually negotiated and to be negotiable again in the future if members find it oppressive. The typical effect of such a successfully negotiated division of labour may not be very different from that of normal family life in terms of observed behaviour; everything depends on what the behaviour is felt to mean. Thus, basic housework can devolve on a 'housewife' without necessarily making nonsense of the commune: 'I am supported by my lover and I work on the place for everyone nearly twelve hours a day. It is a good thing I can as the place needs a lot of work. One other who does quite a lot of work is slightly subsidised by all of us in the hope that his work produces food for us all. This is mildly unsatisfactory but seems to be the best we can do' (R.105). The same woman described the commune in which she was living as a 'minuscule attempt to work out a system which generates and exchanges real wealth without exploitation', and on balance she felt strongly that despite such anomalies as her own commitment to housework the commune was working in that way, that it was 'one sort of genuine alternative to the way the British economy is run'. Her judgement was perhaps confirmed by the

167

fact that when we revisited that commune a few months later, basic housework had been largely reassigned to all commune members on a rota system and the former housewife had taken an outside job. The meals were less excellent, but the relationships had been strengthened. What is involved in solving such problems in general, however, is not necessarily any change in the content of work performed; rather, it is the ability to redefine work relationships.

A good deal of the redefinition tends to be and perhaps has to be highly formal and explicit. This is especially true of matters of ownership. The advantages of communal life for the individual all spring from socially ordered sharing. Precisely what is shared and how are matters that vary from commune to commune. The pattern in any particular commune, whether it is a pooling of incomes, the common ownership of all goods, weekly contributions to a household fund, the drawing of personal allowances from a common account according to need or a more complicated arrangement in which some members contribute income earned outside and others contribute work within the commune, depends largely on how communal the members of any particular group wish to be and on their individual circumstances and opportunities. At one extreme there is the sharing embodied in such places as Postlip Hall, a minimal collaboration governed by considerations of expediency in which middle-class families achieve a higher standard of living than they could do on their own – including a large country house complete with trout stream and a full array of consumer durables – by purchasing and using these commodities in concert. At the other extreme is that type of economic sharing which flows from a comprehensive ethic of cooperation in which sharing is seen as a virtue in itself and strenuous efforts are made to prevent the private appropriation of anything, be it clothes, records or human beings. Somewhere between these poles most actual communes make their economic arrangements. At the very least, some arrangements must be made by all communes to establish known and acceptable terms for the ownership and use of the premises in which the members live. Because uncertainty in this respect gives rise so easily to the sorts of entanglements, bids for power and disruptive personal possessiveness described in the last chapter, there is a tendency, which we see as closely associated with the successful negotiation of communal solidarity, to move towards one or other of two common ways of formalising these primary economic relationships: to form either a limited company or a charitable trust. The limited company tends to be more open-ended; it requires less machinery to construct and administer and can easily contain ventures such as producers' cooperatives or partnerships adapted to whatever work the members of a commune are at any time engaged in; it is therefore the form favoured by secular communes emphasising voluntaristic attachment. The charitable trust permits a fairly high degree of specification of what the commune is about and what its proper internal structures should be; there is a move beyond the simple formalisation of economic relationships towards commitment to a justifying moral purpose. This is the form towards which religious communes typically move. The third obvious device, that of the friendly society specifically in the form of a housing association, although in many ways the obvious and natural economic framework for communal living, is in fact unavailable to groups interested in any serious degree in communality in Britain at present as a result of the particular regulations (requiring self-contained accommodation, prohibiting acceptance of paying guests, and so forth) governing the formation of such associations. There is, as Mark Broido and the Chimera Housing Association, among others, have pointed out for a number of years (Broido (ed.) 1970), a quite unambiguous opportunity here to increase the viability of communal living through fairly simple legal reform; as such, the question is taken up again in chapter 7.

The particular arrangements at which different communes arrive can vary a great deal, as the cases described earlier in this book make clear. Gorman (1971: 100-7) has listed, described and discussed most of the ways in which a commune can go about institutionalising co-operation in relation to both ownership and income. But what matters is not this or that particular scheme so much as the achievement of a situation in which neither ownership nor income can serve as a basis for assigning or appropriating unequal status in personal relationships. Despite the great variation of cases, the principles that drive communes towards certain types of formal economic systems as a condition for solidarity are fairly simple. So far as ownership is concerned, a genuine mutuality of personal relations seems to make it necessary for so direct a source of economic power to be placed on a firmly impersonal basis. And one way or another, the separation of ownership from persons – 'we sought when setting up to exclude control by any one of us; and specifically to extricate ownership from decision-making' (R.057) – involves members of a commune in agreements to establish the commune as a legal entity. Inequalities in initial financial investments, the lingering desire of major contributors to be able to get their money back should the commune not work out as they had hoped, the problems arising when members of the original group leave or of establishing the reality of the membership of people who join later on are solved, and in our view have to be solved, through the creation of such abstract entities. Whether it is a friendly society, a company limited by guarantee or by shares or a trust will depend on the particular circumstances of particular groups at the time when the problem of ownership has to be faced. In each case, however, the commune is turned into a social fact – a fact which at once constrains and liberates, and in which, as many commune members recognise, 'this double action . . . is contradictory in appearance only'.

The limited company is the least elaborate and structured of these forms, and where the commune has no interest in borrowing from public funds and wishes to keep the creation of social structure to a minimum, that is, to do as little as possible to alienate morality from social practice, it is the obvious way to solve the problem of ownership. The movement of particular communes in this direction has been described several times in articles in *Communes,* perhaps most usefully in an account of the Shrubb Family Commune by Peter Cockerton (*Communes,* 40: 17-20). Ownership became a problem in this case because the member who had originally bought the property had decided to leave and wanted to be in a position to withdraw his investment without thereby threatening the existence of the commune. Shrubb Family rejected the idea of a trust as excessively reifying and bureaucratic: 'it did not want the existing structure of the commune to be imposed by but rather for it to be reflected in the constitution of the proposed body'. After a good deal of exploration of possibilities which involved much 'travelling around the country visiting communities to obtain information about different sorts of legal entities' – and the fact that this was necessary itself indicates the curiously fragmented and disorganised condition of the commune movement and the effective isolation in which many communal projects are launched – the minimum requirements became clear: 'to form a legal entity to own the property; to convey the property from the owner to the legal entity; and to give the owner a guarantee of payment for the property by a certain date'. A limited company, Shrubb Family Limited, emerged as the least-structuring way in which these requirements could be met – all the entity entails, apart from the appropriate deed of conveyance and guarantee, is the appointment of a nominal director and secretary and the annual production of audited accounts. The work of setting up the company was carried out from first to last by the members themselves:

> Shrubb Family was able to do all the work involved in setting up the company, arranging the conveyance and issuing the promise of payment without any professional assistance. In fact the document expressing the promise of payment was a debenture issued by the company for the amount of money involved and promising to pay the sum to the previous owner by a certain date. In the event of the amount not being paid, the company could be sued and if necessary wound up to release the required amount. The total cost to Shrubb Family was about £32.00p. This included all the expenses and the registration fees.

However, the distinctive thing about this particular commune was the decision of the members to limit the company by guarantee instead of

170

by shares – and the fact that the extent of each member's guarantee was fixed at five pence. This at once eliminated the residual element of ownership and the problem of ownership in unequal degrees involved in the share system (one example of which was described in the last chapter), and puts the commune on a radically egalitarian basis. But this in turn was only possible, and this is a point not fully brought out by Cockerton despite its great importance, because the members of Shrubb Family were able to agree in advance about their wish to achieve equality and to apply that wish not just to the question of ownership but to the much more immediate and serious matter of income: "With Shrubb Family the total income is pooled and the house will be paid for as a normal expense out of this fund. In a few years time the commune will own the house and succeeding members will be able to come and go without any need for new members to bring large sums of money with them.' Clearly the willingness to pool income wholeheartedly is what makes this particular solution to the problem of ownership possible.

Indeed, intractable as the problem of ownership often proves, its solution is in principle not hopelessly difficult just because a number of standard legal forms for solving it are easily available. In many cases the basic accommodation of the commune is in any case rented, so that the issue of ownership in its severest form does not arise at all – although acute difficulties still do arise over the record-player, the car or the gardening tools.

It seems that common ownership of most things can result in a heightened possessiveness about the few things that remain privately owned – although we were told that this is no more than an unhappy and residual effect of the difficulty the sort of people recruited to communes in Britain have in really freeing themselves from their previous socialisation into bourgeois habits. Be that as it may, the real test of communal solidarity seems to occur in relation to income rather than property: the problem of income is ubiquitous and fundamental, the point at which the coordination of self-interest and mutuality is most precarious and most necessary.

Again there is little point in detailing cases, as the particular ways in which communes can apportion income are endless. But the principles involved in a successful apportionment can be discerned. What has to be achieved and sustained is a shift from inequality of earned income towards equality of used income: a mechanism has to be found for giving practical meaning to the idea that so long as each contributes according to ability each may use according to need – whatever this may mean in terms of redistribution. A total pooling of income and its reallocation through a consensually managed fund is the most whole-hearted way of doing this, but it is a difficult solution to effect unless

171

all the members of the commune have a broadly similar earning power, broadly similar responsibilities and broadly similar work to begin with. Thus the summer population of one commune in Norfolk, about twenty young people, mainly recent graduates, could agree to work a fixed number of days a week each at fruit-picking and harvesting and to have their wages paid direct to the commune. But in the more usual case, members have differing private commitments and interests which they are not willing to sacrifice to this degree. The common compromise therefore is to establish a house fund rather than an income pool. Thus, at Family Farm there is a housekeeping account to which all members contribute an identical sum calculated on the basis of agreed estimates of the total needed for maintenance of the place and its members. Those who are not involved in paid work have their contributions paid by others either directly or as a cost written-in in calculating the total that has to be raised. Thereafter, however, 'those who have an income keep what is left after paying the flat rate; those who have none go without' (Q.118).

Frequently, systems of this kind involve an implicit or explicit notion of an internal wage paid to those members who take on a disproportionate amount of domestic work. Frequently, too, the fund is calculated in such a way that it includes a sum to be drawn on as private spending money by members who do not have independent cash incomes earned outside the commune. The important thing is that the fund is seen as recognising the value of the work of all members, and the importance of all members' working, and as balancing income disparities on that basis. What may matter more than any particular formal arrangement for doing this is the ability of a commune to change its arrangements from time to time in the light of new circumstances so that this principle is preserved. Thus, the Anarchist Commune in Sheffield has moved from an abortive income-pooling scheme to a system of fixed contributions to a system of variable contributions and finally back to an income pool as the commune's needs for cash and the members' own sense of their mutual relationship have changed (*Communes*, 42: 1-7). Their success depends on their adaptiveness in managing the problem of income, not on any one scheme of income management. Gorman (1971: 101) has suggested that income pooling is the arrangement that should come naturally to communes, as, among other things, 'it puts money and material matters generally in perspective, and allows the primary stress to be upon relationships or common purposes within the group'. But in practice this degree of egalitarianism is difficult to achieve and not indispensable. What does seem to be essential is some agreement to work an open-ended, flexible cost-sharing and income-balancing economy which affirms both the private and the collective advantage of communal living for all concerned. From

172

this point of view, perceived equity matters more than formal equality.

It is appropriate to digress at this point to say something of the more obvious economic advantages of communal living, since it is often these which permit communes to achieve an equitable domestic economy even when large disparities in the private sector of members' incomes are allowed to persist. Communal living can be remarkably cheap, and in ways which allow relatively small incomes to seem relatively large. The savings in communal living are almost all a result of economies of scale and are made mainly in relation to the per capita costs of food, consumer durables, services and housing. Savings are also made in respect of income tax in the sense that the total deducted from eight small incomes is likely to be much less as a proportion of gross household income, and can often be a smaller sum than the deduction from one or two large incomes – especially if a large number of children are being supported, if a substantial mortgage is being repaid or if several of the communal incomes are near or below the minimum tax level. Indeed, the advantages of communal living show up most clearly only if some members *are* earning rather low incomes. The economic advantages of communal living must, however, be kept in proper perspective. In many communes, possible economic advantages are deliberately not realised in terms of either income or consumption. Members *choose* to live modestly. There is a deliberate asceticism here, but it is sustained not by a spirit of self-mortification but by a more straightforward rejection of the ethos of consumption as such.

A comparison of the domestic economy of households based on the conjugal family with that of communal households is not easy. The *Family Expenditure Survey* (Department of the Environment 1972: tables 50, 51) suggests that expenditure on housekeeping falls as a proportion of income with each increase in the number of adults in the household, and it is essentially this principle that applies in communes – although the way in which it works is frequently masked by the fact that many members of communes choose to earn far less than they are capable of earning precisely because they want to devote a large part of their lives to the interests and activities of the commune. This voluntary restriction of earnings for the sake of the commune makes it very difficult to discuss communal expenditure in relation to communal income with any real precision or confidence. What matters is the gap between actual earnings and potential earnings, between the sum earned to meet current needs and the sum that could be earned if the agreed definition of needs were to change. The size of this gap is in fact one of the distinctive features of communal economies and is one of the main differences between communal economies and many conjugal economies. Again, the way in which expenditure is

173

analysed in most of the standard statistical sources, such as the *Family Expenditure Survey*, makes it difficult to separate necessary from optional expenditure and to determine that proportion of spending which could be regarded as spending out of disposable income. But in communes, and especially in communes which operate a household fund rather than an income pool, it is this factor which is all-important. The bulk of saving occurs in relation to what can be regarded as basic or necessary housekeeping, leaving relatively large proportions of income to be spent on 'luxuries' (for example, flowers rather than vegetables in the garden) or assigned as pocket money. This is not just a statistical difficulty, of course; we are once more running up against the substantial obstacle that besets every aspect of the analysis of intentional communes – the problem of not knowing where the necessary ends and the optional begins, the confounding of freedom and necessity.

Nevertheless, a comparison of the household budgets of communes and conjugal families does bring to light a number of the peculiar advantages of communal living – advantages which are in our view a significant basis of communal solidarity – and we have therefore attempted it here. We have chosen to compare the income and expenditure of two small family households, one consisting of two adults only and the other of two adults and one child, with that of two communal households, one consisting of six adults and one child and the other of ten adults and four children and both making contributions to a household fund rather than pooling personal incomes as a whole. Both communes were committed to heavy payments in respect of mortgages, and both were groups in which several members were deliberately not earning as much as they could reasonably have expected to earn in order, in one case, to make time to extend and modernise the large Victorian house in which they were living, and, in the other case, to develop the domestic horticulture of the commune to a point where it would be self-sufficient in respect of all fruit and vegetables. The two conjugal households were chosen to be as comparable as possible to the communes in some important respects – owner-occupiers rather than tenants, a high ratio of adults to children, all adults employed or employable in white-collar occupations. The pattern of expenditure of both was in addition quite close to the average for houeholds of their size, type and income as recorded in the *Family Expenditure Survey*. Table 1 presents the gross and net incomes of each of our four households and indicates the degree to which communal living can enhance household income through tax avoidance. In other words, Family A with its two wage-earners was losing 20 per cent of its gross income in deductions, Family B with one full-time and one part-time wage-earner was losing 17 per cent, Commune C with five of its six adults employed

174

was losing 15 per cent and Commune D with seven adults working and two receiving pensions was losing 14 per cent. In both communes the saving was achieved by the combination of a large number of small incomes as the tax base, producing a substantial gross income largely undiminished by deductions.

Table 1. *Weekly income before and after tax and insurance deductions of communal and non-communal households (£)*

	Gross income	Deductions	Net income
Family A (2 adults)	54.20	10.15	44.05
Family B (2 adults, 1 child)	39.80	6.70	33.10
Commune C (6 adults, 1 child)	89.00	13.90	75.10
Commune D (10 adults, 4 children)	239.50	33.10	206.40

On the other hand, if we consider the net income of each household as a resource to be divided per capita among the members of each group, the obvious advantages of a few large incomes reappear. Thus in Family A the sum available per person is £22.02, in Family B it is £11.03, in Commune C £10.72, and in Commune D it is £14.74. Commune C, in which all but one of the wage-earners were receiving very low incomes and thus virtually avoiding tax, suffers considerably when its income is viewed in this way. Commune D, in which three of the seven working adults were receiving incomes above £40 a week, fares better in spite of its relatively large number of children. But beyond this point the economic advantages of communes become a matter of internal income management and good housekeeping rather than of scale on its own. Close comparison between the four households becomes difficult, and comparison between any of them and the averages suggested by the *Family Expenditure Survey* becomes almost impossible, partly because of the distinction between communal (household) spending and private spending that prevailed in both communes but was absent in both families, and partly because some major items of expenditure, such as mortgage payments, are not treated as expenditure for purposes of analysis in the *Survey*. We have followed the categories of expenditure of the *Survey* as far as possible in detailing the spending of our four households in table 2, but some important changes were unavoidable. Thus our 'housing' expenditure category includes mortgage payments, rates and repairs but does not include rent, which none of our households were paying, or any allowance for rateable value. On this basis all four households turn out to be spending a considerably greater proportion of their total household expenditure on housing than the average 12.8 per cent suggested by the *Survey*. Similarly, because spending on clothes, tobacco and alcohol, as well as on private eating and eating out, on holidays and on a number of the items listed as 'other goods' by the *Survey*, were treated as personal matters in both communes and not allowed for in calculating their common household funds, we have, for all four households, placed all such spending in a residual category of 'other' spending. We have done the same with certain types of spending treated by the *Survey* as spending on 'services', for example all expenditure on entertainments, hairdressing and postage, which are again treated as matters of private spending in both communes; what we have included in this category, therefore, is the cost of telephones, radio and television, footwear repairs and certain non-durable goods which the communes did regard as a collective responsibility – cleaning and gardening materials, for example. In effect, then, we are able to make a rough distinction between essential household spending (all expenditure from the household funds) and inessential spending (all 'other' spending). And one of the ways in which the economic advantages of communal living is perhaps best indicated is precisely in the differences that emerge in the relative size of this category of 'other' spending when communes and conjugal family households are compared.

Table 2. *Weekly expenditure of communal and non-communal households (£)*

	Family A	Family B	Commune C	Commune D	All households (%)
Net income	44.05	33.10	75.10	206.40	—
Fund	—	—	49.00	84.00	—
Housing	9.05	5.90	18.80	30.10	12.8
Food	10.40	9.30	14.85	31.00	25.9
Fuel, power	1.90	1.90	3.00	5.95	6.0
Durables	2.90	2.45	4.00	4.20	6.5
Transport	5.20	4.30	5.60	7.20	13.7
Services	2.45	1.70	1.10	2.55	9.4
Total	31.90	25.55	47.35	81.00	74.3
Other	12.15	7.55	27.75	125.40	25.7

Differences in the proportion of total expenditure spent on food perhaps provide the most striking contrast between our four households. Whereas the spending on food increases with the number of mouths in our two conjugal households, from 24 per cent in Family A to 29 per cent in Family B, not only do both communes spend a smaller fraction of their total expenditure on food, but the fraction actually decreases

176

with size, from just under 20 per cent in Commune C to 15 per cent in Commune D. This saving is in large part an effect of bulk buying, self-sufficiency in respect of vegetables and bread and planned catering for communal meals. It is somewhat exaggerated in the case of Commune D by the fact that the members ate a fair number of their meals privately, and perhaps in the case of Commune C by the fact that meat was only eaten once a week. Nevertheless, a significant economy is achieved in both cases. The same economy is evident in respect of spending on fuel, light and power, on durable goods, on transport and vehicles and on services. In each case the most dramatic savings are made by the larger commune, in which, although substantial sums are spent, the proportional spending remains minute. Thus Commune D was well supplied with household durables, a washing machine, deep-freeze, dishwasher and so forth, but was spending only 2 per cent of its total domestic expenditure on these items as compared to the couple in Family A, who were spending 6 per cent to secure the same goods. The effect is even more dramatic in relation to transport and vehicles; while both conjugal families were spending around 12 per cent of their over-all expenditure on these items, Commune C spent only 7.5 per cent and Commune D, as a result of sharing a car and working either at home or very near home, spent only 3 per cent. In respect of services, too, we find that the communes are spending rather less than half the proportion spent by the private households. When we turn to expenditure on housing, the situation is rather different. Both communes were making substantial mortgage repayments, and Commune C was in fact devoting 25 per cent of its total communal expenditure to buying and maintaining buildings in which they lived. Commune D, on the other hand, although spending much the largest absolute sum, was also spending the smallest proportion of expenditure on housing of any of our households – about 15 per cent. The advantage of communal living in this respect is not so much one of absolute cheapness but rather that the general relationship of income to expenditure in communes permits large sums to be spent on the purchase of large houses. It is obviously important for communes that the larger the property, the smaller the unit area cost of accommodation. Finally, we may consider the proportion of the net income of each household devoted to what we have called 'essential' household expenditure – that is, that portion of expenditure met in the communes from the common household fund – the basic costs of co-residence as subjectively agreed within the limits of income. It is here that the economic implications of communal living emerge most clearly. Approximately three-quarters of the net income of each of the conjugal households was consumed on essentials (76 per cent for Family B, 74 per cent for Family A) as compared to 63 per cent in the case of Commune C and 40 per cent in the case of Commune D. Even allowing for the large fraction of 'inessential' spending devoted in each case to essentials such as clothing, such figures leave little doubt that communes represent a significant move towards economic freedom. As it happens, the members of Commune D were spending a very large part of their 'excess' income on personal contributions to the costs of the modernisation of their collective home. It could equally well have been spent on more private purposes. Or, and this is perhaps more important, it need not have been earned at all. The excess income represents the margin within which a successful commune can afford to withdraw from the economy.

The awareness of this possibility, and in at least some cases its actual realisation, is in our view a principal condition and a principal source of communal solidarity. In a sense, everything depends on the willingness of the one or two members who earn large incomes to subsidise the rest. But in the more successful communes it is not experienced like that. To begin with, the principle of equal small contributions to the household fund serves to hide or even to render irrelevant disparities of income and to establish the equal claim of all members on all the amenities of the commune. It constitutes an egalitarian base on which a superstructure of relations of consent can rise. On this base the partially hidden extra cash contributions of some members can, secondly, be offset by the ability of others to make other sorts of contribution in a no less disproportionate way. The sense of equality can be maintained by achieving a balance of different kinds of contribution. For this reason the division of labour in communes tends to be an actively negotiated relationship.

In relatively simple cases a member who is making a large cash contribution over and above his or her basic contribution to the household fund may not be asked to contribute at all in any other way. Thus, Ian at Family Farm lived in virtual privacy within the commune as a whole. Conversely, non-earners or members making only the minimal cash contribution can base their membership on massive contributions of work: 'I am supported by the others and work round-the-clock for them on the house and the garden' (Q.124). Typically such work is not just a matter of household chores but of the decisive contribution that establishes the viability of a major communal project: the shop, the restaurant, the pottery. It is the work that gives the commune its collective individuality. In larger and more complex communes the creation of a mutually affirming division of labour to balance the division of incomes becomes a difficult and delicate task requiring the constant attention of many members. But it is precisely in such communes that the centrality as well as the possibility of such a balance as the basis of communal solidarity becomes apparent.

A viable balance of labour, like a viable balance of income, may be

178

struck in many different ways. When achieved, it is likely to involve commune members in experiencing the abolition of two particularly crippling social categories of normal society: the unskilled and the unnecessary. The affirmation of the value of domestic work is essential from this point of view. It is on that basis that cleaners and cooks, mothers and pensioners can recapture their humanity and live as equals in communes realising skills without which the commune would founder. Thus carpentry, the lifelong hobby of a retired schoolmaster in one of our communes, had become a resource on the basis of which he could continue a working life the value of which was demonstrated in almost daily improvements to the amenities of the life of the whole group. This is not to say that communal solidarity is a matter of ideology or values alone. The point is rather that the devoted practice of essentially domestic skills and the application of non-domestic skills in a domestic setting are real material conditions for establishing the superiority of communal to conjugal living. The distinctive pattern of income management in communes makes this practice possible; but it is the work itself rather than the economic conditions for it that tends to be seized on and cherished in communal value systems.

There is in fact considerable uncertainty among members of the commune movement about the importance of domestic and quasi-domestic skills. Perhaps this is another context in which the core and the fringe members of communes tend to distinguish themselves. We have already quoted Sarah Eno's firm call for would-be members of communes to qualify themselves by first acquiring suitable practical skills. And in the answers to our questionnaire it was very evident that most members of the Commune Movement with any real experience of communal living seemed to echo her views. Of those of our respondents who had lived in communes, all but three stressed the importance of some sort of practical skill as a condition of success for communes. This was in marked contrast to the views of the less-experienced respondents who tended to emphasise broad human qualities such as tolerance, realism and a sense of humour or to insist on the importance of the whole human personality as against any particular characteristics. Some who had tried communal living and failed related their failure directly to their inability to make suitable contributions of practical skilled work: 'I'm going to take a course to train as a farrier and then I'll try again' (R.172). It was often pointed out that one could be too calculating in putting together a set of skills to sustain a commune; for example, 'We have found that in general people find out their natural skills after joining the community – one member joined with agricultural training but became a sculptor' (Q.019). And what emerged very strongly as the general response to this sort of inquiry was a sense of a need for individuals to be willing to learn *some* practical skill and to work hard at it as part of a process of creating a system of mutual aid rather than anything more specific:

People must be willing to work hard at something! The individual needs no one particular skill; but a great variety of skills are needed by the group. Both members who are experts and those who are jack-of-all-trades are invaluable; the specific skills necessary will obviously depend on the set-up of the commune. (Q.129)

I really think that a combination of humility about being willing to learn, confidence that one can learn, and tact about demanding tuition or giving it, matters here. A special skill which makes one able to share the work load in the place, or which makes one employable, bringing in bread, can be a great help; but the essential thing is some realistic understanding of *mutual* aid. (R.009)

The feeling, then, was that people must learn to be useful to one another in practical ways and that it was the realisation of this principle that mattered for communes rather than any particular combination of skills. One could almost say that what is being demanded is that communes should enable their members to experience directly the moral significance of the division of labour: 'We are brought up to be self-seeking individualists without either practical skills or skill in considering our interdependence' (Q.077). But in practice the way in which that is done is by evolving a division of labour in which interdependence is expressed in a delicate balance of skills. For all the reluctance of members of the commune movement to produce recipes for such balances, one of the things any observer of communes is bound to notice is that success (however defined), goes hand in hand with the development of an elaborate network of interdependence based precisely on a division of skills, on knowing who does what for the group and how what each does fits into the miniature economy as a whole. The central importance of such balances in the construction of communal solidarity (a necessary but not a sufficient condition in our view) is perhaps best indicated by the degree of sensitivity, not to say jealousy, with which commune members tend to eye one another in this respect and by the prominence of perceptions of imbalance in many accounts of the failure of communes. A dispute over the importance of work on the garden relative to other contributions was the source of a deep crisis, and the departure of several members, at Family Farm. Two former members of Findhorn made it clear to us that much of their eventual rejection of that community sprang from their feeling that their own hard work in the weaving shed was in fact carrying and subsidising a great deal of incompetence and idleness elsewhere in the craft studios. Ironically, the same people told us in another context that one of the things they came to dislike about Findhorn was the way people were appreciated there for what they did,

180

not for what they were (R.062). This is of course one of the costs as well as one of the conditions of collective individuality.

Sociability and privacy

Our argument is that communal solidarity is one variety of what Simmel (1971: 266) called collective individuality and that as such it involves a subtle and volatile balance between the individuation of the group, achieved by moral and geographical isolation, commitment mechanisms and so forth, and the individuation of its members on the basis of self-interest and self-realisation. For a serious collective individuality to develop among people with a strong sense of personal individuality, the collectivity must be experienced as a valid embodiment of the interests of its members – not least in the sense of establishing the effective separation and differentiation of the *set* of members from the broader mass of society. 'The sociological ambiguity of the family', which Simmel perceived, thus unavoidably pervades the commune, too. We have suggested that for inhabitants of a bourgeois world the striking of a viable communal solidarity is very largely a matter of economic relationships and the division of labour. On this basis, however, the transfer of individuality from the person to the group, or the fusing of personal and group individuality, can be advanced in a number of further ways each involving a significant redefinition of what might be called the normal, taken-for-granted boundaries of *sociability* in non-communal society. For Simmel (1971: 130) sociability occupied a no-man's-land between subjective and objective concerns, representing an emphasis on form which could come into its own only when both of these types of emphasis on the content of action had been relaxed. 'Sociability is, then, the play-form of association. It is related to the content-determined concreteness of association as art is related to reality.' But members of communes live with exceptional seriousness on both an objective and a subjective plane. They are involved in a way of life which is at once a thoroughgoing social project and a profound exploration of self. Dedicated activity of either of these kinds is normally beyond the limits of sociability precisely because its content is so deeply serious. In such a content any concern with form for its own sake, especially with forms of playing, is likely to be seen as frivolous, irresponsible and irrelevant.

But form is itself a kind of content. And something quite close to pure sociability plainly does occupy a great deal of time and attention in many communes. It is a shrewd instinct which leads commune members to sense that the very seriousness of their devotion to the objective and subjective content of communal living itself threatens successful association, on a secular basis anyway, in communes. And that it must

181

be counteracted and alleviated by a proportionate extension of unserious forms, of play, of sociability. Sociability provides a medium in which the serious personal and collective purposes of communes can be pursued the more successfully because they are entangled with enjoyable forms of associating. It is, too, a uniquely apt medium for such projects, because sociability is in itself both an affirmation of sociability and a type of social equality. Both of these aspects of sociability were well understood by Simmel. On the one hand, the 'great problem of association', the problem of 'the measure of significance which belongs to the individual as such in and as against the social milieu', can find a solution 'possible only in sociability', since sociability in its pure form 'has no ulterior end, no content and no result outside itself' and is therefore 'oriented completely about personalities'. It is a mode of interaction governed by Kantian principles of justice:

> Sociability creates, if one will, an ideal sociological world, for in it the pleasure of the individual is always contingent upon the joy of others; here, by definition, no one can have his satisfaction at the cost of contrary experiences on the part of others. Inasmuch as sociability is the abstraction of association – an abstraction of the character of art or play – it demands the purest, most transparent, most engaging kind of interaction, that among equals. It must, because of its very nature, posit beings who give up so much of their objective content, who are so modified in both their outward and their inner significance, that they are socially equal. It is a game in which one 'acts' as though all were equal, and as though he especially esteemed everyone. (Simmel 1971: 133-4)

On the other hand, being a world of forms sustained by the suppression of content, the world of sociability is the only one 'in which a democracy of equals is possible without friction'. It is for this reason that the great amount of time commune members seem to devote to merely associating, to sitting around, to just being together, to conversation, anecdotes and jokes, to play and to games, to interacting for its own sake, must be seen as anything but time wasted. It establishes the crucial reserve of personal value and social equality in relation to which the constraining, demeaning and unequal economic and psychological life of a commune can be safely attempted. 'All sociability is but a symbol of life, as it shows itself in the flow of a lightly amusing play; but even so, a symbol of *life*.'

The distinction between serious and sociable activity is not of course as sharp in practice as Simmel suggested; most serious encounters are coloured by some tinge of sociability, etiquette or protocol; most moments of sociability are no less structured by a background awareness of extraneous properties of ego-involvement or social status. Nevertheless, conventional social life does lend itself with relative ease to a division into serious and sociable episodes and contexts. The peculiarity of communal life is to be found not so much in the wholeheartedness with which sociable episodes are experienced as in the sustained mixing up of the sociable and the serious which they undertake, with the result that a great part of their life cannot be described confidently as either one or the other. There is a systematic blurring of the boundaries of sociability, a persistent transfer of sociability to a great part of the sober objective and subjective content of communal life which is itself a sign that the attempt to construct communal solidarity is beginning to succeed. In religious communes this mixing of form and content with a constant and independent valuation of form is conscious and overt, an immersion of both form and content in ritual, as in the concern for proper modes of talk at Findhorn (almost a matter of cultivating a special Findhorn language) or in the endless touching and kissing at Beshara. In secular communes the most striking evidence of the spread of sociability is found in the transformation of work into play and in the concomitant abolition of leisure. The emergence of leisure and leisure time as separable elements of western culture is arguably one of the more profound expressions of the degree of alienation achieved by capitalism. Communes typically seek to reappropriate the humanness of work and in so doing they tend to obliterate the distinction between work and leisure; play takes the place of both. 'Play culture is turning up . . . let's grow our things . . . let's transform work: work = play + creation' (*Communes*, 38: 27). In an earlier chapter we stressed the role of play in the process of communal self-seeking; it is no less important in the construction of communal solidarity. Such solidarity is a matter of negotiated equality, and just because the concern for equality is so serious it is a great help to treat the activities through which it is negotiated as though they were a game.

Where most families will occasionally treat the eating of a meal as a sociable event, many communes regularly engulf the preparing and clearing away of food as well as the eating of it in sociability. All sorts of games and play-experiments can be elaborated around the collective creation of a meal; whole evenings can be spent in delighted group contemplation of the workings of a communal automatic washing machine; decorating and building projects can be turned into hilarious but curiously efficient group entertainments; shopping can become a matter of fantastic expeditions in which whole car-loads of commune members make an extravagant pantomime of the business of buying groceries, emphasising the extraordinariness of communes and abolishing one bit of the drudgery of the housewife at one and the same time and covering both achievements in a stream of mock-serious talk. Any work done within a commune can be suffused with sociability in this way; indeed, it is difficult for this not happen. Four people quietly

183

gardening, a larger group planning and building a new dining-room, others rehearsing the numbers they will perform at a local club that night, will all in a successful commune be cultivating a pleasant idiom of association as well as getting on with a useful job. But this is the medium, not the essence, of solidarity. It is dependent on the division of labour, of skill and of income within a commune and cannot be nourished on its own as a matter of will. The economy of most communes involves at least some members in earning income for the commune through work unconnected with the commune. For this reason the substitution of play for work and leisure, a complete extension of sociability, is at best partial; and accordingly communes, like other social groups, find a need for episodes of pure sociability, moments when everything is sacrificed to the pleasures of association. Whether these episodes are found in formal meetings, or by sitting talking round the dinner table late at night, in parties, or by going fishing or walking, by drinking or using drugs, by holding encounter sessions or staging revues, is of little importance. What matters is that the episodes are sufficiently frequent and intense to restore the sense of a collectively achieved equality.

It is perhaps for this reason that sociability often takes the form of a constant background of gentle mocking of the commune itself: people at Findhorn offer to 'manifest you a cup of coffee'; 'So much for mind-sharing', one member of another commune observed as we stared solemnly at the last crust in a bread bin. And it is perhaps why commune members generally value humour so highly: 'We'd often hate the sight of each other if the whole scene weren't so funny' (Q.139). Humour permits dissociation and the rediscovery that one enjoys the company of others. It is the pure mode of sociability. But we are still speaking only of modes. Geoff Crowther (1972: 9) has described two forms of sociability which were used to reconstruct the sense of equality by the members of his commune, group encounter games 'particularly one we called "Touching"', and music:

> As the hours went by polarisation often set in and we'd find release by channeling our energies into getting a musical jam together with piano, recorders, flutes, guitars, drums, sitar and all manner of improvised instruments. Those jams used to last hours and hours and leave us incredibly high for days afterwards. Indeed, had I to pinpoint the one thing that held us all together there it was the music.

And yet the music and their other forms of sociability were not in the end enough to hold them together. Specifically, they were not enough to offset the experience of having to work 'like operatives' on other people's machines in order to provide the commune with its basic means of subsistence. Intense and extended sociability remains the dis-

184

tinctive form of communal solidarity: its essential content, however, is a viable and non-exploitative economy.

The obverse of sociability is privacy, and just as the one expresses solidarity directly, so the other provides a vital permissive context (a condition of possibility) for it. Several writers have noted that the very closeness of communal life is itself, if unrelieved, a source of instability and tension (V. W. Turner 1969; Punch 1974). Thus, Punch has argued that the general 'sociological instability' of anti-institutions 'is reinforced by a perhaps more fundamental instability brought about by a widespread need in most humans . . . not only for intimacy, but for privacy and distance as well' (1974: 323). Certainly it is our impression that the successful accomplishment of communal solidarity involves careful provision for privacy as well as for togetherness. It seems, indeed, that there is a basic choice to be made in this respect. Either individuality and solidarity are combined in a tensely balanced dialectic within which both flourish on the basis of a subtle demarcation of the proper territory of each or togetherness engulfs individuality in an encompassing and more or less explicitly religious ideology in which the boundaries of the self and the social are thoroughly confused. A distinguishing feature of the secular commune is precisely the attempt to live together without succumbing to a religion of togetherness – an attempt, as it were, to falsify Durkheim's principle: 'It is indeed a universal fact that, when a conviction of any strength is held by the same community of men, it inevitably takes on a religious character' (1961: 142-3). A vital strategy of this attempt is the creation of acknowledged areas of privacy within the commune. This may be no more than a matter of establishing the sanctity of each individual's own room within the commune. But this is a cardinal resource and a good deal more than individual members of many conjugal families enjoy. We found that the members of our more successful secular communes had a marked sense of the need for privacy within the commune and had over time evolved ways of using the space available to them that gave them as individuals the pockets of private time and space they needed. At Fern Hill William has the pottery shed to himself, and other members have built small cells for themselves on a hillside to which they can retreat to read or think or simply look out over a wide and peaceful valley. At Family Farm it is more a matter of ensuring that each member enjoys effective possession of a room in the house, a place beyond the reach of the society of the commune where one can be oneself, be alone, or cultivate relationships with particular other individuals away from the many-sided communal relationships of the group. Here again, the distinction between the fringe and the core of a commune seems important. The need to counteract togetherness by distance is a need learned over time and one that, once learned, must be met if the commune is to cohere. The core members of Family Farm are well aware of this difference: 'Some of the very young seem to like piling together like kittens in a nest. Anyone as active and aware as I am needs some solitude' (R.181). Often such feelings are expressed as part of a larger concern for the design of communal premises:

> I rather think that both company and solitude could be better in suitable premises so that the overcrowding of a 3-bedroom house and the loneliness of the woman trapped in it could be alleviated: 1 quiet room, 1 TV room, 1 children's room, 1 workshop, 1 laundry could serve several households. The spectrum of human needs could be met if we tried by means of architectural changes and changes in the codes of normal civility and expectations of people. Some of us here have days when we've nothing to say and don't want to listen, and it is possible to get on quietly with some work. (R.022)

This point is simple but fundamental; in Yorkshire, in Northumberland and Norfolk we found communes setting to work to rebuild old farmhouses or rows of cottages to provide the sort of physical environment, the domestic ecology, appropriate to communal living as a balance of privacy and togetherness. That such a balance is crucial to the success of a commune is obvious almost to the point of banality. But these are no suitable available buildings. We simply have not built like that. Once it has acquired its premises a commune inevitably has to reconstruct them. Failing that, members will begin to appropriate the privacy that is essential to them by way of psychological withdrawals which are always disruptive: 'Emma won't talk to me.'

We were impressed by another way in which a commune's physical premises, the place, appear important in the construction of communal solidarity which is worth observing before we leave this topic. The building or perhaps some especially important part of it – such as the carefully decorated meeting hall at Fern Hill in which the members have placed some of the finest products of their several crafts – becomes a focussing symbol of the existence and value of the commune. This is perhaps particularly true, and particularly important, in the early days of a commune's development when the buildings are being actively worked on and when making the commune is largely synonymous with making the place; a group is at that stage realising and defining a social intention within an architectural project. But even in well-established communes the place and the idea of doing things for the place seem to have a critical symbolic function. The building becomes an emblem of an emerging solidarity, perhaps even a source of solidarity in the face of the tensions, conflicts of interest and quarrels of the day. As Durkheim observed in a quite different context, 'the

186

emblem is not merely a convenient process for clarifying the sentiment society has of itself; it also serves to create this sentiment; it is one of its constituent elements' (1965: 262). The use of the place in such a symbolic manner is perhaps especially important in secular communes just because the main concern of the members is so wholeheartedly to confront social relations directly, without the support or mediation of external symbolism. Their life is, one could almost say, deliberately impoverished at a symbolic level in order to allow the members to experience their immediate humanity more directly. The image of the place provides an alleviating counter-force amid the strains of that enterprise. And it is one which stops short of the depth of symbolisation involved in religion. The problem of solidarity in religious communes is more easily solved – but largely because religion succumbs through its distinctive emblems to a dehumanisation of collective life which the secular commune resists.

Communal solidarity and organic solidarity

The solidarity of a secular commune seems to us, then, to be a matter of economics, of sociability and of symbolism. We find that it can be achieved without the transformative influence of personal charisma or religious commitment. Far from resting on a loss of self, we see it as requiring a vigorous personal autonomy on the basis of which the dialectic of the self and the social can be sustained: 'the cooperative society . . . develops in the measure that individual personality becomes stronger', not the opposite. At the other extreme, although the economic arrangements of secular communes often have a strongly contractual quality, contract is not the basis of their solidarity either. It is rather a matter of an ability to overcome two apparent contradictions of ordinary social life. First, there is Durkheim's apparent contradiction of constraint and choice – the contradiction of the institution. And secondly, there is the apparent contradiction, to which he also pointed, of egoism and altruism – the contradiction of the individual. A successful secular commune would master the first of these by refusing to treat the communal institution as an institution at all, at least in its internal social relationships, that is, by establishing a social practice in which the institution was continuously represented as a project of its members: the commune exists only as it is continuously created by individuals. And it would master the second by an equally continuous demonstration of the social sources of individuality: the members exist as they are created by the commune; a meaningful separation of interest is rendered increasingly difficult. These communes are, after all, cooperative, collaborative undertakings in which mutual advantage is not hard to demonstrate and provides the real basis on which a distinctive symbolism, a moral order, a new code of civility, can arise. The two apparent contradictions they have to surmount are in a sense but two faces of a single, deeper but no less illusory contradiction which Durkheim elsewhere (1961: 325) referred to as the dualism of human nature, a dualism that 'corresponds to the double existence that we lead concurrently; the one purely individual . . . the other nothing but an extension of society'. Communal solidarity in other words, is not a special type of solidarity. Rather, it is organic solidarity as Durkheim understood it, in miniature and freed from the chronic abnormalities which prevent its realisation in the larger society. Empirically, however, some sort of community of interest would seem to be prior to the successful division of labour – this is a problem for communes as it was for Durkheim. Communes, which must solve it in practice and not just in theory, do so by the establishment of very tough, even if unacknowledged, criteria of membership, by instituting probationary periods as at Hillside and by developing elaborate rituals of exclusion as at Findhorn.

Our communes are experiments in organic solidarity, that is, in the sort of solidarity that presupposes strong individuals. At the same time they attempt to achieve organic solidarity without an elaborate division of labour, a large population, an intense struggle for existence or any of the other structural conditions which Durkheim associated with the development of solidarity of this type. They seek it within the compass of a small social circle and in societies based on likenesses. The basis of likeness, however, is a shared attachment to the cult of the individual. Insofar as they succeed, it is not by treating the social as a fact but by respecting the essential nature of interaction. This is what makes their reality so hard to grasp. As Turner (1962: 22) puts it, 'Interaction is always a *tentative* process, a process of continually testing the conception one has of the role of the other. The response of the other serves to reinforce or to challenge this conception. The product of the testing is the stabilisation or the modification of one's own role.' In this sense secular communes are encounters rather than institutions. Their dangers are, on the one hand, the reification of the social, and on the other (and more urgently), the reassertion of a possessive individualism. They necessarily exist in a state of endless suspense between these two hazards. Even though we are not sure that we have ever seen communal solidarity securely accomplished – indeed, the idea of security is perhaps incompatible with that sort of accomplishment – we have seen the idea of such an accomplishment close enough to being realised to feel that secular communes are something more than merely utopian projects. Their value is that they hover on the brink of constructing organic solidarity on the basis of an uncompromising assertion of the moral autonomy of the individual.

188

7. Communes, sociology and social policy

To every individual in nature is given an individual property by nature not to be invaded or usurped by any; for every one as he is himself, so he has a self property, else could he not be himself, and of this no second may presume to deprive any of without manifest violation and affront to the very principle of nature and of the rules of equity ... between man and man.

Overton, *An Arrow against All Tyrants*

Overton's words are quoted by C. B. Macpherson (1962: 140) to illustrate the peculiar moral and political philosophy which in his view has dominated western culture since the seventeenth century – possessive individualism. We have tried to show that the communes we visited, which we think to be broadly representative of the commune movement that emerged in Britain in the late 1960s, may be thought to embody that culture insofar as they are strongly moved by possessive individualism and experience its distinctive dilemmas. The heart of possessive individualism as Macpherson describes it 'is found in its conception of the individual as essentially the proprietor of his own person or capacities'. The individual is seen 'neither as a moral whole nor as part of a larger social whole, but as an owner of himself'; the human essence, accordingly, 'is freedom from dependence on the wills of others and freedom is a function of possession'. In modern market societies however, such an ideal of self-property or self-possession becomes, as Macpherson so clearly shows (1962: 275), the source of a cruel dilemma: individuals can be human only to the extent that they possess themselves; but the conditions of the society in which they find themselves, and which establishes that very image of humanity, deny the possibility of actual self-possession. 'The individual in market society *is* human as proprietor of his own person. However much he may wish it to be otherwise, his humanity does depend on his freedom from any but self-interested contractual relations with others.' The secular communes we have studied are above all attempts to create pockets of freedom within such market societies but sufficiently insulated from society for the ideal of possessive individualism to be realised without contradiction.

We have looked at these communes as experiments in self-creation and as experiments in the construction of organic solidarity. We have examined a number of ways in which, either implicitly or explicitly, communes speak to a range of contemporary social problems – of the family, the generations, women and so forth. In order to draw our arguments together and to achieve some sort of conclusion it is necessary at this stage to distinguish firmly between social problems, the designated issues of the day, and what might be called problems of society, the anomalies and contradictions of structure and meaning that constitute the existence of whole social orders. Like any other social phenomenon, communes must be explained with reference to both social problems and the problems of society if they are to be adequately explained. In our view, the theme of possessive individualism provides a key with which both levels of explanation may be unlocked and also a bridge by which they may be linked. We may begin at the level of social problems.

At the heart of the set of problems with which communes are involved stands the family. Philippe Aries (1962) has traced the development of the conjugal nuclear family as a social institution of the western middle class constructed as part of that larger and more essentially bourgeois creation, private life. The fashioning of such a family, on the basis of an 'essential withdrawal by the household from the outside world', was also of course the fashioning of a new mode of individual property: the family becomes more definitely the possession of the head of the household. As such, the withdrawn family, as we might call it, is the enemy not only of a larger sociability but also of a larger, more open and unpossessive individualism. It militates against both. So it is perhaps not surprising that as women and children come to feel that they, too, are human, and that the ethos of possessive individualism therefore gives them rights as well as men, they should feel urged to rebel against the family. And as they do, of course the family must become less and less satisfactory, more and more problematic, for men as well. Possessive individualism has to break out of the shell of the conjugal family once all the members of the family have become individuals. But how successful can such a rebellion be?

It is a rebellion to create a family milieu in which one can fully possess oneself without possessing or being possessed by others. In the first chapter we argued that one could see communes as having a relevance for seven social problems. Of these, the problems of identity and the family are the most important for commune members themselves. But if these could be solved, solutions to other problems would begin to emerge: women would be freed, the generation gap would be closed, the distinction between work and leisure would blur, and the demonstration of all this within communes would slowly revolutionise the larger society. The virtue of such a strategy was that it seemed to offer immediately and comparatively easily realisable goals. And within rather strict limits appearances were justified. It *did* prove possible to create domestic settings in which familial relationships and the experience of self were significantly freed from conventional modes of possession. Provided a group had the resources to seclude itself a little from the pressure and demands of the economy around it, and provided its members were selected from a fairly narrow range of possible backgrounds and circumstances, a non-possessive familism could be achieved. Of course these conditions are already somewhat compromising; they lead communes rather quickly to exclude the damaged, the disabled and the demanding and those who are potentially so. But it is when one tries to move from such a base towards a resolution of other social problems that the real difficulties of communes appear.

To begin with, the structures (or encounters) that were developed did not ensure the greater freedom of women, although they did not prevent it, either. The refusal to let communes develop the fixity and facticity of a social institution is also a refusal to let communal living guarantee any particular social effects – even such effects as a dependable freedom. It is manifestly not enough to tell the visiting sociologist that 'the women here have become so liberated that the men are slaves' as the men troop off to the pub leaving the women cooking tea for the children, even if one man is also left behind because it happens to be his turn to make the evening meal. But so long as one insists on treating freedom as though it is exclusively a question of the individual, sexless, classless, owner of a self and socially unlocated, one can only be baffled by one's failure to do better. And the members of communes are baffled by that failure just as they are perplexed by their normal inability to achieve more than a partial solution to their second fundamental problem, the problem of identity. We have argued (in chapter 4) that the same determination to minimise structure that makes it so difficult for communes to guarantee women a more liberated experience also makes the process of communal self-seeking highly precarious, variable and indeterminate. The combination of an ethos of possessive individualism with a rejection of social structure works its distinctive effects here too: one man's absence of structure is another man's social fact. Lesser planets must circle around a commune's sociometric stars to reflect the full intensity of their being. The full individuation of some members of a commune, usually the core group, tends to depend upon the, usually unacknowledged, stunting of the individuation of others. The conditions for sustaining the achieved identities of the core members become obstacles around which the self-seeking of other members cannot, after a while, find a way. Thus, one member of one religious commune told us how he had explained to the leaders of that group, when he was negotiating his own entry, that he thought the commune was a place in which he could grow. And so up to a point it had proved. But two years later he was experiencing the commune, and in particular its leaders, as an overwhelming constriction on his growth. As the commune was inseparable from its leaders, he then left.

It is not always the fringe members who lose out in the struggle for identity. Since other people have to be seen as 'only individuals like us' it is difficult for a commune to close its doors to newcomers – a difficulty compounded by the obvious advantages of size. Heavy traffic in and out is a constant feature of intentional communities. And it quite often happens that the newcomers prove more determined in their efforts to create identities within the commune as they find it than the core group are to sustain identities within the commune as it has become. This is of course only another way of demonstrating the extreme difficulty of reconciling the two projects. Paradoxically, although those who are attempting individuation within a commune and those who have achieved it must live in a state of close mutual dependence as models and audiences for one another, the probability is that the nature of their underlying individualism will lead them to find each other mutually intolerable. Whether in any particular case it is the core members or the newcomers who decide to go away, the capacity of communes to act as forcing-houses of identity is plainly both dramatic and ambiguous. Commune members themselves tended to explain the odd performances of communes in this respect in one of two ways. Some attributed it to the fact that there were, 'as yet', so few communes and so many would-be members of communes. As the commune movement spreads and communes diversify, it was argued, there will begin to be a wide enough range of types of commune to satisfy and contain all individual projects. Others pointed to the ways in which family relationships, education and the whole process of personality formation experienced by an individual in societies such as contemporary Britain before he or she can enter a commune pervert and distort the sensibility, engaging one specifically in a possessive individualism, so that one is effectively disqualified in advance from living communally. Both of these views shift the discussion away from the level of social problems and towards the level of problems of society. Both raise the issue of the *possibility* of communes within advanced capitalism.

When the chain of personal and social transformation breaks, and typically it breaks early on, well before even the most essential and pressing social problems have been mastered, attempts are made to

192

reassemble it. A possible conclusion in the face of the limitations communes are found to have as instruments of transformation would be to
assert the need for a more directly instrumental and more explicitly
political revolutionary commitment. In practice this conclusion is very,
very rarely drawn by members of British communes. Much more
common is the decision that what is needed is a still more thorough
exploration of the possibilities of strictly private life – in settings which
are either more intimate (encounter groups) or more carefully regu-
lated (religions). The political conclusion is not unknown. It is not
impossible to conclude that communal living needs to be caught up in
a larger revolutionary process and to be reconstructed as an essential
part of that process. Most of the examples, however, are not British
ones. Reichert has given us an account of one exceptionally articulate
version of such a development in the case of Kommune 11 in West
Berlin (Fairfield 1972: 143). The members of this group believed that
the revolutionary struggle must permeate the whole of a revolutionary's life. Refusing to confine politics to the public domain, they
demanded a total revolution pervading and uniting the public and the
private life in a new whole: 'integrate the whole personality in the revolutionary struggle'. But even in this case the essentially private logic
of communes ended up working against, and overcoming, the essentially public logic of revolution:

> [The fusion of the two] within the given political context of the
> time turned out to be far more problematic and protracted than
> the Kommune members had bargained for. The group (whose
> membership is constantly changing) then began to withdraw more
> and more from political activity. They could not agree on a
> common project; moreover, once the psychoanalytical sessions
> began, they claimed the entire attention of the members. To com-
> pound these difficulties there was no revolutionary methodological
> development of psychological theory for the individual and the
> group.

In the course of our own research one of us did visit one similar group
in the south of England, but our welcome ran out after twenty-four
hours. They seemed to be living in the grip of an extraordinarily tight
notion of how revolution and communal living could be put together.
Their revolutionary activity was of a very limited kind. Their tolerance
for alternative proposals was virtually non-existent. And the modern
revolutionary with whom they claimed most sympathy was Marcuse;
their leader was proud to announce that one of their number had studied under him in the United States. This is perhaps not surprising. As
Colletti (1972: 140) has rightly pointed out, the distinctive feature of
Marcuse's marxism is that 'Marcuse acclaims "the interior space of the
private sphere"; he invokes that "isolation in which the individual, left

to himself, can think and demand and find"; he acclaims the "private sphere" as the only one which can "give significance to freedom and independence of thought".' His is a revolution of the possessive individual against possessive individualism. A Leninist conception of revolution, by contrast, calls on the revolutionary to combat and overcome the private sphere: a professional revolutionary party cannot be composed of friendship cliques. From such a point of view, communes can only divert potential revolutionaries. If a commune is successful in providing a rich world of relationships for its members, it is that much less likely that they will be impelled by their situation to undertake political work outside the commune. To the degree that a commune protects and insulates its members from the oppressive realities of society, its members are unlikely to be outraged or harassed to the point of action by those realities. The theory of a demonstrative revolution to which so many commune members adhere lets them escape that particular dilemma; but it does so by drastically diminishing the idea of revolution. The brand of marxism that flourishes in some communes envisages no more than a revolution of private life.

And the end of that road is personal salvation, not social change. Those on the fringes of communes who achieve a measure of individuation attempt to consolidate their good fortune in projects of their own, to live in primary-group situations which cultivate their gains. Conversely, when a commune begins to break down or runs into difficulties, the call for harder relationship work, for more personal candour face to face, saps any outside activities. And as we do not typically experience social structure, or in this case the absence of social structure, directly, the structural reasons which make communes such precarious undertakings come to the surface as matters of personality – of someone being immature or domineering or, most ironically of all, possessive. So what is learnt from the collapse of these moral adventures is a lesson about human nature, not a lesson about social structure. Those who do not despair set out to find a new gathering of better individuals. It is at this point that the eclectic religious communities such as Findhorn or those based on creeds such as Sufism which stress that there are many simultaneous paths to True Being come into their own. It is in such societies, or as Richardson et al. (1972) have observed more spectacularly in the United States in the communes of the Jesus Movement, that those who have understood that selves are created with others but who cannot rid themselves of the idea that the self is a possession make their last stand.

But all this begs the question. Why does this socially produced demand for individuality take the form that it does? Why are almost all communal groups impelled to live introspectively? As we have said, the social problems that communes are 'about' indicate the problems of

194

society. In particular they indicate the problems of our society as experienced by the petty bourgeoisie. They seek to resolve those problems from the point of view of the distinctive predicament of that class. The moral force of the commune movement no less than the practical disasters of communes springs from the impossibility of the situation of the petty bourgeoisie. The broad features of that situation were indicated long ago by Paul Sweezy (1968: 314):

> Instead of a growing solidarity of interests expressed in closer organisational unity and more conscious and effective political action, we find among the middle classes the utmost confusion and diversity of interests and aims. An objective basis for organisational unity and consciously oriented policy is lacking except in the case of relatively small groups which are too weak to be effective and often work at cross purposes into the bargain. Hence it is the fate of the middle classes in the period of ripening capitalist contradictions to be squeezed between the extortions of monopoly capital on the one hand and the demands of the working class for better conditions and greater security on the other hand; this much, at any rate, they all have in common, and it is this which determines the basic attitude characteristic of nearly all sectors of the middle classes . . . hostility to both organised capital and organised labour which manifests itself in seemingly contradictory ways. On the one hand the middle classes are the sources of various degrees of non-proletarian anti-capitalism; on the other hand of Utopias in which all organised class power is dissolved and the individual (i.e. the unattached member of a middle class group) becomes the basic social unit as in the lost days of simple commodity production.

Within this general experience of the middle classes, the petty bourgeois experiences a devastating loss of control of his social relationships. In Poulantzas' account (1973: 27-54) the petty bourgeoisie is composed of two sharply distinguished economic groups who nevertheless constitute an ideological and political unity. There is a traditional group engaged in small production, trading and craft work and experiencing a steady decline in both numbers and status; a group whose increasingly desperate attempt to protect its distinctive mode of individualism through the deliberate cultivation of ever more skilled activity that is ever more socially useless has been finely traced in Christopher Caudwell's analysis of the English poets (1937: 73-122). And there is a modern group thrown up by the inner technological revolutions of capitalism and found particularly now in the communication industries, the educational system and cultural institutions (the 'ideological apparatuses' in Poulantzas' terms), a group experiencing the peculiarly uncomfortable predicament of being both constantly faced

195

with obsolescence, status-withdrawal and loss of income and constantly replaced by new equivalents of itself. The real inability of these groups to withstand or shape the processes in which they are caught up is hardly assuaged by the readiness of some social scientists and politicians to describe the indignities they experience as a matter of our all becoming middle-class now. The destiny of the petty bourgeoisie has an iron presence; what we observe in the commune movement is a double flight of some petty bourgeois from that destiny. There is a flight, first, from occupations in the 'modern' sector of the class to more or less serious attempts to live in the 'traditional' sector. And secondly, there is a flight from the supposedly 'modern' nuclear family formation to the supposedly 'traditional' relationships of the extended family (and in some cases explicitly of the tribe). Is it inappropriate to call the symbolism of such a movement reactionary? Or is it fanciful to see the insistence of the commune movement on the tyranny of things over people, and their efforts to rescue the individual from a world of things, as expressing the crisis of a social group whose most cherished values have been outraged by the discovery that their own life-work and being are for others no more than commodities?

The connection between the commune movement and certain wider social and political movements is interesting in this context. The links with Anarchism, with Release, the Peace Movement and the National Council for Civil Liberties serve to locate communes in a curiously exact way. The connection with the Campaign for Nuclear Disarmament is perhaps the most revealing instance of the entanglement of communes with this whole complex of movements and agitations – a complex which Parkin in the best study of CND aptly identified as middle-class radicalism (Parkin 1968). Many of the older members of communes were directly active in the marches and meetings of CND and recall the nights in sleeping bags, the days in court and 'all those pacifists spoiling for a fight' as the record of a golden past (R.004; R.019; R.061). But there is a more general, indirect link between the two movements as a whole which is a matter of style and tone and of what is perceived as the significant act. Both movements were about the affirmation of freedom by individuals. Andrew Rigby, who has himself been active in both, has analysed the problem of revolution in a way which both would immediately accept (he was in fact writing in *Communes* on the basis of a paper presented at a conference on peace research): 'The major problem facing revolutionaries in modern industrial societies is surely not so much the social question . . . but the question of freedom: the need is to instil into individuals the positive desire for freedom to take control of their own lives and to realise themselves' (Rigby 1971: 3). The commune movement, like CND, and like middle-class radicalism in general, is in the last analysis an expressive radicalism (to use Parkin's terms) rather than an instrumental radicalism; it eschews both the compromises and the commitments of mundane organised politics in order to proclaim the integrity of a symbolic posture. But in reality that is all the petty bourgeois *can* do in a world they have already lost.

Expressive radicalism allows one to substitute the universality of a moral crusade for the specification of class or culture. It thus recreates the world of individuals which is the desired but non-existent petty-bourgeois ideal: in the face of the Bomb we all become mere individuals; the distinctive 'honesty' of communes consists in the same way of nothing but the recognition that there are only individuals. In elaborating his own account of expressive radicalism, Parkin cites a curiously apt analysis of the functions of certain kinds of attitudes by Daniel Katz:

> Satisfactions also accrue to the person from the expression of attitudes which reflect his cherished beliefs and his self-image. The reward to the person in these instances is not so much a matter of gaining social recognition or monetary rewards as of establishing his self-identity and confirming his notion of the sort of person he sees himself to be. Just as we find satisfaction in the exercise of our talents and abilities, so we find reward in the expression of any attributes associated with our egos. (Katz 1960: 173)

The various quasi-political causes sustained by the petty bourgeoisie all have this character. They give the world, and therefore the members of the movement concerned, a ringing account of the moral importance of an essentially individualistic critique of the world advanced by given individuals. And they do so in a way which carefully avoids examining the practical implications of the critique as a matter of status or class or party. Many members of CND denied the existence of classes just as they affirmed the irrelevance of parties; many members of communes would do no less. There are of course moments of truth. One commune member described to us the way in which she saw through the Committee of 100 and turned to communes instead: 'Going on these demonstrations I suddenly realised that no one else was a poverty-stricken old widow on social security with three kids, going on a supporting thing, never mind a going to jail thing, and anyway, well ...' (R.118).

If these movements share a common tone and style, they are no less at one in sharing a common source of members. Parkin found that the bulk, not just the leading members, of CND were drawn from the educated middle class employed in non-profit organisations in the welfare, educational and creative professions, from 'that stratum whose social position and life chances rest primarily upon its intellectual attainments and professional qualifications, and not upon the ownership of

197

property or inherited wealth', a stratum for which the educational system and the development of personal skill have 'provided the means for achieving high placement and the social and economic security which property provided for the traditional middle class'. Hence, as distinct from the traditional, genuinely bourgeois, middle class, 'they are in a sense freer in their choice of political allegiance in so far as their talents and their expertise are at a premium in highly industrialised societies, and their rewards and privileges are more or less guaranteed, no matter what the reigning political ideology' (Parkin 1968: 179). Within the compass of this relative freedom, they can cultivate the distinctive ethos of their stratum, the ethos of the free, self-realising individual. Their choice of profession was an initial affirmation that that was what their lives were about. They joined CND not so much because of the discrepancy between their material rewards and their felt social status as because the movement afforded a further affirmation of the same point. As Parkin puts it (1968: 192), 'the welfare and creative professions provide acceptable sanctuaries to those who wish to avoid direct involvement in capitalist enterprises by affording outlets for the exercise of their talents which entail no compromise of political ideals'. There is here a dovetailing of self-selection and natural selection in which these individuals who have remained eager to champion individualistic values end up in organisations tolerant of such values while organisations intolerant of such values train their individual members to be more appropriately realistic.

The difference between CND and the commune movement is, of course, that the latter is not really a movement. In all significant respects it is a private, not a public, assertion of individualism. By comparison with CND it lacks leadership, structure, focus and even a clearly defined cause. It is a retreat rather than a challenge, making sense in the context of the drastically worsened situation of the lower middle class in 1970 as compared to their situation in 1960, and in the context of the closing off of opportunities for genuinely political action which had occurred in the same decade. CND has been called a cause without an ideology; the commune movement is perhaps an ideology without a cause. The expression of petty-bourgeois individualism which comes nearest to qualifying as a genuine social and political movement in this period, and hence as a true successor to CND and indeed as an improvement on it in that its cause is presented in the terms of a general ideology, is surely Women's Liberation. The commune movement shares with the Women's Liberation Movement that curious reaction which Baudelaire called 'la grande maladie de l'horreur du domicile', but once again, while the latter has entered the arena of public action, presenting an increasingly formidable case for the general destruction of private life as a realm of masculine power,

198

the former has for all practical purposes remained within the private sphere; it is a movement of those petty bourgeois for whom the self is really all that matters. Communes are, within the terms of this culture, heroic enterprises in which a drama spun from the themes of identity, freedom and individuality is acted out. In Durkheim's terms, they attempt to form a social cohesion in which altruism and egoism are both simultaneously fully realised. They are for the present the best and therefore the most pathetic expression of the logic of petty-bourgeois culture. Our research files are crammed with statements of the ideal mutuality – accounts of a possible world of possessive individualism. And they are equally packed with accounts of the insufferable inability of others to rise above their own possessiveness. One of the most dedicated, considerate and giving commune members we met understood perfectly clearly that 'communes are pitched right into this conflict', and told us again and again of her own experience of it:

> We have just had two lads here who roused all my objections, and scuppered our plans to do something a bit generous by telling us to be generous while themselves contributing less than their basic share. Three of us saw it this way. others liked them and took against me. So the fundamental division that has bedevilled us was acute – people versus things. What really impressed me is that the others of us who have *used* me in every way were totally unable to face the fact and acknowledge it. 'Only give what you want to', Jenny said and no one argued. So that's what I'm doing instead of responding to the needs of others till I'm drained. So they feel the place is disintegrating now and hasn't a dynamic. (R.020).

Most commune members experience the same problem but in a much less articulated way: 'I still believe in communes; it's just that I'm completely pissed-off with the people living here' (Q.134). The dilemma is plain but insoluble: 'In a genuine community individuals gain their freedom in and through their association' (Marx 1959: 64), but so long as individuality is impelled to realise itself in possession it destroys association. The only fundamental obstacle to successful communal living is the sort of people who want to live communally.

The individualism of market societies, as Macpherson discreetly calls them, is both their glory and their tragedy; and it impinges to set the stage for movements such as the commune movement in two main ways. All the disruptive innovating activity needed to drag a market society from the womb of a feudal society is legitimated by the ethos of individualism. But the actual circumstances of a market society, that is to say, of a formally free market in both capital and labour, transform the ideal world of equal individuals into a real world of powerful owners of capital and powerless owners of mere labour-power who

199

cannot realise their own individuality in their labour because they are impelled to sell it on terms dictated by others. The only means to redress this real inequality is combination; that is, the abandonment of individualism and the creation of an alternative ethos of solidarity. Communes are an attempt on the part of those who have belatedly and unexpectedly discovered their true situation in market society to follow the example of the working class and construct a little bit of power through combination. But it is an attempt made on distinctively petty-bourgeois terms, from *within* the ethos of individualism and denying the profound contradiction between that ethos and the requirements of effective combination. Hence innumerable 'practical difficulties' constantly frustrate the efforts of the commune movement to generalise and spread the alternative economic relations in which commune members believe. There is an endless watching and checking to make sure that one is not being exploited by the very people with whom one is trying to combine, an endless sad discovery that others cannot or will not give enough.

The second way in which individualism decisively conditions the commune movement is a more subjective counterpart to the first. The real situation of the petty bourgeois now is that they are not possessors of their own capacities but rather, like any proletarian, must sell their labour-power in order to subsist. But the very being of petty-bourgeois man is conditional upon possession of *something*. As everything else eludes one, the impulse to possess at least that immaterial essence, the self, can only be intensified. The ways in which the powers of the individual are expropriated in our society are not, typically, seen for what they are – to do so would be to be forced to recognise that the petty bourgeois is indeed in many ways a proletarian. Instead the problem is perceived as one of the incomprehensibility of complex society (Durkheim), of the obliteration of spontaneity by routine (Weber) or of the fragmentation of whole men by the division of labour (Jung). Against all this, it becomes overwhelmingly important to reconstruct whole persons, a 'something to call my own' that one has indeed created heroically in the face of an iron world. The investment in self-projects – whether in the form of sociologists desperately trying to find at least some tiny enclave of freedom in which people can authentically be themselves or in the form of the varied adventures (whether they be affairs or trips or crimes or communes) to which less academic people commit themselves – assumes a life-or-death urgency. But any such project, such as a commune, which requires the collaboration of other people involves peculiar hazards. Simmel understood quite well that the more people relate to one another as whole persons, the more at risk they are: the greater the probability that any dispute between

200

them will also engage the whole person, exploding the relationship in crises of total personal being. For him, this explained the savagery that can well up in domestic quarrels, bursting into the most tender and intimate of relations. But he understood this as an effect of the wholeness of the form of such relationships, not, as we do, as a peculiar consequence of the fact that the identity typically sought in such relationships in our kind of society is primarily a matter of possession: a possession-identity. We were endlessly surprised, as we have reported, by the degree to which members of communes felt themselves fundamentally threatened by disputes over territory or tools or household tasks or consumable objects. Trivial as these matters were usually seen to be in retrospect, at the time they signified a precarious achievement of self.

What those in communes do is to try to create social entities in which people can possess themselves as full, rich, unique and hence, given the culture within which they move, egocentric beings. Their chief concern is reflected in their argot: at the time we did our fieldwork, to be 'together', that is, whole, was praise; to be 'spaced-out', that is, disjointed, was condemnation; at one commune sadly disintegrating on a bleak Yorkshire farm, we were told that 'at least the dog seems to be together now'. In a slightly different dimension of meaning, it was desirable to be 'cool', undesirable to be 'hung-up'; the best rendering of coolness is of course precisely self-possession; hung-up individuals are troublesome because, lacking self-possession, they encroach on the self-possession of others.

Communal projects are commonly inspired by profoundly generous instincts; commune members often described their involvement to us in statements such as 'I'd like to be able to give myself to everyone, even though it does mean getting hurt in the end.' But the generosity is in practice checked by a wary guarding against the actual probability of being hurt. To be able to give yourself you must first securely possess yourself. Being hurt in this particular context is a matter of discovering that what you thought was yours to give, others have been treating as theirs to use. Such a dilemma only makes sense, is only possible, in the setting of an encompassing culture of possessive individualism in which the self is a uniquely real, uniquely precious and uniquely fragile object. It is also of course a peculiarly odd type of object. It is an object, of contemplation and action, for oneself but not for anyone else. To all others it must be inviolably a subject, absolutely not to be treated as an object. In such a world the carrying through of individual plans becomes entangled intimately with the sense of identity, of how individuals define themselves. And as Berger, Berger and Kellner (1974: 74) have pointed out, a consistent identity is exceptionally hard

201

to grasp in such a world just because the structure of consciousness that makes self-possession an imperative value develops against the background of institutional structures which leave the individual largely undefined and problematic:

> On the one hand, modern identity is open-ended, transitory, liable to on-going change. On the other hand, a subjective realm of identity is the individual's main foothold in reality. Something that is constantly changing is supposed to be the *ens realissimum*. Consequently it should not be a surprise that modern man is afflicted with a permanent identity crisis, a condition conducive to considerable nervousness.

The attempt to master the issue of identity through the practice of mutuality is in these circumstances anything but trivial. But the same circumstances also make it anything but easy. As one of the things that members of communes bring with them to the communes they join is, almost invariably, a sense of the problem of identity as a problem of possession, as what they are looking for is a form of possession-identity, and as this sense of the problem (even though it is often consciously understood as a bourgeois residue) is almost impossible to dispel since every actual move towards mutuality is bound to reactivate it, the collective search for identity turns all too easily into a zero–sum game. What some have others have to be denied. If the core members of a commune are to appropriate a unique communal individuality, others, sadly, must either embrace just that form of individuality or go elsewhere. Nor is this all-or-nothing dénouement simply an unhappy incidental outcome of particular projects, or a matter of the particular personalities who chanced to come together in certain groups. It is much nearer to being a necessary condition for the sort of individuality that is being sought. In this respect communes reenact in miniature and at the level of personal relationships the socio-economic logic of the larger society; one class of people derives its position and well-being from the exploitive domination of another:

> Do you know of any communes in London or within daily travelling distance of it that are looking for new members? If there is a choice I would prefer one as big as possible. I have had experience of the other kind, which you get into by accidentally sleeping with somebody else's wife and mother, and want one that is flexible and not tied either to that sort of love–hate situation or to the rigid political–social–sexual philosophy of one or two people – usually with the cash and therefore the power. You know, not like most communes are but like they are supposed to be. (*Communes*, 38: 22)

Possessive individualism reduces identity to a question of power.

The close connection of power and individuality has of course been remarked in a good deal of writing concerned with the issue of identity. Thus, in *The Undiscovered Self* we find Jung arguing that, as power is concentrated in the state, the high official of the state enjoys a unique opportunity for individuality: 'He is thus the only individual or at any rate one of the few individuals who could make use of their individuality' (1974: 15). In a somewhat more banal manner, behavioural social psychology is riddled with demonstrations of the positive relationships between such properties (apt term) as 'ego-strength', 'competence', 'self-esteem', and 'leadership'. H. S. Sullivan built his system of inter-personal psychology very largely on the assumption of the linkage of subjective self-confidence or security and the power motive: as his student Mullahy put it, 'to gain . . . security, is to have power in interpersonal relations' (Mullahy (ed.) 1952: 244). Among sociologists, the same conception of individuality is particularly noticeable in the writings of Max Weber, for whom, on the one hand, power is quite simply a matter of an ability to impose one's will on others in spite of their resistance, while, on the other hand, individuality is most fully realised in those charismatic persons whose power breaks down not only personal but also institutional opposition. The tribute accorded to the individuality of the charismatic leader is the surrender of individuality on the part of his followers. Freed from its spurious association with science, the fundamental cultural assumption behind these views emerges most clearly and obviously in the conception of heroism which has dominated all western art forms for two centuries; whether as Prometheus or as Shane our heroes are real individuals because they are powerful because they are individuals.

Perhaps the most striking illustration of the way in which communes serve as settings for the creation of possession-identity is provided by the experience of many therapeutic communities. The irony is only superficial. If individuals are to be restored 'cured' to our sort of society, they must of course be equipped with the most essential and inalienable property of individuality in such a society – a possessed self. Therapeutic communities differ from the general run of communes in that the core and fringe members are explicitly identified as such: as the sane and the sick, or the helpers and the helped. The core members offer individuality by way of an interpretation of the world which, among other things, affirms and validates the previously troublesome past experience of the fringe members. The acceptance of this interpretation of things is a basic step towards being defined as cured. The interpretation may be more or less radical, more or less centred on the idea of the opposition of individuality and the social order. But even in its most extreme forms, well represented by the work of David Cooper, the conception of self advanced in therapeutic communities fails to transcend the limits of possessive individualism. Thus Cooper (1971:

67) ends his advocacy of communes with an oddly revealing piece of rhetoric – if it is more than rhetoric, it is simply the more revealing: 'What we want, in short, is not to chew our loaf but to consume the system so that at last we might get a taste of ourselves.' Everywhere else in his writings the idea of consuming is associated with the idea of greed which in turn is for him the epitome of bourgeois possessiveness. More generally, what the core members of most therapeutic communities seem to do is to offer to their peculiarly helpless and dependent fringe members to validate *their* identities as therapists as a condition and possession, in terms of which they can act meaningfully in at least some sort of social world. But the keys of meaning are cut and held by the core members. However helpfully, generously, affirmatively or of course therapeutically they may reveal or implement their power, the whole project turns on the way in which the core members oblige the fringe members to validate *their* identities as therapists as a condition for acquiring new identities of their own as individuals who have been cured. As in other communes, the gaining of an identity by a fringe member is likely to result in his or her departure. In therapeutic communities the implications of departure for the relationship between the core and fringe members as common members of a commune are concealed under the agreed statement that the fringe member is leaving because he or she is cured. We were, nevertheless, given a number of insights into the realities behind these departures in the course of our research. Perhaps the most direct was an unguarded conversation one of us had with the leader of a group in London which aims to rehabilitate recently discharged psychiatric patients. He was very frank about the benefits of such work for him personally; he worked with his hands (most of the rehabilitation work was carried out in a workshop); his conscience was clear, as he was not exploiting or living off other people; and his ego enjoyed the additional boost of knowing that he was doing good while giving full expression to his own personality and wishes. He exemplified this situation by talking about the relationship within the group between the 'workers' (that is, the therapists such as himself) and the 'members' (that is, the patients): 'It really ends up with me telling them what to do. They have been so conditioned that they cannot think for themselves. When they start arguing back I say that they are getting better and it is time for them to leave.' This frankness about the realities of power and individuality in therapeutic communities is not in fact unique among the dominant members of such groups. Consider again the case of David Cooper. From one point of view, the point of view of the therapist or simply of the outsider, the way in which he writes about 'the positive centre of the experience of the community' seems extraordinarily humane, egalitarian, power-free. He speaks of the community as 'places for people to *be*, not to *be*

204

treated, as places where the distinction between psychiatrist and patient vanishes and 'there are simply people'. But consider all this from the point of view of the people who know perfectly well that they are also patients. Cooper's suggestion that the essence of community is the 'guarantee that some other person will always accompany one on one's journey into and through one's self', that some non-interfering person will be there as one goes through 'experiences of personal disintegration and then reintegration', surely now takes quite a different aspect. It is perfectly clear who is the 'one' and who is the 'other' in this script. There is no suggestion that the 'other', that is, the therapist, is also going to experience personal disintegration and reintegration. Self-evidently, his self is quite adequately achieved in advance. From this point of view, the community is at best a field of psychic voyeurism. At worst, it is, in a quite old-fashioned sense, a system of exploitation in which the strong enjoy their selves at the expense of the weak.

But therapeutic communities are an over-dramatic example of communal living in general. And are we not in danger of over-dramatising anyway? Are not the members of most communes united at a much more mundane level by simple material interest, the calculable ways in which each member sees the others in the group as contributing to his or her well-being? Obviously, at a place like Hillside interest is a significant basis of solidarity from day to day, and the issues of power and possession are far from intrusively present. Moreover, the notion of personal well-being in such a commune is not at all narrowly conceived; it includes the possibility of others' causing one pain or distress, a cost fairly incurred in the development of the whole person. Yet what the experience of such communes reveals in the end is just that this passive being-with-others is not enough to satisfy most members of communes as individuals. The material advantages of communes consistently fail to meet the spiritual needs of commune members – for the former are rooted in sharing while the latter presuppose possession. As Durkheim pointed out so forcibly in his criticism of Spencer, personal interest really is no basis for social cohesion: 'There is nothing less constant than interest. Today it unites me to you; tomorrow it will make me your enemy. Such a cause can only give rise to transient relations and passing associations' (1933: 172). It is one of the ironically distinctive features of individualism that a common attachment to its values by no means provides a condition for social cohesion; rather, 'if it turns all wills towards the same end, this end is not social' (*ibid.*). The ideological unity of communes insofar as it derives from ideas of personal interest cannot be mirrored in a structural unity; rather, it must go hand in hand with an endless loosening of structure, the encouragement of all centrifugal forces.

The whole point of communes is to live in terms of something more

205

worthwhile than interest, however. But equally it is to live in terms of something a lot less self-denying than commitment. The valued middle ground between interest and commitment is found, ideally, in the idea of mutuality, of giving. It is precisely the attempt to realise this ideal, the ideal of personal life as something one constantly gives freely to others, that in our view makes secular communes important projects – however often and calamitously they fail. The ideal is easy to understand and to talk about. It is a matter of living in such a way that from moment to moment in each new episode of one's life one makes a free gift of one's self to others who are equally making free gifts of their selves to you. But in practice the line along which such an ideal could be realised, the line between relationships of interest and relationships of commitment, between the market and the marriage, is incredibly thin – often to the point of being almost invisible. Commitment and interest, far from being extensions of support for the spirit of mutuality, are thus in a sense equally antitheses of it – and yet, as we have tried to show, it is to the less fully human solidarity of either interest or commitment that communes are well-nigh invariably driven in the face of the stupendous emotional and practical difficulties experienced by people such as these in a society such as this when trying to grasp an authentic, lasting mutuality. In chapter 2 we suggested that communes could usefully be understood as attempts to institutionalise the ideal of friendship proclaimed by Aristotle and Cicero. We could perhaps now conclude that that ideal is likely to be especially attractive to the petty bourgeoisie of advanced capitalist societies, because for people to whom possession is the quintessence of being it promises an enormous affirmation of the only real possession they can hope to enjoy, their selves. But by the same token it is an ideal uniquely difficult to realise for such people in such societies because of the manner in which they are driven endlessly to weigh the affirmation of others which is the cornerstone of friendship against the nightmare hazard of possible further alienations of self.

The problems of identity and association which can be seen vividly in communes are, although probably incapable of solution by them, capable of variation. So far in this chapter we have assumed that the groups we are discussing are both secular and small in size. But religious communes and communities can become both big enough and sufficiently bonded to escape at least some of the inter-personal difficulties we have looked at. Yet the implementation of religious belief, if it is to work in this way, must clearly carry with it certain limitations on the personal freedom of those involved. The gains resulting from an increase in size are offset by losses resulting from an increase in commitment. Thus, core members of such groups will successfully resist the attempts of more marginal members to build their own identities on the personal appropriation of religious competence. In one very large religious community, for example, we found that although the diffusion of the group's basic religious skill – communication with deities through the medium of automatic writing – had been overtly welcomed and predicted by the core members, those very members made the most determined efforts to prevent such a diffusion from actually occurring. Even though the newly competent members did not seek to challenge the overall supremacy of the core group or to overthrow in any way the beliefs to which the community as a whole was attached, their claims to religious competence were vigorously invalidated by the group's established leaders. False accusations, supposedly of divine inspiration, were made, during our own visits, against two such emergent automatic writers by the dominant seer. Up to that point these two members had believed without question in the spiritual authority of the seer. But the certain knowledge that the charges brought against them were false shattered their faith in the community as a whole. Separately but equally passionately, they denounced the leaders of the community and left. In a sense their departure was a triumph both for them and for the community. They had broken through, or so it seemed to them in retrospect, to an autonomous individuality which they could win only by freeing themselves from the dominant individualities of the leaders of the community. But at the same time their departure was interpreted within the community as an affirmation of the integrity and solidarity of those who remained. Periodic denunciations, expulsions and rejections of this kind served, it seemed, to reinforce the cohesion of the group around its original core. Powerfully sanctioned interpretations refashioned the reasons actually given for leaving (talk of the hypocrisy or paranoia of the core) into accounts that served to tighten the attachment of those who remained (talk of many ways to the truth or of the need of those who had left to learn through error).

Within the religious groups we were able to study, many of the difficulties of secular communes were dissolved away on the strength of an implicit or explicit belief in the existence of a hierarchy of religious competence. Thus, the confusing dilemmas of individuality associated with notions of secular equality or uniqueness were generally avoided in religious communities in the light of the understanding that the creation of a truly valuable self within a religious project is not something that is immediately open to everyone but on the contrary is something to be won patiently through self-denial, discipline and submission. The existence of an acknowledged hierarchy of personal development also serves, of course, to partially blur the realities of economic control and moral domination enjoyed by the core members of such communities. And this, together with the much more closed ideological systems developed in these groups, tends to give them a degree of cohesion unattainable by secular communes. At the same time the larger size which this form of organisation permits – and size is often striven for as an indicator of success as well as a source of income – requires the institution of something like a rational division of labour in which everyone is used to the best advantage of 'the community'. The skill demanded of any particular member may not be one he or she particularly enjoys using, but, despite the rigours of this discipline, a good many members do manage to appropriate the elements of an identity of their own within the permitted fields of specialisation. At the very least they have the opportunity to develop in the shelter of cliques or work-groups within the main community and to reinterpret or rework the beliefs of the core members insofar as they judge them extreme, bizarre or inappropriate. Some of the religious groups we encountered manage to tolerate quite a high degree of internal eclecticism in this way. Greater size and a more elaborate division of labour really do seem to permit these groups to combine individual diversity with a rather firm solidarity based on the reestablishment of society, on the idea of the community as an external dominant entity. Phenomenally, these large variegated and persistent religious groups appear to many observers to be the most successful type of project within the whole field of communal organisation, coming closest to what many sense to be the spirit of community.

We ourselves reject this impression. We do so not because we find the moral order of religious communities fraudulent – although we do indeed hold that from a humanistic point of view there is an unavoidable element of fraud in any religious project – nor because in practice so many religious groups turn out on close examination to consist of people engaged in nothing but a more ambitious version of the struggle to possess oneself through the possession of others which looms so large in secular communes, but because the most basic principles of social bonding involved in religious communities are such as to make their whole experience irrelevant for the type of project which is at the heart of secular communes. The depth and diversity of spiritual experience that are possible within the limits set by a metaphysical commitment have to be weighed against the fact that it *is* commitment rather than giving that holds such communities together – a lesson constantly being learned by many of those who join them, struggle within them and finally either surrender their selves so as to be reborn on someone else's terms or leave. It is precisely the struggle to prevent mutuality from being transformed into commitment that gives secular communes their value and, as we argued in chapter 6, the religious reconstruction of commitment is from this point of view a kind of failure.

208

But is it not possible to combine the advantages of size and division of labour with a secular and humanistic ideology? Although we have argued that there are powerful material and cultural reasons why such a combination is highly improbable in Britain now, there plainly are conditions under which it can be achieved, as the kibbutzim have shown. Unfortunately, the kibbutz is itself largely an irrelevant form of organisation so far as British communal experiments are concerned. Even if the kibbutz is not, as so many kibbutz members believe, the essential and central institution of Israeli society, it clearly is an institution that has received formidable moral, economic and political support from its surrounding society and one that enshrines values which are distinctively of that society rather than at odds with it. Furthermore, the energies and emotions of kibbutz members were throughout the long formative period of kibbutz history turned firmly away from problems of individuality by the much more pressing demands of the external and collective issues of economic and military survival. And thirdly, this suppression of the issue of individuality was of course powerfully consolidated by the fact that such a very high proportion of kibbutz members were recruited from a culture marked by collectivistic traditions and had, within the framework of that culture, developed an explicit and often passionate socialism. As Durkheim put it, 'we can only re-animate collective life . . . if we love it: we cannot learn to love it unless we live it' (1961: 235). On both counts the founders of the kibbutzim were qualified for communal living in a way which, as they are often harshly aware, most members of British communes are not. This of course raises again the question we discussed in chapter 6 of the moral basis of social solidarity at the level of individual meanings. Solidarity is not an artefact of certain kinds of social arrangements; it is a construct of people who are disposed to be solidary.

Yet the experience of the kibbutzim does have an indirect relevance for communes in Britain. Following Talmon (1972), recent studies of the kibbutz have made much of a supposed revival of 'familism' among younger generations of kibbutz members – a growing movement to strengthen the bonds between parents and children and to make the family home more of an autonomous sphere of life. Some observers have gone so far as to suggest that such a development is an almost inevitable reassertion of the naturalness and functionality of the nuclear family, something that was bound to occur once the worst pressures of war and economic survival were eased. This strikes us as a profound misunderstanding of the kibbutz as a social system. To begin with, as Gerson (1974) and others have shown convincingly, there has hardly been a significant revival of familism anyway: it would seem that the extent to which the present generation of kibbutz parents want to construct strong private family units of parents and children is in fact no greater than that of earlier generations. Thus, only about 12 per cent of all kibbutzim have adopted the practice of allowing children to sleep in their parents' houses, and certainly in the kibbutzim that we visited this practice was seen very much as a concession to the older generations rather than as a demand of the young. Moreover, we found a very clear understanding of what familism meant for the kibbutz and of which aspects of it were accordingly acceptable and which unacceptable. Familism as a whole is undoubtedly a regressive theme within the kibbutz, strongly associated, for example, with the wish to restore segregated sex-roles and to emphasise the home-centred propensities of women. But the essence of the kibbutz is not this or that ideological stance about sex-roles or child–parent relationships; it is the construction of an economy in which the family as an emotional unit is firmly prevented from becoming a significant economic unit, either of production or of consumption. And in this respect familism seems not to have been allowed to dilute the kibbutzim at all. So long as the removal of kinship relations from the communal economy is maintained, strong family attachments between spouses and between parents and children can flourish without threatening the collectivity. The remarkable achievement of the kibbutzim in their present stage of development is to have found ways of cultivating these private relationships while continuing to resist any reconstitution of the family as a distinct economic entity. By contrast, the problem of western communes is plainly that it has hardly anywhere been possible to destroy the economic reality of the component families and thus develop a thoroughgoing communal economy. The kibbutzim had the advantage of *having* to put economic considerations first; they started with a problem of survival, whereas the commune starts with a problem of the family. In almost all cases in communes, behind the patterns of economic sharing that are achieved, the nuclear family, or the private individual, persists as the fundamental economically self-interested unit. The commune tends to be a federation of family units, whereas the kibbutz is more directly a society; the standard of life of its members depends on the economic performance of the community as a whole, not on the performance of particular breadwinners to whom particular dependants are attached. If one were really concerned to advance communalism in Britain, an essential step would be to create the conditions for communal economies in which individuals related directly and exclusively to the commune as a whole. What is important is not the destruction of familism but the creation of a situation in which the family as a private emotional world is separated from the economy – a situation in which, among other things, economic dependence, advantage or responsibility would cease to be reasons for forming private relationships or for keeping them in being.

Implications for policy

An institution which touches a range of social problems as intimately as communes do might be thought to be of interest from the point of view of social policy. One of the things one is asked when applying for grants to the Social Science Research Council is what implications for policy, if any, one's research is likely to have. And at the start it did seem probable to us that communes would turn out not only to be reflecting certain social problems but also to be resolving them in some interesting and valuable ways. The claim that that was so was being made from within the commune movement before we began our research, and it is being made as we finish writing this book (Saunders 1975). However, doing the research has changed our minds. Crudely put, it now seems to us that the best thing the state could do for communes is to leave them severely alone. We are speaking here of communes as ends, as experiments in mutuality as such, rather than of communal organisation as a means. Nothing that is valuable about communes in the former sense will be enhanced by their entanglement, however well intentioned, with the agencies of social policy. In this sense at least, the instinct which leads members of the commune movement to see communes as 'an alternative' is a sound one. The conditions for realising the type of friendship to which communes aspire may well not exist at all in our sort of society, but there is some value at least in breaking cleanly from some of those features of the society which militate most actively against communality. Over the past ten years the commune movement has found ways of insinuating itself *as an alternative* into the fabric of British society – perhaps most remarkably in the sorting out of viable legal frameworks for communal action of the kind produced by the Laurieston Hall community or the People-in-Common group and reported in *Alternative England and Wales* (Saunders 1975: 302–20). But these are proposals for more effectively detaching communal projects from the world of rationalised organisation of which social policy is part, not for drawing them into it. Voluntarism may not be enough to sustain friendship, but it is an unavoidable first step.

We will come back to this argument shortly. But communalism does not have to be an end in itself. It is in fact much more commonly treated as merely a device to serve other ends. And in this respect there are perhaps slightly more positive connections between communes and social policy. Communal organisation as a means does

211

appear worth considering in relation to some social-policy purposes – so long as it is understood that such uses of communal organisation may not have any substantial value from the point of view of the development of communal values as an end in their own right. Then again, communes do, as we have argued throughout this book, *indicate* both the nature and the urgency of a number of social-policy problems even if they also make clear that these problems are unlikely to be solved within communes.

Of the social problems for which communes have such indirect implications there is one to which we have kept returning, and which indeed impressed itself on us with ever greater force as we visited communes – the problem of 'mothers alone'. Such women form probably the largest single category of people wanting to live communally and a noticeable, but much smaller, proportion of the actual members of communes. Unfortunately, those already in relatively well-established communes are far too accurate in their understanding of the costs to themselves of accepting such people. Even if the commune does not have financial problems – and unsupported mothers are not likely to be wealthy – a deserted or rejected mother will need exceptionally sensitive attention – with all the additional giving, and strain, that that means for the group. Many commune members were quite emphatic and open about their coldness towards the needs of unattached mothers. In their view only the most remarkable single mother could be expected to give to the commune anything like as much as she would take out. And yet in principle communal living quite obviously is a rational and humane way of meeting the needs and restarting the lives of these women. Dennis Marsden has charted the loss and deprivation suffered by mothers in this situation with an unblinking candour. For the middle-class women attracted to communes desperate poverty is unlikely to be the sharpest form of the calamity they experience – although their economic hardships are still real enough – but they have lost, too, 'economic support, companionship, a sexual relationship for the mother, an audience to which to play her role, a child-minder, a craftsman about the home, an authority figure or goal-achiever, a model as father and worker, a playmate for the children, an initiator of adult roles, a unit in the family and neighbourhood networks and so on' (Marsden 1973: 166). They may never have enjoyed all these things within the dead or dying relationship behind them, but they look hopefully to communes to supply them. And why not? This image of communes presented by the Commune Movement does suggest that this dispersed many-sided support is just what communes are all about. More simply, communes surely offer accommodation and a chance for mothers to be with their children, and according to a survey carried out by *Mothers in Action*, these are,

212

above all, what unsupported mothers are looking for – and what impels them to take posts in domestic service. All of which makes it doubly annoying that actual communes are so reluctant to admit actual unsupported mothers. But if private-enterprise communes will not risk opening their doors to such women, perhaps one or two sensible local authorities might think about the obvious advantages, either as a permanent arrangement or as a half-way house, of communal residence for groups of women who want to go on being mothers without having to give up being people. No one would suggest that provision of that sort is likely to be fulfilling or profoundly valuable in the long term but as a staging-post in the management of personal disaster it would be a lot better than nothing. There are plenty of mothers willing to make such an experiment with or without public support:

I am an 'unsupported mother' aged 32, with 3 children, girl 11, 2 boys 7 and 3. As I have no remunerative skills, we live on social security. Not surprisingly, perhaps, communes aren't exactly falling over themselves to have us join them. Yet we badly need to belong to some sort of community. From the letters to the Communes Journal I see that there are a good many women in this situation. Why don't some of us get together and start a commune ourselves? A commune full of nothing but women and kids is not my ideal, and I don't suppose it's anyone else's either – but at least it would be a start. Other people's communes seem to form, disperse and re-form with such rapidity that they aren't very suitable for families with older children anyway. Maybe we could create something more stable. (*Communes*, 40: 22)

The sensible idea in such a statement would seem to be the idea that 'at least it would be a start', rather than the hope for stability. Stability is probably no more likely in groups of unsupported mothers than in any other type of secular commune – not least because sooner or later the group will have to face up to the wish of some of its members to embark on new relationships with men. Whether a group accepts this development or resists it, as some have done, by turning the commune into a militant base for one or other of the many battles in the war to liberate women, the original project will be profoundly changed, and at least some members will find the change profoundly disconcerting. On the other hand, a start, a significant move towards the winning of a new personal equilibrium, is something that an episode of communal living plainly can offer – and not just to unsupported mothers. It is in this sense that the idea of communal organisation as a means would seem to have a rather wide relevance for social policy. In the field of housing some local authorities have already taken steps to legalise squatting. Riddled with contradictions and ambiguities as they are, therapeutic and geriatric communities are on balance more honest and

213

humane ways of coping with great personal dependency than most of the more institutional alternatives. If the social process of mothering is ever to be detached from the biological fact of motherhood – which arguably should at least be an available option for those women that want it – that, too, will be best done on a communal basis. In sum, the attempts which many unsupported mothers are already making to win a communal way of life for themselves rest on a sound understanding of the subjective side of the crises of isolation that lurk within a great range of social problems – and on an equally clear grasp of the sorts of social interaction which by reconstructing a significant world make it possible for particular individuals to master such crises. Being alone is a problem that can only be solved by being together. The banality of the observation should not blind us to its originality in the context of social policy.

We are suggesting that there is room for a broader extension of the principle of communal organisation in the field of social policy. This is not at all the same as suggesting that communes will in any sense solve social problems, let alone the problems of society which they obscurely indicate. The creation of a network of communes for unattached mothers would not even begin to undo the deep-rooted exploitation which makes such women socially problematic in the first place. Nor would the proliferation of loving communities of the kind advocated by David Cooper begin to prevent the possessiveness or irresponsibility or general emotional mauling that initially give us the frightening rates of mental sickness with which such communities try to cope. In this sense communes deal with social problems at the level of personal troubles, not at that of public ills. But this is an argument for keeping communes in their place, not for ignoring them. Extreme dependency is, after all, realised as a personal trouble. And it is the sort of trouble which can be genuinely eased by just that sense of involvement in a social project which communes do, however fleetingly, achieve. Indeed, there are many situations in which communes, for all their difficulties, are likely to prove a good deal more protective and considerate of the troubled individual than either families or Social Service departments. One of these, which particularly impressed us, is the situation of marital breakdown. In a small but interesting number of cases the communes we visited had provided settings for the disintegration of a conjugal relationship – usually ending in the departure of the man while the woman and children remained within the commune. In almost all of these cases it seems that the marriage was in quite deep trouble before the couple joined the commune. Indeed, it was their very difficulties, which they interpreted as caused by the structure of their relationship rather than by the parties to it as persons, which drew them toward communes in the first place. The typical condition of such

214

marriages is best described as one of excessive sensitivity, a state in which the partners constantly enact small dramas in which they challenge each other to affirm or invalidate the meaning of the relationship. In the solitude of their own homes, couples can become thoroughly caught up in implicit conspiracies to live in terms of such dramas. Before the larger and sharper-eyed audience provided by a commune, the element of self-deception at the core of such performances is quickly brought to light. Some couples then create a new basis for their relationship. A larger number, having 'seen through' their fraudulent past, and helped no doubt by the immediate opportunity for new relationships which communes offer, seem to drift apart. Commonly, in the cases we encountered, the dissatisfied man moves on. He can do so more easily, of course, because the woman and children he abandons are, after all, now surrounded by friendly others to whom they can turn.

That this sort of thing happens in communes should not be construed as a weakness on their part but, if anything, as a strength. It is surely beneficial that hollow and unhappy relationships can be ended with a minimum of pain and guilt for the participants – and that is what sometimes happens in the supportive atmosphere of the secular family commune. Even if the liberation of women is not attained within communes, their oppression can be made more bearable; as individuals they can be less totally constrained by the fact that they are women. Indeed, in one or two cases, we have watched the sort of situation we have just described work itself out to a genuinely radical dénouement. The most striking instance in our experience was one in which a group of women, having struggled through variously fractured marriages and a male-initiated move towards communal living, found their consciousness of sexual oppression so intensified that they evicted the men, formed a new commune of women and children only, and plunged vehemently into the militant politics of women's liberation.

In the course of our research we came upon several groups of this kind in which a shift from communalism as an end to communal living as a means had occurred. In most of the resulting groups, the problems of sustaining satisfying relationships within the commune had been firmly subordinated to the pursuit of an external political objective. The lives of the members became immersed in work on behalf of such causes as shelters for battered wives, squatters' action, the Claimants Union, Gay Liberation, community action projects and various branches of the women's movement. At the same time the arrangements they made domestically to care for one another's children and run the house in such a way that no one of them was tied to domesticity seemed to us to generate a consciousness of the social situation of women and of the possibility of solidary action by women which was considerably sharper and more practically informed than that typical of the women's movement as a whole. Whether it was their forcible break from family life with men or their experience of communal living that produced this effect it would be hard to tell. On the one hand, their freedom to participate fully in the political world was seen by them as made possible by their communal life. On the other hand, communal living was not for them a field of significant problems. If personal relationships within the commune were awkward, if the home itself was, as it often was, something of a neglected mess, these were at least minor irritants in lives that were centred elsewhere. Communal living as a means – whether to liberating women, rehabilitating the disturbed or finding a true religion – can be a viable instrument of policy because the state of the commune is not the members' prime concern.

But this brings us back to our more important argument – that so far as communes as ends are concerned the right policy for communes is to have no policy for communes. The distinction between communes as ends and communes as means is, however hard it may be to draw in any actual case, especially important here. To live communally in order to do something else may be a perfectly rational measure, a sensible policy for all sorts of supportive, protective, transformative or libertarian purposes. Groups involved in such projects, whatever their official or unofficial standing, may reasonably press for public recognition of the advantages of communal living as a means to their several ends, and the degree of support they receive will no doubt be related to judgements about the value of those ends which different powerful persons or institutions decide to make. The Department of Health and Social Security has recently moved towards the idea of encouraging 'alternative' patterns of care for the elderly and disabled. *Alternative England and Wales* lists an enormous number of mystical groups, some with very substantial resources behind them, seeking to develop along communal lines. We ourselves would like to see much more active support being given to therapeutic communities, to squatters' communes and to communes for unsupported mothers. As long ago as 1970 the Chimera Housing Association collected a good deal of support for a set of proposals designed to ease the provision of communal accommodation by Housing Associations. Specifically, they urged the Minister of Housing to encourage local authorities to 'cooperate with and to lend in connection with communal housing schemes and with schemes providing communal facilities, on exactly the same basis as any other schemes prepared by Housing Associations', and to modify appropriately any existing legislation or Statutory Instruments which might prevent such cooperation. In making a case for this proposal Chimera reviewed the demand for communal housing at length and stressed in particular its benefits in relation to the care of children and old people, its cost-effectiveness in terms of the optimal use of housing stock, especially larger properties, and its more general value as a means of providing 'a grouping of people larger than the nuclear family which will stand between families and the impersonal world'. These proposals were perhaps particularly concerned to clear the ground for the development of caring communities on more genuinely communal lines, and they have been echoed subsequently by bodies such as the Richmond Fellowship and the Simon Community. More recently, People-in-Common have devised a set of model rules for a flexible type of Housing Association providing for a high degree of communalism and have successfully collaborated with local authorities in Lancashire to provide housing for the homeless along these lines.

The commune movement as a whole, however, and especially those involved in secular family projects within it, have been curiously quiet about the possible implications of communes for social policy. Many commune members would probably shy away from the mere posing of such an issue as at best a form of one-dimensional thinking, at worst 'an attempt to coopt communes and their members into the prevailing system' (*Communes*, 37: 17) – the prevailing mood of getting as far away as possible from any sort of formally organised social action is indicated, too, in the fact that for some years many commune members have found even the extremely loose framework of the Commune Movement oppressive, a feeling which culminated early in 1975 in a decision to set up the Commune Network as an alternative to the Commune Movement: in contrast to the minimal constitution of the Commune Movement, the point about the Commune Network is that it 'has no constitution'. Nevertheless, the issue of the policy relevance of communes is discussed, not least in the pages of *Communes*, and the usual outcome of such discussions is the view that although any initiative by the state to promote communalism would be flawed hopelessly by the state's unavoidable interest in maintaining its own power, the cultivation of mutual responsibility and attachment which is such an essential feature of communes is, somehow, a true basis for social policy – if only one could have social policy without the state. It is perhaps for similar reasons that Safilios-Rothschild (1974) finds so little room for communes in her review of 'social policies to liberate marriage and the family'. The extensive development of communal living would require collaboration with the state, a collaboration which would be bound to contaminate rather than to liberate. However much sponsored and protected communes might feel like contexts of self-realisation from within, one could never be quite sure that they were not means of 'containing the deviants' from without. The value of communes turns on an authentic autonomy of the communal group which is seen as effectively removing communes from the field of public policy.

The attempt to live communally in order, simply, to live communally must, in short, be seen, in a capitalist society and despite commune members' own distaste for conflict, as *essentially oppositional*. Communes spring from rejections of the existing social order which, however one-sided they may be and whether they are put as a matter of values or structures, are fundamental. The difficulties of such communes are not fortuitous; they result from the very fact that such communes are deeply at odds with all the powerful tendencies of the society – a tension that persists even within the personalities of the most dedicated members of communes. Such communes, finally, are worthwhile to the extent that they achieve, however insecurely, social relationships which are abnormal if not unattainable in the surrounding society and adumbrate a genuinely different social order.

How could one have a policy for such undertakings? All their value springs from the self-creation involved in struggling against a world that is hostile or indifferent to them. Insofar as they do achieve an alternative reality, they do so because they have forcibly separated themselves from the common reality. We are not recommending tribulation for its own sake. The radical antithesis that exists between communal aspirations and the bourgeois culture within which they are born but from which they must break free really does imply a strenuous practice of opposition. And opposition and policy do not easily mix; opposition tends to subvert and unmask policy; policy tends to confuse and contaminate opposition. So we reach the possibly odd view that although, for example, many of the difficulties of communes could be overcome if communes were larger, richer or more legally secure, it would in fact be a disservice to communes to try to provide these benefits from outside. From the point of view of what communes stand for, genuinely social social relations, the constant failures of unsupported struggling communes may be more important than the possible successes of sponsored communes would be.

Indeed, even the successes of some unsupported communes are enigmatic. There is an ironic possibility that in pursuing their ideals in their own way communes will in fact come to succeed by mirroring the very society from which they wish to escape. Perhaps, as Weber thought, there is an inexorable drive towards rationalisation that engulfs *everything* about capitalist societies – even the alternative societies that struggle to emerge within them. Thus, as we finish writing this book the most visible developments within the commune movement are developments in apparently contradictory directions. There is the attempt to move still further away from any sort of concerted inter-communal social action, a retreat from the idea of a commune movement. But at the same time individual communes are establishing themselves more firmly on the basis of greater wealth, greater size and much more carefully elaborated formal organisation; there is an intra-communal embracing of social structure. The most remarkable development of this kind – apart from the Laurieston Hall *Legal Frameworks Handbook* – is perhaps the Crabapple Community near Shrewsbury (*Undercurrents*, 1975: 12). This group, which already contains refugees from some of the family communes we visited, is consciously and explicitly modelled on the rationalised community projected by B. F. Skinner in *Walden Two*, and is complete with a meticulously egalitarian and legally complex financial structure, an interest in 'behaviour modification through positive reinforcement', a labour credit system (child care 1.1 points; washing up 0.8 points) and a rota of 'planners' and 'managers' to make and implement policy (the labour manager assigns jobs; intending visitors should contact the visitor manager). The purpose of this precise structural definition, a communal bureaucracy in effect, is of course to forestall the destructive wrangles about work and mutual responsibilities that have indeed eroded the hopes of many family communes. But it remains to be seen whether projects such as Crabapple which seek to apply the logic of bureaucratic society to communal living are a new departure in the social construction of friendship or merely a sour epitaph for a fading vision. In any event the commune movement seems to have travelled a long way since that moment four years previously when one of the people now at Crabapple told us that the most positive attraction of communal living was 'the abolition of roles'.

We end this book as we began it, as sympathetic outsiders. We have certainly not made light of the ambiguities and shortcomings of communes. But we have tried also to recognise their seriousness as a criticism of the society in which we live, their relevance to the problems of that society and their value, chimerical though they may be, as a tentative statement of how ordinary lives might actually be different. Above all we have tried to recognise their humanity and the enduring, defiant patience with which members of communes go on trying to treat one another as persons. The culture in which we find ourselves is one which in a profound way denies the possibilities of social life. Yet critics of that culture, from Marx onwards, have found it strangely difficult to give an account in any practical depth of what a more authentic existence would be like. By attempting to practice such an existence, communes begin to give us that account. Both their value and their dilemma were shrewdly anticipated by Durkheim:

> For morality to have a sound basis, the citizen must have an inclination toward collective life. It is only on this condition that he can become attached to collective aims that are moral aims par excellence. This does not happen automatically; above all this inclination toward collective life can only become strong enough to

shape behavior by the most continuous practice. To appreciate social life to the point where one cannot do without it one must have developed the habit of acting and thinking in common. We must learn to cherish these social bonds that for the unsocial being are heavy chains. We must learn through experience how cold and pale the pleasures of solitary life are in comparison. The development of such a temperament, such a mental outlook, can only be formed through repeated practice, through perpetual conditioning. If on the contrary, we are invited only infrequently to act like social beings, it is impossible to be very interested in an existence to which we can only adapt ourselves very imperfectly (1961: 233).

Appendix

On informed consent

The *Statement of Ethical Principles* of the British Sociological Association urges sociologists to adopt the principle of 'informed consent' in the relationship between a researcher and the subjects of his research. So far as possible, that is to say, the subject should understand why he is being studied and should on the basis of that understanding agree to make his life available as a matter for research and report. We found it difficult to comply with this principle in our own research. Members of communes seemed to have all too clear an understanding of why we wanted to study them and were, almost without exception, willing to let us make our observations and publish our findings in any way we thought fit. They were, in other words, quite adequately informed about what we were doing and about why we thought it important. But both during the research and especially when we showed them what we had written, we were left in no doubt that consent was a far more problematic question. In the strongest sense of the word, it is probable that none of the people we have written about really consent to what we have written. Members of the communes we have described in detail have agreed that our accounts are 'amazingly accurate' or have achieved 'remarkable insight'. But that is not really the point. They have in effect *assented* to our work while denying it any real validity. They have not consented to sociology. We were repeatedly told that if our professed concern for communal aspirations had any substance we would stop writing and start living instead. They refused to consent to the externality of our interest in them. They raised an ethical issue which it seemed to us it was impossible for the sociologist to overcome. If their relationships bothered us so much, the morally responsible thing to do was surely to join in, to relate directly ourselves and try to help. To observe and go away and make judgements was by comparison something less than human. In fact of course we did join in a little – one of us did, for example, sit up all night talking to a particular member of one commune who was desperate about the way her most valued relationship was being torn apart. In such ways we did perhaps contribute infinitesimally to that social breadth which is the great value of communes. But the force of the criticism

221

remains. What sort of concern is it that culminates in the writing of a book rather than in the living of relationships? The issue has been put to us quite bluntly by people who in no way deny the accuracy of our reports:

This little episode has confirmed views I've been tending towards about sociology; that sociologists are people who don't live lives; they study them instead. Why not come out from under the protection of your course or your career and your professor (or is he really the worst, sending you out to take the, metaphorically speaking, dirty pictures for him to slaver over in the comfort and security of his study?) and take up with someone and grow potatoes and sweep the floor and catch buses just like living people?

Others have made the same sort of point rather more gently; they are puzzled and troubled by our ability to keep our distance. Unfortunately, explanation imposes distance. And we were therefore doomed to achieve something less than informed consent from the commune movement; informed indifference, perhaps?

Methods and materials

Our most ambitious and most naive attempt to study communes involved the distribution of a questionnaire to all known members of the Commune Movement. Seven hundred of these questionnaires were sent out; 245 came back completed in whole or part. These are filed and when referred to in the text are cited as Q.001–Q.245. The questions on which we have principally drawn, apart from standard data on education, occupation and so forth, are questions about 'what communal living offers you personally', about 'the main strains and difficulties of communal living' and about the 'advantages/ disadvantages of communal living for women and children'. In the event, the most useful part of the questionnaire turned out to be the blank pages we added at the back and on which we invited respondents to make any comments they felt might be relevant to an understanding of communes. This elicited a great deal of comment, including some very long and detailed analytical essays. One respondent described the process of completing the questionnaire as a form of 'intellectual masturbation', and several others indicated their strong sense of the shallowness of this sort of inquiry. Nevertheless, we did find the replies we received helpful both in an indicative and in a confirmatory sense.

We invited and received a very large number of letters, life-histories, stories and other personal documents from members of communes. We have filed and cited these as L.001–L.320 and have drawn upon them at length throughout the book. And then we had the mass of transcripts of tape-recorded conversations and interviews and of our own reports and diaries (R.001–R.262) which in the end were to prove our principal resource. The first 67 of these items (R.001–R.067) are accounts of our initial visits to the 67 communes or communal projects which we ended by studying in some detail; subsequent items in this set are either reports of initial visits to communes to which we did not return or accounts of our subsequent visits to those to which we did return. When making our first visit to any commune we planned to organise our observations in relation to a common checklist of questions, and insofar as we were able to do this our reports do have a loose similarity of design. We began in each case with a description of the physical location of the commune, the type and size of the dwelling and an attempt to map the distribution of areas of activity within it. We then tried to identify by name, sex, age, occupation and length of membership all those living in the commune at the time of our visit, making at this stage only a cursory attempt to determine actual or ostensible relationships between members. Our third concern in these initial visits was to obtain some account, from as many members as possible, of the history of the commune, the occasion and reasons for its founding. Was it an original foundation, the upshot of an earlier unsuccessful commune or of a split within another still-existing commune? Who were the founders of the commune, and were they still living there? Next, we sought to determine some of the basic structural features of each commune: how were the premises acquired and how were they now owned; how were household tasks organised; did the commune have any sort of attached enterprises, a farm, pottery, shop or other business, and if so how was that organised and related to the commune as a whole; and had the commune developed regular procedures for making policies and decisions, and if so what were they and how had they been established (we found that a useful way into this issue was to ask how the decision had been made to permit our own visit)? We then tried to obtain information on the commune's relations with the outside world, including social movements, the local community and the personal friends and relatives of individual members. Perhaps the most difficult category on our checklist to do anything about during these initial visits was the one concerned with the financial arrangements of the commune; we were told a good deal about day-to-day budgeting but little or nothing about the larger sources and allocation of resources. Finally, we tried to form an impression of the prevailing ethos or ideology of the commune, the extent to which a common ethos was being articulated and the sorts of values on which it was centred.

Our object at this stage was to gather a body of basic information about the extent, distribution and nature of the commune movement in

223

Britain. Using our checklist, we therefore visited as many communes as we could in a very short period of time with a view to organising them into a range of types and revisiting some examples of those types that seemed important from the point of view of our original research interest later on. It was interesting to observe the subsequent collapse of this tidy research strategy.

In our application to the SSRC we had outlined three main areas for investigation in the context of which we hoped to be able to make judgements about communes as alternatives to the nuclear family. We argued that some sense of a commune's viability as an alternative to the family might be found in its ability to provide (1) a setting for strong and stable adult relationships, (2) a setting for child rearing and (3) a setting in which women could lead more 'satisfying' or 'liberated' lives. These central concerns were derived from what we had read and heard about communes in the preceding months. As we pursued our other objective, that of gathering broad sociographic information about the commune movement as a whole through our initial visits and the use of the checklist, it became clear that the phenomenon represented in the literature and gossip that had first aroused our interest was only a tenuous and partial manifestation of the reality. To begin with, the Commune Movement and indeed any sort of extensive connection between communes hardly existed. Most communes had knowledge only of a handful of others; some knew of none at all. The mere locating of communes proved a slow and laborious business. Many of the addresses we were given had been abandoned by the time we arrived at them. Fruitless hours and days were spent tramping around London to find houses from which the occupants had been evicted or had simply moved on or at which it was firmly denied that the residents constituted a commune. A day's hiking across the Northumberland moors north of Hadrian's Wall in swirling November mists brought us to a derelict farmhouse with only a few mystical daubings on the door to support the claim of one of our informants that it had, in better weather presumably, housed an exceptionally thriving commune. To a large degree we found that the commune movement consisted of rumours of communes; 'I've heard of one in the West of Scotland but I don't know exactly where it is' was to be something of a leitmotiv of our field-work. Secondly, once the communes were located, it turned out that our two research tasks – to map the commune movement as a whole and to explore the alternative-family theme within communes – were not at all complementary in the way we had expected. It is perhaps one of the advantages of participant observation and the unstructured method that research can be redirected as one goes along on the basis of what one is discovering. This allows for the assertion of the particularity of the world being studied,

224

but it also means that there is a strong element of unpredictability about the whole procedure. As other advocates of this method have frequently pointed out, so much is played by ear that although the research may well be highly sensitive to nuances it can be equally susceptible to red herrings. Pat Gore, who did a very large part of the early work of tramping around commune-hunting, described the situation we had created after the first six months of our research as follows:

Alternative family communes are but one type amongst many and it seems that by concentrating solely on this aspect we will give the communes movement a false emphasis and distorted perspective. It has become clear that there are many communes that hold all sorts of ideas about how one should or should not bring up children but nearly every one of these has no children. Likewise many of the communes that do have children maintain a nuclear family structure with the biological mother always being the person who has the main share of responsibility for her children. With the results of our questionnaire showing that a quest for an alternative to the nuclear family is the basis of many people's interest in communal living it now seems that there are two main types of communes – those that are dreamt of and those that actually exist. The latter only ever seem to be rather shaky approximations to the former, especially so far as experimenting with the family is concerned. In retrospect it is clear that our own preconception of what communes are about and what they are doing was necessarily a speculative one. Our emphasis on the family aspect of communes has created a strong tension between what is being looked for and what is being found. (R.170)

Nevertheless, as we have reported, we did find a very powerful demand for communes to function as alternative families outside communes themselves, especially among unsupported women with children. And we did find an appreciable number of communes in which the cultivation of friendship was part of an admittedly rather diffuse ethos of replacing the family. And so we were able to redirect our research, making it a study of that particular type of communalism within the commune movement as a whole and of its actual or possible relationship to the larger demand for family communes. The second stage of visiting accordingly consisted of relatively protracted stays in communes of a single type, the secular family commune as we have described it in chapter 2. The character of the research at this stage was much influenced by the personal relationships that developed between us and individual members of particular communes. We tended to proceed on the basis of a mutual inquisitiveness, long conversations in which as much was asked about us as we asked about them. Almost without exception, the family communes made it clear that they wanted to play down our role as researchers and to get through to us as people, and we invariably did our best to keep the formal aspects of our presence as researchers in the background and to fit in with the pattern of life already in train in the commune. This meant that our questioning and observing had to be somewhat disjointed and fragmentary, interrupted by the need to do our share of communal work, and that we tended to be thrown into the company of some members of the group more than others. One result of this was that a number of quite close friendships developed with one or two members of a number of communes. And this in turn raised its own difficulties. On the one hand we tended to be given more detailed, intimate and probably reliable information by our friends. But on the other hand the human and ethical implications of using such information became increasingly problematic, as did the implications of either remaining neutral or being partisan when those with whom we had such close relationships became entangled in conflicts with other members of their group. There is a sort of moral paralysis which afflicts the human being committed to social science in this type of predicament. We can record it, but we did not find any way of overcoming it.

On sharing data

The research materials discussed in the previous section are obviously not of a type which could usefully be deposited in any sort of Data Archive. We are aware, however, that we did gather an enormous amount of information about the commune movement which has not been used substantially in this book. The materials have been 'cleaned' to the extent that it is impossible to work back from them to particular individuals (which often means to particular groups as well, of course). In some cases we have made specific commitments not to make information available to anyone else without the explicit permission of those who gave it to us. Subject to those conditions, the material we have collected may be consulted by anyone sufficiently interested in the problems of communal living to wish to do so.

226

Bibliography and references

Abrams, P., and McCulloch, A. (1974), 'Men, Women and Communes'. Paper read at British Sociological Association Annual Conference, Aberdeen. To be published

Aries, P. (1962), *Centuries of Childhood*. Jonathan Cape, London

Aristotle (1953), *Ethics*, ed. J. A. K. Thomson. Allen & Unwin, London

Armytage, W. H. G. (1961), *Heavens Below*. Routledge & Kegan, Paul, London

Becker, H. S. (1960), 'Notes on the Concept of Commitment', *American Journal of Sociology*, 66: 32-40

Bennett, J. W. (1975), 'Communes and Communitarianism,' *Theory and Society*, 2: 63-94

Bennis, W., and Slater, P. (1968), *The Temporary Society*. Harper & Row, New York

Berger, B., Hackett, B. M., and Millar, R. M. (1972), 'Child Rearing Practices in the Communal Family', in H. P. Dreitzel (ed.) (1972)

Berger, P. L., Berger, B., and Kellner, H. (1974), *The Homeless Mind*. Penguin, Harmondsworth

Berke, J. (ed.) (1971), *Counter Culture: The Creation of an Alternative Society*. Hillary, New York

Bestor, A. E. (1950), *Backwoods Utopias: The Sectarian and Owenite Phases of Communitarianism in America*. University of Pennsylvania Press, Philadelphia

Boguslow, R. (1965), *The New Utopias: A Study of System Design and Social Change*. Prentice-Hall, Englewood Cliffs, N.J.

Bookhagen, C., Hemmer, E., Raspe, J., and Schultz, E. (1973), 'Kommune 2: Childrearing in the Commune', in Dreitzel (ed.) (1973)

Broido, M. (ed.) (1970), *Communal Housing*. Chimera Housing Association, London

Bronfenbrenner, U. (1963), 'The Changing American Child', in N. J. Smelser and W. J. Smelser (eds.), *Personality and Social Systems*. Wiley, New York, pp. 348-59

Buber, M. (1958), *Paths in Utopia*. Beacon Press, Boston

Burtt, E. A. (1932), *The Metaphysical Foundation of Modern Science*. Doubleday, New York

Carter, N. (1974), *Something of Promise: The Canadian Communes.* Canadian Council on Social Development, Ottawa

Caudwell, C. (1937), *Illusion and Reality.* Lawrence & Wishart, London

Clarke, T., and Ingle, D. T. (1973), *Toward a Radical Therapy: Alternative Services for Personal and Social Change.* Gordon & Breach (Interface), New York

Cockerton, P. (1972), 'Shrubb Family Limited', *Communes,* 40: 17-20

Cohen, S. (1974), 'Dionysus Revisited', *Guardian,* 11 Nov. 1974

Cohn, N. (1957), *The Pursuit of the Millennium.* Secker & Warburg, London

Colletti, L. (1972), *From Rousseau to Lenin.* New Left Books, London

Commune Movement (1970), *Directory of Communes and Commune Projects, Tribes, Crash Pads and Related Phenomena in Great Britain and Europe.* BIT, London

Commune Network (1975), *Network.* Huddersfield

Communes, Journal of the Commune Movement, nos. 23-42 (1969-73)

Community Service Committee (1938), *Community in Britain: A Survey of Community Thought and Activity.* London

Cooper, D. (1971), *The Death of the Family.* Allen Lane, The Penguin Press, London

Corrigan, P. (1975), 'Dichotomy Is Contradiction: On Society as Constraint and Construction', *Sociological Review,* 23 (2): 211-43

Crowther, G. (1972), 'The Elms', *Communes,* 40: 5-14

Cuber, J. F., and Haroff, P. (1965), *Sex and the Significant Americans.* Penguin, Baltimore, Md.

Dahrendorf, R. (1958), *Class and Class Conflict in Industrial Society.* Routledge & Kegan Paul, London

Daner, F. (1975), 'Conversion to Krishna Consciousness', in Wallis (ed.) (1975)

Dawe, A. (1970), 'The Two Sociologies', *British Journal of Sociology,* 21 (2): 207-18

Department of the Environment, United Kingdom Government (1972), *Family Expenditure Survey: Report for 1971.* HMSO, London

Diamond, S. (1971), *What the Trees Said: Life on a New Age Farm.* Dell, New York

Dreitzel, H .P. (ed.) (1972), *Family, Marriage and the Struggle of the Sexes.* Collier-Macmillan, New York

(1973), *Childhood and Socialization.* Collier-Macmillan, New York

Durkheim, E. (1933), *Division of Labour in Society,* trans. G. Simpson. Free Press, New York

(1938), *The Rules of Sociological Method*, ed. G. E. C. Catlin, trans. S. A. Solovay and J. H. Mueller. Free Press, New York

(1961), *Moral Education*, trans. E. K. Wilson. Free Press, New York

(1965), *The Elementary Forms of the Religious Life: A Study in Religious Sociology*, trans J. W. Swain. Free Press, New York

Engels, F. (1951a), 'Socialism Utopian and Scientific', in Marx and Engels (1951)

(1951b), 'The Origins of the Family, Private Property and the State', in Marx and Engels (1951)

Eno, S. (1972a), 'Spring Waits for No Man', *Communes*, 41: 1-6

(1972b), 'Signposts on the Road to Communes', *Communes*, 41: 16-22

Epstein, A. L. (ed.) (1967), *The Craft of Social Anthropology*. Tavistock, London

Erikson, E. H. (1963), *Childhood and Society*. Norton, New York

(1968), *Identity: Youth and Crisis*. Faber & Faber, London

Fairfield, R. (1972), *Communes Europe*. Alternatives Foundation, San Francisco

Fairweather, G. W., et al. (1969), *Community Life for the Mentally Ill – An Alternative to Institutional Care*. Aldine Press, Chicago

Findhorn, *Findhorn News* (1969–73). The Findhorn Foundation, Forres

(1969a), *Moving into the New Age: Blending the Generations*. The Findhorn Trust, Forres

(1969b), *The Findhorn Story*. The Findhorn Trust, Forres

(1969c), *The Findhorn Garden*. The Findhorn Trust, Forres

(1971), *The Significance of Findhorn*. The Findhorn Trust, Forres

(1972), *The Transformation of Findhorn*. The Findhorn Foundation, Forres

Firestone, S. (1971), *The Dialectic of Sex: The Case for Feminist Revolution*. Jonathan Cape, London

Flacks, R. (1971), *Youth and Social Change*. Markham, Chicago

Freeman, J. (1972), 'The Women's Liberation Movement: Its Origins and Ideas', in Dreitzel (ed.) (1972)

Fromm, E. (1955), *The Sane Society*. Holt, Rinehart & Winston, New York

Gerson, M. (1974), 'The Family in the Kibbutz', *Journal of Child Psychology and Psychiatry*, 15: 47-57

Gil, D. G. (1970), *Violence against Children*. Harvard University Press, Cambridge, Mass.

(1973), 'Violence against Children', in Dreitzel (ed.) (1973)

Goffman, E. (1959), *The Presentation of Self in Everyday Life*. Penguin, Harmondsworth

229

Gorman, C. (1971), *Making Communes*. Whole Earth Books, London (1975), *People Together: A Guide to Communal Living*. Paladin, London

Green, A. (1946). 'The Middle-class Male Child and Neurosis', *American Sociological Review*, 11: 31-41

Hawthorne, N. (1962), *The Blithedale Romance*. Dell, New York

Hedgepeth, W., and Stock, D. (1970), *The Alternative: Communal Life in New America*. Collier-Macmillan, London

Hill, C., and Dell, E. (eds.) (1949), *The Good Old Cause: The English Revolution of 1640-60*. Lawrence & Wishart, London

Hillery, G. A. (1968), *Communal Organizations: A Study of Local Societies*. University of Chicago Press, Chicago

Holloway, M. (1966), *Heavens on Earth: Utopian Communities in America*. Dover Books, New York

Hostetler, J. A. (1974), *Communitarian Societies*. Holt, Rinehart & Winston, New York

Houriet, R. (1971), *Getting Back Together*. Coward, McCann & Geoghegan, New York

Huizinga, J. (1955), *Homo Ludens: A Study of the Play Element in Culture*. Beacon Press, Boston

Ineson, G. (1956), *Community Journey*. Sheed & Ward, London

Jensen, A. E. (1963), *Myth and Cult among Primitive Peoples*. University of Chicago Press, Chicago

Jerome, J. (1975), *Families of Eden*. Thames & Hudson, London

Jones, R. K. (1975), 'Some Sectarian Characteristics of Therapeutic Groups', in Wallis (ed.) (1975)

Jung, C. (1959), *Researches into the Phenomenology of the Self*, vol. 9 of *The Collected Works of C. G. Jung*, ed. R. Adler, M. Fordham, and H. Read. Routledge & Kegan Paul, London (1974), *The Undiscovered Self*. Routledge & Kegan Paul, London

Kanter, R. M. (1972), *Commitment and Community*. Harvard University Press, Cambridge, Mass. (1974), *Communes: Creating and Managing the Collective Life*. Harper & Row, New York

Katz, D. (1960), 'The Functional Approach to the Study of Attitudes', *Public Opinion Quarterly*, 25: 170-86

Keniston, K. (1971), *Youth and Dissent: The Rise of a New Opposition*. Harcourt Brace Jovanovich, New York

Klapp, O. E. (1969), *Collective Search for Identity*. Holt, Rinehart & Winston, New York

Kluckhohn, F. (1965), 'Dominant and Variant Value Orientation', in C. Kluckhohn et al. (eds.), *Personality in Nature, Society and Culture*. Knopf, New York

Kryananda, S. (1968), *Cooperative Communities: How to Start Them, and Why*. Ananda Publications, Nevada City, Calif.

Laing, R. (1961), *Self and Others*. Tavistock, London
(1971), *The Politics of the Family and Other Essays*. Tavistock, London

Leach, E. (1968), *A Runaway World*. The Reith Lectures for 1967. BBC Publications, London

Legal Frameworks Handbook – For Communes and Collectives (1975). Laurieston Hall, Castle Douglas

Lockwood, G. B. (1905), *The New Harmony Movement*. Appleton, New York

Macpherson, C. B. (1962), *The Political Theory of Possessive Individualism*. Clarendon Press, Oxford

Marcuse, H. (1964), *One-dimensional Man: Studies in the Ideology of Advanced Industrial Society*. Routledge & Kegan Paul, London

Marsden, D. (1973), *Mothers Alone*. Penguin, Harmondsworth

Marx, K. (1959), *Economic and Philosophical Manuscripts of 1844*. Foreign Language Publishing House, Moscow
(1975), 'Contribution to the Critique of Hegel's Philosophy of Law', in *Collected Works of Marx and Engels*, 3, pp. 3-129. Lawrence & Wishart, London

Marx, K., and Engels, F. (1939), *The German Ideology*, ed. R. Pascal. Lawrence & Wishart, London
(1951) *Selected Works*, I and II. Foreign Language Publishing House, Moscow

Melville, K. (1972), *Communes in the Counter Culture: Origins, Themes, Styles of Life*. Morrow, New York

Mills, R. (1973), *Young Outsiders: A Study of Alternative Communities*. Routledge & Kegan Paul, London

Mitchell, J. (1971), *Woman's Estate*. Penguin, Harmondsworth

Morton, A. L. (1952), *The English Utopia*. Lawrence & Wishart, London

Mullahy, P. (ed.) (1952), *The Contributions of Harry Stack Sullivan*. Hermitage House, New York

Mungo, R. (1970), *Total Loss Farm: A Year in the Life*. Bantam, New York

Murry, J. M. (1952), *Community Farm*. Peter Nevill, London

Musgrove, F. (1974), *Ecstasy and Holiness*. Methuen, London

Natanson, M. (1970), *The Journeying Self: A Study in Philosophy and Social Role*. Addison-Wesley, London

Nearing, H., and Nearing, S. (1970), *Living the Good Life*. Schocken, New York
(1971), *The Maple Sugar Book*. Schocken, New York

231

Neville, R. (1970), *Playpower*. Jonathan Cape, London

Nordhoff, C. (1965), *Communistic Societies of the United States*. Schocken, New York

Otto, H. A. (1972), 'Communes, the Alternative Lifestyle', *Saturday Review* (New York), 24 April 1971

Parkin, F. (1968), *Middle Class Radicalism: The Social Bases of the British Campaign for Nuclear Disarmament*. Manchester University Press, Manchester

Parsons, T. (1949), 'The Social Structure of the Family', in R. Anshen (ed.), *The Family: Its Function and Destiny*. Harper Brothers, New York

(1971), *Social Structure and Personality*. Free Press, New York

Peace News (1972), 'Communes in Britain'. Special issue of 28 Jan. 1972, ed. A. Rigby. London

Polsky, N. (1971), *Hustlers, Beats and Others*. Penguin, Harmondsworth

Poulantzas, N. (1973), 'On Social Classes', *New Left Review*, 78: 27-54

Punch, M. (1974), 'The Sociology of the Anti-institution', *British Journal of Sociology*, 25(3): 312-25

Ramey, J. W. (1972), 'Communes, Group Marriage and the Upper Middle Class', *Journal of Marriage and the Family*, 34(2)

Richardson, J. T., Simmonds, R., and Harder, M. (1972), 'Jesus People', *Psychology Today*, 12: 269-81

Rieff, P. (1968), *The Triumph of the Therapeutic*. Harper (Torchbooks), New York

Rigby, A. (1971), 'Communes and Social Change in Britain', *Communes*, 37: 12-14

(1974a), *Alternative Realities*. Routledge & Kegan Paul, London

(1974b), *Communes in Britain*. Routledge & Kegan Paul, London

Roberts, R. E. (1971), *The New Communes: Coming Together in America*. Prentice-Hall, Englewood Cliffs, N.J.

Robinson, P. A. (1973), *The Sexual Radicals*. Paladin, London

Rogers, C. (1972), *Becoming Partners: Marriage and Its Alternatives*. Delacorte, New York

Roszak, T. (1970), *The Making of a Counter-culture*. Faber & Faber, London

Rowbotham, S. (1972), 'Women's Liberation and the New Politics', in M. Wandor (ed.), *The Body Politic*. Stage 1, London

Ryder, A. (1967), 'Compatibility in Marriage', *Psychological Reports*, 20: 807-13

Safilios-Rothschild, C. (1974), *Women and Social Policy*. Prentice-Hall, Englewood Cliffs, N.J.

Sagarin, E. (1970), *Odd Man In: Societies of Deviants in America*. Quadrangle Books, Chicago

Saunders, N. (1975), *Alternative England and Wales*. Nicholas Saunders, London

Schmalenbach, H. (1961), 'The Sociological Categories of Communion', in T. Parsons et al. (eds.), *Theories of Society*, 1. Free Press, New York

Shaw, N. (1935), *Whiteway: A Colony in the Cotswolds*. Daniel & Co., London

Simmel, G. (1955), *Conflict: The Web of Group Affiliation*. Free Press, New York

(1971), *On Individuality and Social Forms*, ed. D. N. Levine. University of Chicago Press, Chicago

Simpson, G. (1966), *People in Families*. Meridian Books, New York

Skinner, B. F. (1970), *Walden Two*. Macmillan, London

Skolnick, A. (1973), *The Intimate Environment*. Little, Brown, Boston

Slater, P. E. (1970), *The Pursuit of Loneliness*. Beacon Press, Boston

Speck, R. V. (1972), *The New Families: Youth, Communes and the Politics of Drugs*. Tavistock, London

Spiro, M. E. (1963), *Kibbutz: Venture in Utopia*. Schocken Books, New York

(1965), *Children of the Kibbutz*. Schocken Books, New York

Sprague, W. D. (1972), *Case Histories from the Communes*. Lancer Books, New York

Sugarman, B. (1975), 'Reluctant Converts: Social Control, Socialization and Adaptation in Therapeutic Communities', in R. Wallis (ed.) (1975)

Sweezy, P. (1968), *The Theory of Capitalist Development*. Oxford University Press, Oxford

Talmon, Y. (1972), *Family and Community in the Kibbutz*. Harvard University Press, Cambridge, Mass.

Thompson, E. P. (1967), 'Time, Work-discipline and Industrial Capitalism', *Past & Present*, 38: 20-38

Thompson, O. (1970), 'Norfolk Commune', *Communes*, 33: 9-13

Turner, R. (1962), 'Role-taking: Process versus Conformity', in A. Rose (ed.), *Human Behaviour and Social Processes*. Routledge & Kegan Paul, London

Turner, V. W. (1969), *The Ritual Process: Structure and Anti-structure*. Penguin, Harmondsworth

Undercurrents (1975). Undercurrents Ltd., London

Van Velsen, T. (1967), 'The Extended Case Method and Situational Analysis', in Epstein (ed.) (1967)

Vidich, A. J. (1974), Review of J. Scherer, *Contemporary Community: Illusion or Reality*, in *Contemporary Sociology*, 3(4): 333

Wallace, A. F. C. (1956), 'Revitalization Movements', *American Anthropologist*, 58(2): 264-81

Wallis, R. (ed.) (1975), *Sectarianism*. Peter Owen, London

Webber, E. (1959), *Escape to Utopia: The Communal Movement in America*. Hastings House, New York

Weber, M. (1968), *Economy and Society*, ed. G. Roth and C. Wittich. Bedminster Press, New York

Whitworth, J. K. (1975), 'Communitarian Movements and the World', in Wallis (ed.) (1975)

Woodcock, G. (1947), *The Basis of Communal Living*. Freedom Press, London

Yablonsky, L. (1965), *The Tunnel Bank: Synanon*. Macmillan, New York

Zablocki, B. (1971), *The Joyful Community: An Account of the Bruderhof*. Penguin, Baltimore, Md.

Zicklin, G. (1973), 'Communal Child-rearing: A Report on Three Cases', in Dreitzel (ed.) (1973)

Index

Hill, Christopher, 3
'Hillside Community', 61–72, 188, 205
hippies, 88–9, 91, 109
'Hollingsworth problem', 93, 94, 103, 118–19, 120
housing associations, 169, 216

identity, development of, 110–11, 112, 113–14, 117–18, 126, 151, 192, 204–5; problem of, 191
identity and youth, 107–20, 118–19
ideology, 72, 84–5, 90, 132, 137, 141, 146, 149, 161, 162, 179, 185, 198, 205, 223
income, apportionment of, 171–3
individualism, 8, 35, 36, 71, 92, 93, 94, 98, 130–1, 152, 153, 167, 185, 187, 195, 198, 200, 201; possessive, 93–4, 188, 189–90, 191, 192, 193, 199, 202, 203; problem of, 142, 187, 189, 192, 193, 199–200, 201–2, 205
individuation, 109, 110, 112, 113, 114, 116, 120, 181, 191, 192, 194
industrial cooperatives, 106
inequality, 199–200
intentional community, 162
intentional villages, 106

Jerome, J., 26, 29, 32, 33
Jesus Movement, 194
Jones, R. K., 51
Jung, C., 11, 109, 119, 120, 162, 200, 203

Kanter, R. M., 3, 35, 36, 51, 93, 151, 153, 154, 155, 160, 161
Katz, D., 197
Keniston, K., 108, 109, 110, 113, 114, 116
kibbutz, 93, 209–10
Kingsway Community, 50
Kluckhohn, F., 20
Kommune II, Berlin, 193

Labour Party, 142
Laing, R. D., 113, 115, 122, 123
Laurieston Hall Community, 211, 218
Lawrence, D. H., 129, 162
Leach, E., 122
leadership, in communes, 43–5, 46, 83, 85, 87, 203
Lee Abbey, 39
leisure, see play
limited company, 168, 170
Little Gidding, 49
love, 6, 28, 29, 31, 60, 67, 81, 83, 85, 89, 95, 96, 97–9, 100, 101, 112, 116, 129, 131, 152, 155, 164, 209; kinds

of, 139–40; moral economy of, 115, 122
love and family life, 114–15
love and identity, 115–16, 140
love-nexus, 123, 147
love and work, 97–101 passim, 106, 108, 114

Maclean, Dorothy, 86
Macpherson, C. B., 189, 199
'manifestation', 84–5, 86, 89
Marcuse, H., 123, 124, 193
marital breakdown, 214–15
marriage, types of, 157
marriage and communes compared, 156–9
Marsden, D., 212
Marx, K., 1, 22, 159, 163, 164, 167, 199, 219
marxism, 123, 193, 194
Mead, G. H., 7, 154
Melville, K., 3
middle classes, 42, 50, 63, 68, 87, 117, 127, 141, 168, 190, 195, 198, 212
Mill, J. S., 113
Miller, R. M., 12
Miller Family Commune, 125
Mills, R., 33, 34, 159
Mitchell, J., 145
Morton, A. L., 2
mothering, 5, 15, 19, 136–7, 144–5, 148, 149, 213–14, 224, 225
mothers, single, see single parents
Mungo, R., 32, 33
Musgrove, F., 3, 6
mutuality, 6, 38, 39, 40, 43, 96, 97, 102, 110, 119, 120, 154, 157, 167, 169, 171, 199, 202, 206, 208, 211
myth about communes, 3–4, 16, 19–21 passim

Natanson, M., 11
New Age, 86, 88, 90, 92, 145, 146, 149
nuclear family, 81, 115, 116, 117, 121–5, 136, 137, 142, 144, 147, 151, 190, 210, 216, 224, 225

openness, communal, 12–15, 50, 84, 90, 102, 106, 112, 122, 137, 143
ownership, 168–71 passim

pacifism, 162, 196
pair relationships, 57, 68, 125, 128, 138, 145, 150
parenthood, surrogate, 68, 149–50
Parkin, F., 196, 197, 198
Parsons, T., 122, 167
People-in-Common, 211, 217

237